The Government of
Japan

The Government of JAPAN

Ardaih W. Burks

RUTGERS—THE STATE UNIVERSITY

CROWELL COMPARATIVE GOVERNMENT SERIES

Thomas Y. Crowell Company

NEW YORK   ESTABLISHED 1834

Library of Congress Catalog Card Number: 61–15524

Series design by Joan Wall

Manufactured in the United States of America
by The Colonial Press Inc.

EDITOR'S FOREWORD

In our time the study of comparative government constitutes one of many fields or specialities in political science. But it is worth recalling that the most distinguished political scientists of the ancient world would have had difficulty recognizing the present-day distinction between the study of comparative government and study in other subject areas of the discipline. Think of Plato, for example, whose works abound in references to the political systems of his own and earlier days. Or consider Aristotle, whose *Politics* and related writings were based on an examination of more than one hundred constitutions. Twenty centuries after Aristotle the comparative emphasis continued strong in the work of Montesquieu and Rousseau, among others. In the nineteenth century the comparative tradition entered upon a period of decline, but there are signs that the merits of comparative political analysis are once more gaining recognition. At many colleges and universities, the introductory course in political science is no longer focused exclusively on American government. The comparative approach—in politics, in law, in administration—is becoming increasingly important in the political science curriculum.

This booklet, one of a series, is designed to reflect that approach, without, however, marking a sharp departure from the substance and method of most comparative government courses. With one exception (Arnold J. Heidenheimer, *The Government of Germany: West and East*), each booklet deals with one national government, but the booklets are distinctively comparative in at least two senses. Most of them include material descriptive of other political systems, especially that of the United States. In addition, the booklets follow a common outline, so far as possible, and are designed to promote comparative treatment. Of course, there is nothing to keep the instructor or student from treating a particular governmental system in isolation, if he chooses to do so. On the other hand, his approach to political institutions and functions can be as comparative as he wishes.

A further advantage of this series is that each booklet has been written by a distinguished scholar and authority in the field; each author is personally and professionally familiar with the political system he treats. Finally, the separate booklets make it possible for the instructor to design his course in accordance with his own interest or the interests of his students. One booklet may be substituted for another or any booklet put aside for one semester without affecting the others. The booklets, in short, unlike most one-volume textbooks, give the instructor maximum freedom in organizing his course. This freedom will be virtually unlimited as the forthcoming titles in this series complete a survey of representative governments of the world.

But to return to Aristotle once again, it remains true that the best judges of the feast are not the cooks but the guests. I have tried to indicate why, in my view, the recipe for the series is a good one. Let all those who teach comparative government, and all those who take courses in that field, proceed to judge the booklets for themselves.

ARNOLD A. ROGOW

INTRODUCTION

This booklet describes the government of Japan, with emphasis on the period of readjustment since the peace treaty of 1952.

A generation ago, governments and politics of the Far East were relegated to picturesque appendices of standard treatises on more familiar Western states and political behavior. A handful of American scholars equipped with Asian languages were then only laying down the foundations for the understanding of unfamiliar cultures, in which the governments and politics of East Asian countries were and are rooted. To understand the dynamic changes inherent in the modernization of Asia and particularly of Japan, this generation of observers has had to go into the field to see the transition firsthand, to break across orthodox disciplinary boundaries and, indeed, to begin to hammer out a whole new approach to the politics of developing areas.

After a brief sketch of historical background, this booklet picks up Japan's politics where the quiet but amazing Occupation of Japan (1945–1952) left off. The Occupation drama has, with few exceptions, been treated with Americans pictured in an active and Japanese in a passive role. Such an ethnocentric approach has, in any case, now been rendered completely academic because the Japanese, since 1952, have once again set about rediscovering their fading past, matching it against their dynamic present, and speculating about their uncertain future.

In this generation and the next, there need be no explanation for inclusion of a booklet on Japan in a series devoted to foreign governments. The reason is simple. To quote Kipling: He who only England knows, knows not England!

This booklet is essentially a distillation of the author's experiences: twenty years' study of East Asia; five years' involvement in civilian and military intelligence projects devoted to wartime Japan; a decade of teaching graduate students, undergraduates, and in-service teachers about postwar Japan; and,

finally, four trips to East Asia, two (1952–1953 and 1958–1959)
involving extended residence and research in the contrasting ways
of life found in agrarian, rural and in commercial, urban en-
vironments within post-treaty Japan.

For support during the two most recent trips, the author is
grateful to the Social Science Research Council; the University
of Michigan Center for Japanese Studies (specifically, to Professors Robert B. Hall, John W. Hall, and Robert E. Ward); the
United States Educational Commission in Japan; the Institute of
Humanistic Studies, Kyoto University (specifically, to Dean
Kosaka Masaaki and Professors Sakata Yoshio and Horie Yasuzo);
and the Research Council and Calm Fund, Rutgers University.

In Japan the author has run up an enormous debt of grati-
tude: to Director Tanabe Sadayoshi, Tokyo Institute of Municipal Research (as well as his son, Tanabe Tatsuro, International
House); to former Rutgers students, Professor Shibata Tokue and
Mr. Takizawa Nobuo, for various data; to Mr. Toda Morikuni
(in 1958–1959, Counsellor, Foreign Service Training Institute
and member of the U.S. Educational Commission), for materials
on the *Gaimusho;* to Dr. Richard W. Rabinowitz and Judge
Tanabe Koji (Japanese Legal Training and Research Institute),
for materials on courts and law; and to Messrs. Kanagawa Buichi
of the Liberal-Democrats, Fujimaki Shumpei and Kamigura Tetsu
of the Social Democrats, for party materials.

Along with a generation of "Mishigan" researchers, the au-
thor is proud to have become an honorary citizen of Okayama
Prefecture. Such acquired rights do not wipe out long-standing
obligations: to Governor Miki Yukiharu, Mr. Araki Eietsu, and
Mr. Ueda Chikao of the Okayama *Kencho;* and to Kawahara
Yukuo of the Okayama *Shiyakuso.*

Back here in America, the author has regularly relied upon
the services of the Japanese Consulate General, New York (and
particularly, Mr. Alan Smith, Information Office) for numerous
materials.

For opportunities both to listen and to sound off, the author
has been fortunate in affiliations with the Council on Foreign
Relations study group on Japan, 1956; with colleagues in the
New Jersey Seminar on Asian Studies, 1960–1962; and with neigh-
bors in the University Seminar on Modern East Asia: Japan,
Columbia University. He has profited from several successive
graduate seminars at Rutgers (specifically, from work by his
Korean graduate student, Mr. Lee Soon-won, and by Mr. Frits

Levenbach, who continued study at the University of Michigan).

Several of the author's colleagues—Professors John Brush, John Hall, Eugene Meehan, Bennett Rich—read parts of the booklet; Dr. Nobutaka Ike, Stanford University, read the entire manuscript. All contributed valuable suggestions but none is in the least responsible for errors.

The reader should note that in citing Japanese names, the author has used Japanese style: the family name followed by the given name.

The author's wife, Jane Burks, typed the manuscript and, following Editor Arnold Rogow's precedent, helped the author to keep the dogs, Sumi-e (who has been to Japan) and Anzu (her *nisei* daughter), from tracking on the copy. To Riki-*chan,* who made his first trip to Japan in 1958–1959 and became the author's skillful guide, this book is dedicated.

A.W.B.

New Brunswick, N.J.
June, 1961

CONTENTS

FIGURES

TABLES

The Government of
Japan

1 - Background I:
The Japanese Rediscover Their Past

Not long ago the Japanese public was startled by the dramatic protest of Prince Mikasa, 45-year-old youngest brother of Emperor Hirohito. The prince, a popular professor of orientology at a women's university in Tokyo, strode out of a general meeting of a historical society in disgust when a motion he had made was ruled out of order. His motion expressed opposition, originally circulated in a magazine (*Nippon Bunkazai*), to the revival of a holiday called *Kigensetsu* (National Foundation Day).[1]

Sharp critics of the prince suggested that he should have voiced his opposition only after he had relinquished his title of Imperial Prince. The prince himself said that as a member of the imperial family, a former army officer, and a scholar, he had a responsibility to denounce the prewar holiday as "without historical foundation." A close friend said the prince had worried over the fact that the emperor system had been exploited in prewar concepts of education. He was thinking more seriously than anyone else about the future of the Japanese imperial family.

[1] In prewar Japan, before the frowns of Occupation authorities, February 11 had always been set aside to celebrate the day in 660 B.C. when, according to Japanese mythology, the first Emperor Jimmu ascended the throne eternal. Later, the prince compiled and sponsored a book of essays entitled *The Dawn of Japan*, written by twenty leading scholars including some who supported revival of the holiday even though they did not subscribe to the mythology. My distinguished colleague, microbiologist and Nobel Prize winner, Dr. Selman Waksman, told me that the last time he enjoyed a long talk with Prince Mikasa, the latter's burning interest in ancient history had led him into the study of Hebrew, so that he might read Biblical literature close to the original.

Despite these questions, emanating from a member of the family, gala *Kigensetsu* celebrations have been revived, particularly at the Kashihara shrine near Nara.

Origins

What the squabble involving Prince Mikasa may obscure is, in fact, the strong sense of continuity the Japanese continue to derive from their own history. The 1,200-year-old view of history —indeed, the 3,000-year-old prehistory, protohistory, and history of Japan—still casts a spell over the Japanese mind. The appeal is to the emotions rather than to the intellect and can be explained more easily in sociological terms of religion than of political science. Since the Japanese have never, save under alien prodding, separated religion from government, the semi-religious myth of Japanese origins obviously has had a persistent effect on politics. And, disregarding for the moment the plodding process of proving or disproving the legends, Japan is beyond doubt the country with the oldest continuous government in the world.

Most Japanese now recognize that the *Kojiki* (Record of Ancient Matters) and the *Nihon Shoki* (Chronicles of Japan), both compiled in the eighth century, were pieced together from tradition in obedience to an imperial command. In other words, the aim of this first historical writing was to establish cultural and educational policy on the basis of loyalty to the imperial family. In general thereafter, Japanese writing of history was regarded as too important an undertaking to be left merely to historians. As in China, historiography in Japan was regarded as a significant political instrument of the state itself. Space does not permit a survey of the 1,200-year pageant of Japanese written history, and so citation of one or two trends must suffice. Motoori Norinaga (A.D. 1730–1801), for example, successfully undertook a review of early Japanese classics with remarkably scientific method. Nevertheless, his *Commentaries on the* KOJIKI also contributed to the sanctions of nationalism and gave the ancient classics the authority of scriptures.[2]

It was not until after the Meiji Restoration in 1868, in theory a restoration of power to the throne, that Western historiography

[2] Motoori Norinaga, *Kojiki-den* (Commentaries on the *Kojiki*). For a convenient overview of the spectrum of historical analysis, see Hugh Borton, "A Survey of Japanese Historiography," *American Historical Review*, XLII (October, 1937 and July, 1938).

was introduced in Japan. A scientific view of history was usually reserved to the educated few, however, and popular understanding of history underwent no drastic change. Later in the age of militarism, Western culture which, on the one hand, enabled scholars to take a detached view of the past, strengthened, on the other hand, the power of the state as a menace to academic freedom. With Japan's surrender in 1945, a reaction to the official view of history set in and it became popular to debunk the glory of Japan and the imperial family. It has been gratifying to note, after the treaty of peace in 1951, that the Japanese have now set about the rediscovery of their past with a more mature attitude.

One difficulty lies, of course, in the fact that now Japanese biologists, anthropologists, and archaeologists debate fiercely the complicated ethno-historical origins of the Japanese people. After a careful survey of the wealth of new data, Professor Richard Beardsley came up with a tentative but useful chronology of ancient Japan:

Dates	Period	Characteristics
? B.C.–2500 B.C.	Early Prehistoric	Nonagricultural
2500 B.C.–250 B.C.	Middle Prehistoric (*Jomon*)	Nonagricultural; handmade pottery
250 B.C.–A.D. 250	Protohistoric (*Yayoi*)	Rice cultivation; social classes; copper, bronze, iron
A.D. 250–A.D. 750	Semihistoric; Historic (*Tomb*)	Earth-mound tombs; iron weapons; Buddhism; Chinese script [3]

Since 1949, when stone implements were unearthed in the loam of Gumma Prefecture, it has been considered safe to push back Japan's prehistoric curtain to the Pleistocene epoch. The finds indicated chipped but not polished stone, no ceramics and, doubtless, no agriculture. Beyond this, knowledge of early prehistoric Japan is hazy, but speculation does hint at both Siberian and Southeast Asian origins of the stone implements. It may be that the waves of migration out of the cultural heartland of Asia had already begun piling up on coastal areas and even spilling over into Japan.

The earliest Neolithic pottery culture, called *Jomon* (literally, "rope-mark"), was also of two distinct types, possibly emanating from Northeast and Southeast Asia. Among the some 15,000 Ainu in Hokkaido and Sakhalien are still some faint echoes of

[3] Richard K. Beardsley, "Japan Before History: A Survey of the Archaeological Record," *The Far Eastern Quarterly*, XIV, No. 3 (May, 1955), p. 320.

remains associated with *Jomon* but, as Dr. Beardsley has pointed out, it is entirely too simple to identify *Jomon* solely with Ainu culture.[4] Certainly by the middle prehistoric period (*circa* 1000 B.C.), Japanese culture was well advanced. Then, about the third or second century B.C., began the first of those great and dramatic confrontations of culture which have successively reshaped Japanese life. Indirectly, the influence of the powerful Chinese Han dynasty (206 B.C.–A.D. 220) was felt in Japan. The relatively primitive nomadic peoples watched the intrusion of migrants who engaged in rice culture and who were metal experts. The two strains fused to provide the stuff of protohistoric (*Yayoi*) culture. Its main base was in Kyushu, closest to the mainland, but the early literary classics also illuminate socio-religious rites and a secret society complex somewhat similar to those found in Melanesia. Similarly, the earliest *taro* or yam culture appears to be connected with the South Seas. In any case, over the edge of Japanese history came the familiar rice paddy field, the root of Japanese culture.

Already too there began to appear the familiar outlines of Japanese social structure: father domination of the family; marriage outside the clan; village organization built around age and class; growth of Altaic languages; and even the myth of *Amaterasu,* the Sun Goddess. By the third or fourth century of our Christian epoch there had clearly emerged a people with considerable political genius, with a society built around a patriarchal clan (*uji*), with marked occupational specialization and slaves, with clan gods (*uji-gami*) and, most significant, with the legend of a chief clan god. Among the various myths which have obviously political characteristics the most important is this story of a deity who conquered the "middle land." It forms the basis for the assertion of sovereign rights of the oldest imperial family in the world. Beyond doubt, it partially accounts for the publicity given the criticism voiced by Prince Mikasa of the doubtful historical foundations of the myth itself!

It seems that a grandson (*Ninigi*) of the Sun Goddess descended from heaven. (Although it is embarrassing to remind the Japanese of this, there is a close parallel here to the so-called Tankun myth of the founding of Korea.) The story merges with the myth of the Emperor Jimmu, whose existence is also problem-

[4]*Ibid.,* p. 318. See also *Japan: Its Land, People and Culture,* Compiled by Japanese National Commission for UNESCO (Tokyo: Ministry of Finance, 1958), pp. 116–118.

atical and who is supposed to have conquered and ruled the realm of Yamato. Beyond doubt a monarchy was established in Yamato, surrounding present-day Nara, by the fourth century. Thus was formed the oldest political tradition of Japan, the tradition of imperial rule under the *Tenno* (literally, the Sovereign of Heaven).

Techniques and Myths

Anthropologists have demonstrated that peoples everywhere are marked off, not so much by characteristics acquired through so-called racial strains, but by their differing social organizations. They are also distinguished by their differing systems of belief, their ideologies. These important weights on the scale of culture have been referred to by Professor Robert M. MacIver as techniques (for example, of governing) and myths (for example, of religion and politics). Incidentally, in this sense a myth is not necessarily an untruth. It is an entirely valid symbol possessing emotional appeal for a large group of people, or an unstated belief, the significance of which may or may not coincide with its historical origin.[5] It is, of course, not the purpose of this book to recount in detail the political history of Japan.[6] Before turning to modern Japanese government and politics, however, it will be useful to summarize some of the persistent and surviving Japanese techniques and myths for the governing of men.

It is obvious from the archaeological and legendary evidence, recounted above, that almost from the beginning, Japanese felt most comfortable when organized in the family and clan, or in what looked like the family and clan. The corollary is the tradition which dictates that Japanese will feel uncomfortable when forced to rely on individual initiative, when expected to operate an impersonal political party, when employed by a detached company, or when precipitated into what is called class struggle.

[5] See Robert M. MacIver, *The Web of Government* (New York: Macmillan, 1947).

[6] This job the author has done in a collaborative comparative study of systems, historically applied: Paul M. A. Linebarger, Djang Chu & Ardath W. Burks, *Far Eastern Governments and Politics*, 2d ed., Part 2, "Japan" (Princeton: Van Nostrand, 1956). In the broader field of literature, humanities and thought the teacher's and student's opportunities to read from original sources (in translation) have been immeasurably expanded by publication of *Sources of Japanese Tradition*, compiled by Ryusaku Tsunoda, William T. deBary, and Donald Keene (New York: Columbia, 1958).

It should be added here, since Japan almost from the beginning
was agrarian, that from ancient times there has been a strong
tradition which runs counter to individual land ownership.

What distinguishes Japanese from Western, more particularly American, society is the fact that the family group is traditionally larger and the web of rights and duties among members
more tightly woven. To understand this phenomenon we must
look in Japanese history, not to the individual or even to the
small family, but to the household. The house (*ie*) thus becomes
a useful bridge upon which we can cross from the family itself
—always a significant training ground for politics—over to the
family as a symbol for the entire society.

Familism in Japan is a product not only of traditional
family structure but also of Japan's 250 years of isolation and
experience with feudalism, from the early seventeenth to the
mid-nineteenth century. As Professor Robert Scalapino pointed
out, in his brilliant analysis of the failure of party democracy in
modern Japan, feudalism set up points of profound influence
and also of resistance.[7]

Influence, in that feudalism strengthened the hierarchical
nature of the family and integrated it into larger social, economic
and political units. Resistance, in that feudalism saw the family
blend into the larger social units, but it never saw the family
completely absorbed by them. Where familism has not broken
down, the side-effects of inequality, hierarchy and family structure on political behavior are striking. Even where it is in the
process of crumbling, under the blows of industrialization, urbanization and atomization, there is a lag in the systems of belief
behind the rapidly changing social organization. "In short,"
wrote Jean Stoezel in a remarkable UNESCO study,[8] "Japanese
culture has no real place for the concept of individualism."

Concepts of family, therefore, have provided the foundation
for myths of social structure and political behavior. They have
had a powerful influence on the myth of the state and on the
techniques of government. How did the latter first appear in
Japan?

[7] Robert Scalapino, *Democracy and the Party Movement in Prewar Japan:
The Failure of the First Attempt* (Berkeley: University of California, 1953),
esp. pp. 130–133.

[8] Jean Stoezel, *Without the Chrysanthemum and the Sword: A Study of
the Attitude of Youth in Post-war Japan* (New York: Columbia University
Press for UNESCO, 1955). The allusion in the title is, of course, to the wartime classic by Ruth Benedict, *The Chrysanthemum and the Sword: Patterns
of Japanese Culture* (Boston: Houghton Mifflin, 1946).

According to partially provable history, Japan's first so-called constitution was written by a prince, Shotoku Taishi (A.D. 573–621). Little more than a policy statement, the prince's code actually rested on moral exhortation and contained no clear idea of a peculiar political structure. The words state and emperor were used, but the emphasis was interestingly upon superior and inferior officials rather than upon existent clan chieftains. In other words, by the sixth century Japanese were already reworking Chinese ideas.

In the seventh century, Japan felt the full impact of the cultural irradiation of a mighty Chinese dynasty. This time it was the T'ang (A.D. 581–618), one of the world's greatest empires, which inspired the Japanese to lay down the foundations of a state. The Taika reform (646) was a blueprint for a structure which was supposed to endure for years. In brief, it called for (1) the nationalization of clan-controlled property; (2) centralization of government; (3) registration of the population; and (4) taxation in kind for the benefit of the Imperial Court. The Taiho code (702) more practically and effectively provided detailed specifications for a Chinese-type system of public administration. Japan acquired, for the first time, departments of religion, war, treasury, and justice, a council of state, controlling boards, and counselors. The basic principles were both Chinese and Japanese, Chinese in organization of the bureaucracy and Japanese in the unique theory of sacred sovereignty. For these reforms were carried out in the name of successive emperors, although not necessarily by their personal acts. The system established was, of course, mongrel and was gradually revised in light of Japanese experience. Yet to this day some features of government can be traced back to their origins in this code: [9]

If government on the T'ang model is considered the first government of a truly civilized and literate Japan, the long period of shogunal government can be considered the second major governmental form.[10]

[9] In 1868–69, for example, the *Jingikan* (Bureau of Shinto worship) took precedence over the *Dajokan* (Council of State), even with modernization of government. In postwar Japan, the older Imperial Household Ministry has became a subdivision of the Premier's office. Two other human examples will suffice: Prince Saionji, last of the elder statesmen, and Prince Konoe, last Japanese prime minister of noble (*kuge*) rank, were actually family descendants of the early bureaucracy, as well as its political heirs. See Chap. 11, "The Japanese Model of a Chinese Empire," Linebarger, Djang, Burks, *op. cit.*, pp. 272 *ff.*

[10] *Ibid.*, p 289.

Between these forms a peculiar Japanese brand of dualism
in government had already appeared, in the years from the
seventh to the twelfth centuries, and a concomitant feudalism
which was to become firmly rooted in Japanese national character. The technique of putting aside the perfect, faultless reigning
instrument, and establishing very practical, administering tools
of government on the other side of perfection, was initiated with
a civil regent (called *Kampaku*). The regency was, in theory, a
spokesman for the emperor himself; as a matter of fact, from
the tenth century on, this post too was inherited, by a member
of the famous Fujiwara family. This phenomenon represented
the persistence of clan politics. It also marked the beginning of
characteristic dualism in government.

Add to these developments the collapse into order of the
old, nationalized land system—with the rise of the characteristic
Japanese *shoen,* or manorial estate—and the economic under-
pinnings of the Taika-Taiho reforms crumbled as well. Japan,
unlike almost every other Asian state, was about to enter upon
her long experience with feudalism.

The establishment by Minamoto Yoritomo of a military
headquarters at Kamakura, a little city south of Yokohama,
marked the beginning of shogunal government and the emergence
of feudalism. In 1192, Yoritomo received the coveted commission
of *Sei-i Tai-shogun,* the barbarian-subduing generalissimo. Here
was Japan's first, frank "tent government" (*bakufu*). Civil dictatorship had merged into military dualism, with which Japan was
to experiment off and on, until 1945. Meanwhile, in effete and
detached Kyoto and in theory, the emperor continued to reign.
The Kamakura era (1185–1338) was the dawn of Japanese feudalism; the Tokugawa period (1600–1868), the zenith and sunset
of the system.

There is today a popular as well as Marxist notion, particularly encouraged by Chinese Communists on the mainland, that
any political and economic system before socialism and capitalism
is feudal. Territorial and personal relationships of a true feudal
character, however, have been rare in the West and in East Asia.
The late Asakawa Kannichi, formerly of Yale University and
an outstanding authority on feudalism of a Japanese or Western
variety, was a good deal more specific. Feudalism, he wrote, has
the following characteristics: a ruling class chained together by
links of loyalty, supported by a divided class structure reflecting
tenures of land, wherein such land holdings condition the exercise of public rights and obligations— ". . . that is, in govern-

ment, in finance, in military affairs, and in the administration of justice there should be a complete confusion or coalescence of the public and the private." [11]

Feudalism did, as we have seen, accentuate Japanese familism and underlined rigid codes of conduct, social inequality and hierarchy. After a brief fusion of imperial tradition and shogunal power in Kyoto (in the Muromachi era, 1336–1600), marred by more than a hundred years of civil war, the Tokugawa family established (at Edo, modern Tokyo) an even more ruthless military dictatorship. Japan was cast in the unyielding mold of what its historians themselves call centralized feudalism, almost a contradiction in terms. Indeed, so well articulated was the Tokugawa *Bakufu* that doubt has been cast on the wisdom of using the term feudal for the system. Perhaps the most significant result, on the debit side, was that for 250 years Japan was practically isolated from the rest of the world. In truth many modern Japanese are unconscious heirs of one of the world's most autarchic and most efficient police states, Tokugawa Japan.

And yet in Japanese feudalism itself may lie significant clues to the political discipline and the strong emphasis on certain legal rights and obligations in Japan to this day. Japan developed a far stricter concept of law than did Old China, for example, because society as well as government rested entirely on the maintenance of feudal rights and obligations. Such historical factors have led Professor Edwin O. Reischauer shrewdly to guess that therein lay part of the explanation of the great difference between the Japanese and Chinese response to the Western challenge and process of modernization. [12]

Careful research, by Western and Japanese scholars alike, is just beginning to awaken an appreciation of the constructive side of the long Japanese feudal experience. Space permits only a sampling of the findings. American historians, for example, who have tried to account for Japan's spectacular rise as a modern power, have usually begun their narrative with the arrival of

[11] Honjo Eijiro, *Nihon shakai-keizai shi* (Japanese socio-economic history) (Tokyo: Kaizosha, 1928), Chap. 5, Part I, *"Hoken no igi"* (The meaning of feudalism); Asakawa Kannichi, "Some Aspects of Japanese Feudal Institutions," *Transactions of the Asiatic Society of Japan*, XLVI (August, 1918), pp. 78–79. Professor Asakawa divided Japanese feudalism into three stages: (i) 1185–1338 (Kamakura); (ii) 1336–1600 (Muromachi); and (iii) 1600–1868 (Tokugawa).

[12] Edwin O. Reischauer, *The United States and Japan* (Cambridge: Harvard, 1950), pp. 166–167. Part 3, "The Japanese Character," is a thoughtful summary.

Commodore Perry's black ships; or they have continued with the largely fictitious account of the barbarian (Consul Harris) and the geisha. To overemphasize the role of the impact of the West is, however, to neglect dynamic changes which occurred in the latter half of the Tokugawa, changes which directed the emergence of Japan as a modern state.[13]

A most important change, so far as effect on government is concerned, was the steady shift of attention on the part of the *Shogun, his Bakufu* headquarters, the local lords *(daimyo)*, and even the *samurai,* from the military arts to those of civil administration. The appearance by late Tokugawa of modern budgetary techniques and the influx into government service of experts, many with a nonmilitary background, meant that Japan had already built up a reservoir of skills and leadership required to run a modern state.[14] Significantly, the last functions to be developed were those concerned with the conduct of foreign relations and diplomacy. But even in those fields, Japan came up to the Restoration in 1868 with a corps of dedicated, experienced negotiators, already tested under fire in dealing with the sea-borne barbarians. The modernization of Japan, as we shall see, was not a sudden or simple process. It is dangerous, in the case of Japan, to assume that the word Westernization can be a substitute for the more complex idea, modernization.

The Modernization of Japan

It is true that, from the sixteenth century onward, dynamic change in Japan as in all of Asia was increasingly paced by the steady intrusion of the Western, secular, nation-state system. To the Japanese themselves, however, the division between the Tokugawa (1600–1868) and Meiji (1868–1912) eras is not therefore as sharp as it has appeared to Westerners, who have been fascinated by the clash of two worlds from the nineteenth century on. Furthermore, as we survey this long and involved process, we cannot avoid the overwhelming impression that what finally occurred in the nineteenth century, so far as it was partially a product of Western influences, was more a Japanization of alien

[13] One of the first reconnaissance studies, lately subject to challenge and revision, was E. Herbert Norman, *Japan's Emergence as a Modern State: Political and Economic Problems of the Meiji Period* (New York: Institute of Pacific Relations, 1940).

[14] Professor John W. Hall, to illustrate this thesis, made a study of *Tanuma Okitsugu, 1719–1788: Forerunner of Modern Japan* (Cambridge: Harvard, 1955).

influences than a Westernization of Japan. In this sense, Japan's emergence from feudalism reflected a tradition of assimilation of Chinese influences in the past; it forecast an absorption of American influences in the future.

This process of modernization was so complex, in Japan, and is today so significant, for all of Asia, that we can safely say that we do not yet have a fully satisfactory interpretation. Japanese scholars themselves admit that their research until now has been occupied with isolated aspects of this transition. Not a few of their works have lacked objectivity, owing to prevailing ideologies. As cases in point, prewar studies concentrated on an emperor-centered historical point of view; many prewar and postwar treatises adopted wholesale dogmas of economic determinism and of the class struggle. There have been available monumental Japanese studies of government leaders and even of the leaders of the democratic movement which opposed the government. Only recently have Japanese scholars begun to study the so-called subleaders in Japan's modernization, the men who interpreted and promoted government policies and who channeled the creative energies of the people into official policies.[15] American scholarship too is increasingly dedicated to an interpretation of this critical process. Here we can only briefly summarize some of the conclusions drawn from the mounting literature on modernization.

The arrival of Russians, British, and Americans from the early to the mid-nineteenth century constituted the occasion for lifting the long seclusion, not the basic cause. Finally, the *Shogun* on November 9, 1867, submitted his resignation to the young Emperor Meiji and this event opened the famous Meiji Restoration. On April 6, 1868, the Emperor took the famous Charter Oath,[16] which seemed to promise establishment of a deliberative assembly. In the years following, a clause in the oath was exploited by those who were to advocate a popular, elective assembly.

Political and economic unification was indeed the great

[15] "A Prospectus for Research and Publication on the Characteristics and Peculiarities of the Modernization of Japan, under the direction of Dr. Kosaka Masaaki, Director," mimeographed. (Kyoto, n.d.). This is the plan for the interuniversity, interdisciplinary *Kindaika* (modernization) seminar, with which the author was privileged to be affiliated during 1958–59, in Kyoto. He has described it for his American colleagues in *"Kindaika," PROD* (Political Research: Organization and Design), II, No. 5 (May, 1959), pp. 3–6.

[16] Reading No. 2, Arthur Tiedemann, *Modern Japan; a Brief History* (Princeton: Van Nostrand, 1955).

accomplishment of the Meiji Restoration. As we have seen,
however, there had already existed in Japan a strong tradition
of a nation-family and even the irregular growth of central
authority. On the other hand, former feudal leaders and their
ideologies strongly colored the transition. A by-product was
modern Japanese bureaucracy. In fact, some authorities have
referred to the new administration as the *Sat-Cho* Shogunate,
named after leaders drawn from the Satsuma and Choshu domains.[17]

Perhaps the most decisive step on the road to centralization
of power and modernization of the nation was the abolition,
in August, 1871, of the old feudal domains (*han*) and their rapid
conversion to new prefectures (*ken*).[18] Parallel to this development and equally significant was the land legislation of 1872–73,
incorporating tax reform (*chiso kaisei*), which led in turn to the
certification of private land ownership. In the 1870s, over 80
per cent of the regime's revenues was derived from the land.

Changes now came with bewildering speed, in the field of
education, in the building of a modern peasant-conscript army
and in the establishment of a navy.[19]

In the 1870s and 1880s, the Meiji oligarchs stripped off the
shells of ancient Chinese nomenclature and got down to the
kernels of Western-type governmental departments. In 1885, the
central administration was completely overhauled and a cabinet,
designed on the Prussian model, was formed with the famous
Ito Hirobumi as the first premier.

The authoritarian prejudices of the oligarchs, their traditional fear of factionalism in the state, coupled with their pre-

[17] Robert A. Wilson, *Genesis of the Meiji Government in Japan, 1868–1871*
(Berkeley: University of California, 1957). The appendices, identifying burea-
cratic personnel, are invaluable.

[18] For a detailed case study, see my "Administrative Transition from
Han to *Ken:* The Example of Okayama," *Far Eastern Quarterly*, XV, No.
3 (May, 1956), pp. 371–382.

[19] Two Japanese monographs originally contributed to the *Kindaika*
seminar, mentioned above, dealt with earlier American and later German influences on educational reform; with the conscription system modeled first
on the French and later the German type; and with the British influence on
the navy: Motoyama Yukihiko, "Mori Arinori no kokkashugi to sono kyoiku
shiso" (Nationalism and educational ideas of Mori Arinori), *Zinbun Gakuho*
(*Journal of Humanistic Studies*), VIII (March, 1958); Umetani Noboru, "Meiji
ishin guntai no kensetsu tosho ni okeru Furansu-shugi no saiyo to Jubusuke
no koken" (The contributions of duBousquet and the adoption of French
principles at the beginning of the establishment of an army during the Meiji
Restoration), September, 1958.

occupation with military readiness and pressing problems of industrialization from the top down, led them to turn—if they turned outward for models—to German theories of the supremacy of the state. They completely rejected theories of representative government. Nevertheless, an opposition built around disaffected *samurai* did make an appearance. In 1874, Itagaki Taisuke organized the first political association and in 1875, representatives of *samurai* and other dissatisfied groups formed the first national party, the *Aikokusha*. Later, the Liberal Party and the Progressive Party entered the lists, but by 1885 the democratic movement had been effectively checked by the oligarchs. While it was not completely destroyed, it never regained its earlier effectiveness.[20]

The capstone of this early modernization was the Meiji Constitution, which was drafted in preparation for the first session of parliament, in 1890. The oligarchs moved slowly, considering the ideas of Kido Koin and his gradualist approach; and those of Okubo Toshimichi, who leaned toward imperial absolutism. The real architect was, however, Ito Hirobumi, who spent the years 1881–1883 in Europe studying Western, chiefly Prussian, constitutional theory. Professor George Beckman has given us an up-to-date account of the drafting:

> While the oligarchs made important political concessions to those groups that demanded a national parliament, the Meiji Constitution was essentially a carefully formulated legal justification of a government in which the oligarchs had only a minimum of responsibility to the people. By the Meiji Constitution, the oligarchs established a body of authoritarian political principles in Western forms as the ultimate defense of their dominant position in the government.[21]

Finally, on February 11, 1889, the emperor, in a court ceremony, promulgated Japan's first modern organic law. Only then did the public learn of its provisions.

The Religions of Japan

Before turning to Japanese political problems of the twentieth century, it will be useful—with some defiance of chronology—to take brief note of Japanese religions as they have developed

[20] See Nobutaka Ike, *The Beginnings of Political Democracy in Japan* (Baltimore: Johns Hopkins, 1950).

[21] George M. Beckman, *The Making of the Meiji Constitution: The Oligarchs and the Constitutional Development of Japan, 1868–1891* (Lawrence: University of Kansas, Social Science Studies, 1957). p. 84.

in the past and to note their present political influence. It is obvious that the *ethos* of a people is intimately related to their public behavior.

SHINTO. Before the introduction of Confucianism and Buddhism from China there was probably no religion in Japan. There was an indigenous cult, a kind of primitive animism, which is often erroneously identified with Shinto (literally, the Way of the Gods). We know, however, that the latter is a word of Chinese origin, first used in Japan of the eighth century. The indigenous cult merged into ancestor worship and Shinto, which, as retranslated across the centuries, fused into the *Yamato-damashi*, the spirit of Japan, the amorphous, many-sided national cult. Along with the underwriting of the claim by the *Tenno* of divine ancestry, there were corollary moral principles: imperial benevolence, mutual affection, the people's welfare and veneration of ancestors.

As influenced by Confucianism—originally not a religion but an ethical system—Japanese came to agree with their Chinese brethren that morality, religion and politics ought to be one in the cultural whole. Dominated by the clan concept, Japan twisted Confucian doctrine to suit its ideas and recognized the superiority of pedigree. Finally, Japanese came to accept literally what Chinese meant figuratively, namely, that the emperor was the source of benevolent government.

Shinto came back into its own with the Restoration in 1868 and the re-emergence of the imperial family as a symbol of power. Striving to appear as citizens of a modern state, the Japanese wrote a constitutional guarantee of freedom of religion. By administrative decree, however, Shrine Shinto (*Jinja Shinto*) was distinguished from Sectarian Shinto (*Shuha Shinto*), and the former drew governmental support.

This official view was reversed in December, 1945, when the Supreme Commander for the Allied Powers directed the Japanese government to abolish official support of Shinto shrines. The new constitution of 1947 guaranteed unqualified freedom of religion and Shinto presumably became just another religion. As such it is difficult to measure in simple terms of number of adherents.[22]

Since the peace treaty, the legal problem of state aid to the

[22] The number of pilgrims to the Ise shrine dropped from a prewar high of 8,000,000 to a low in 1947 of 800,000 and then rose again in 1950 to 2,000,-000 and in 1952 to 3,500,000. One authority placed the number of adherents of *Tenri-kyo* (the most influential sect) at 1,500,000. William K. Bunce, *Religions in Japan* (Rutland: Tuttle, 1955), also, Kuroda Kazuo, "The Cult of the Sun Goddess," *The Japan Times*, March 21, 1959.

Ise shrine has been raised again. To press the issue to the extreme might however place the emperor in an embarrassing position. He can neither disassociate himself entirely from the cult of the Sun Goddess, nor can he actively link himself with any state-inspired revival. Since the emperor renounced claims to divine lineage (by rescript, January 1, 1946), he has identified himself with the new constitution (May 3, 1947), in which he has become the symbol of the state and of the unity of the people, with whom sovereign power resides.

BUDDHISM. The role of Buddhism in Japanese politics is hard to define precisely. From the time of Prince Shotoku (seventh century) and for about 1,000 years, Buddhism was accepted by the court and, more vitally, by the people at large. As a center of learning and a reservoir of literate scribes, it was of great significance. Buddhism has given tremendous inspiration to Japanese art; it has inspired Japanese literature; its impact on the spirit of government is profound. And yet it contributed less than Confucianism or Shinto to the technical processes of government.[23]

Even the casual tourist in Japan after the war has been struck by the museum-like unreality of the great Buddhist temples, in Kyoto for example. Increasingly, the traditional sects have become separated from the main currents of modern life. In the countryside, there is no doubt that the Occupation-inspired land reform dealt a body-blow to Buddhist temples. Buddhism still numbers its adherents in the millions, but increasingly these are the old folk; the youth of Japan are largely indifferent.

"NEW GODS." Christianity is certainly not a new religion in Japan, but perhaps it can be treated here as outside the more traditional faiths. Indeed, Japan's first contact with Christianity dates from the sixteenth century and, by the early seventeenth century, the number of converts approached a half million. In the nineteenth century, scientific rationalism and materialism seemed to offer a better solution to the problem of how Japan can become Westernized without becoming Christianized.[24]

After the surrender in 1945, there was a brief and somewhat artificial fad of Christianity parallel to the interest in *demokura-*

[23] Random statistics drawn from the appendix of Bunce, *op. cit.*, list adherents of sects as follows (1946): *Jodo,* 4,520,535; *Hokke,* 459,987; *Nichiren,* 897,984; *Shingon (Koyasan),* 4,221,110; *Tendai,* 1,137,671; *Zen (Soto),* 6,408,622.
[24] Robert S. Schwantes, "Christianity versus Science; A Conflict of Ideas in Meiji Japan," *Far Eastern Quarterly,* XII, No. 2 (February, 1953).

shi. After the peace treaty, Christianity continued to grow but the rate of increase has slowed down. Recent estimates place the number of Catholics at 250,000, alongside an equal number of Protestants. Today Christianity is a strong influence but one confined to rather specific islands of culture: the right-wing of the Socialists, Moral Rearmament adherents, the Rotary International, and the Y.M.C.A.

When the ninth International Congress for the History of Religions met in Tokyo, in 1958, foreign scholars showed excited interest in the so-called "new religions" (*shinko shukyo*), which have been springing up all over post-treaty Japan. Although followers of all these number not more than eight million (less than one-tenth the population), this figure compares favorably with the membership of the Japan Communist Party (estimate, 40,000). The new religions range from the lunatic fringe, with leaders claiming to be reincarnations of deities, to the philosophically pretentious, including references to Christian Science, psychoanalysis, and nuclear physics.[25]

2 - Background II: Japan in the Twentieth Century

The present and the future are everywhere, of course, products of the past. Japanese editors of a UNESCO-sponsored encyclopedia have correctly applied this universal truth to modern Japan. What is truly remarkable in the cultural attitudes of Japanese, they concluded, "is the coexistence of exclusive and receptive tendencies." [1] The exclusive side is best represented

[25] The religion with the most spectacular success is the revived *Soka Gakkai* (Value Creation Academic Society), with a claimed membership of 1,500,000. As an important political influence, it is further discussed below (Chap. 4); Ueda Haruo, "Unique Buddhist Organization Now a Political Factor," *Mainichi,* July, 24, 1959.

[1] *Japan: Its Land, People and Culture,* compiled by Japanese National Commission for UNESCO (Tokyo: Ministry of Finance, 1958), p. 3.

by the persistence of a way of life which is purely and peculiarly Japanese. Parallel to this tendency is an open-mindedness toward foreign influence, a quality rare in other peoples.

Japan entered the twentieth century already well along the road to conversion from an agrarian, tradition-centered political system to an industrial, modern constitutional monarchy. Yet traditions were not entirely lost. Japan re-emerged in the 1950s, prodded along the road to conversion from a complex oligarchy to a modern, parliamentary democracy. The successive transitions, with occasional reversion to tradition, provide the major theme in Japanese politics of the twentieth century.

The Meiji and the MacArthur Constitutions

Since the late nineteenth century, the drama of Japanese politics has been performed before the backdrops provided by two startlingly different constitutions. The first was the constitution of the empire (*Teikoku Kempo*), or so-called Meiji Constitution, drawn up in 1889 by the oligarchs and promulgated in the name of the emperor. The second is the new constitution of Japan (*Nihonkoku Kempo*), or so-called MacArthur Constitution, drawn up in 1946 largely by American officials in the Government Section of the Headquarters, Supreme Commander for the Allied Powers (SCAP), and promulgated by the emperor in the name of the Japanese people.

The Meiji Constitution was said to have been granted to the people by the emperor and could, therefore, be amended only by him. It purported to define the essential nature of the national polity—the *kokutai* in Japanese jargon[2]—traditionally regarded as located in the "line of emperors unbroken for ages eternal" (Chap. I, Art. I). In the famous phrase of Baron Hozumi Nobushige the organic law embraced theocratic, patriarchal constitutionalism. To all save the most naive Japanese, the emperor's position differed from that of a God in the Western sense. Nevertheless, the Meiji Constitution accurately reflected the widespread view that "the emperor is sacred and inviolable" and is the "head of the empire, combining in himself the rights of sovereignty" (Chap. I, Arts. 3, 4). It is also true that traditionally others exercised this authority. Yet until 1946 the theoretical supremacy

[2] *Kokutai no Hongi; Cardinal Principles of the National Entity of Japan*, trans. by John Owen Gauntlett and ed. by Robert King Hall (Cambridge: Harvard, 1949).

of the emperor was never challenged. With the possible exception of constitutions of certain German monarchies, the Meiji was potentially the most autocratic constitution in the world.

Government under the Meiji Constitution did not, however, have to be absolutist. Japanese mythology had been tempered by the European theory of *Rechtstaat*, which actually brought liberalizing tendencies to Japan. The written constitution itself was an entering wedge. The emperor, by indicating the governmental channels through which his authority was to be exercised, was himself bound. That powers were defined at all implied limitations. The constitution even allowed, in 1912, a major debate over an organic theory of the state.[3]

In sharp contrast, the MacArthur Constitution is revolutionary to the extent that, in theory, it was issued by the Japanese people. In good American phrases, the preamble begins, "We, the Japanese people, acting through our duly elected representatives . . . do proclaim that sovereign power resides with the people and do firmly establish this Constitution." Professor Kazuo Kawai, of Ohio State University, has concluded:

These are most explicit expressions of the doctrine of popular sovereignty, a doctrine completely alien to Japanese thought.[4]

The Meiji Constitution, as we have seen, described an unbroken line of sacred and inviolable emperors (Chap. 1, Arts. 3, 4) under whose benevolent rule subjects' welfare was promoted "according to the provisions of the present Constitution" (Art. 4). The emperor was placed above and beyond inadequate administration, always the responsibility of his ministers of state (Preamble).

Under the MacArthur Constitution, the emperor presumably becomes "the symbol of the state and of the unity of the people, deriving his position from the will of the people with whom resides sovereign power" (Chap. 1, Art. 1). In one sense, the imperial rescript of January 1, 1946, which renounced the "false

---

[3] The Organic Theory (*Kikan Setsu*) debate revolved around the views of two Tokyo University law professors: Uesugi Shinkichi argued in essence that the emperor was the state, thus justifying absolute rule behind the complex institutional screen; Minobe Tatsukichi argued that the *Tenno* was an organ of the state, like the privy council, the cabinet, or the diet. Finally, Minobe suffered under a charge of *lèse majesté* and was forced to resign from the House of Peers. Nonetheless, the mystique of the *Kokutai* had been weakened by constitutionalism.

[4] Kazuo Kawai, "Sovereignty and Democracy in the Japanese Constitution," *American Political Science Review*, XLIX, No. 3 (September, 1955), p. 663.

conception that the emperor is divine," was a prelude to the constitutional provisions; in another, it more accurately stated the fact that "ties between us and our people have always stood upon mutual trust and affection."

Turning to the distribution of powers, the Meiji Constitution provided for the execution of laws and ordinances by the emperor's ministers of state (Chap. 1, Art. 6; Chap. 4, Art. 55), who were responsible to him. Beyond doubt the constitution favored the executive; yet gradually, up to the 1920s, the cabinet came to be a political battleground; the Diet and even political parties gained as vehicles for public expression. The revival of dualism in the 1930s, with constitutional and extra-constitutional supremacy of military over civilian agencies, came to characterize the executive. In constitutional theory, the emperor legislated with the consent of the Imperial Diet (Chap. 1, Art. 5). Thus the Diet could deliberate on laws; it could not determine them. In the opinion of Prince Ito, architect of the constitution, the upper House of Peers (Chap. 3, Art. 34) was designed to protect the organic character of the state; the lower House of Representatives (Art. 35) was to speak for the state as a whole. Overshadowing the operations of both houses and ranking alongside legislation were imperial ordinances (*Meirei*), recognized in the constitution itself (Chap. 1, Arts. 8, 9). The ordinance power was greater than that to be found in any constitutionally guided state of the time. In Prince Ito's words, "It must be remembered that the ultimate aim of a state is to maintain its existence." [5] There was, of course, no judicial review. The courts (Chap. 5, Art. 57) were also administrative organs operating in the name of the emperor.

Under the MacArthur Constitution the Diet, composed entirely of elected representatives, acts as "the highest organ of state power, and shall be the law-making organ of the state" (Chap. 4, Art. 41). It thus inherits the powers stripped from the emperor and exercised by the former executive. It consists of a lower House of Representatives, elected every four years or upon dissolution; and a House of Councillors, whose members sit for six years, half being elected every three years. Executive power is vested in the Cabinet (Chap. 5, Art. 65), which is collectively

[5] All commentaries on the Meiji Constitution return eventually to the basic source, Ito Hirobumi, *Teikoku Kempo koshitsu tempan gikai* (Commentaries on the imperial constitution and the imperial house law) (Tokyo: Maruzen, 1935), an article-by-article analysis. Sections on the constitution were translated into English by Ito Myoji, *Commentaries on the Constitution of the Empire of Japan* (Tokyo: Chuo Daigaku, 1931, rev. ed.).

responsible to the Diet (Art. 66). The "whole judicial power" is vested in a Supreme Court and inferior courts (Chap. 6, Art. 76); the American process of judicial review is provided (Art. 81).

The summary of "Rights . . ." in the Meiji Constitution appears, at first glance, to incorporate many points of modern democratic theory; but favored over rights were the ". . . duties of Subjects" (Chap. 2). Furthermore, rights were subject to the public order and, specifically, could be controlled by legislation. In an emergency, especially war, the sovereign right of the emperor was supreme (Chap. 2, Art. 31).

The longest section (Chap. 3, Arts. 10–40) of the MacArthur Constitution spells out the rights and duties of the people and these are not limited by legislation. The list goes far beyond even the American Bill of Rights, including, for example, rights of academic freedom, collective bargaining and employment.

Formal changes of the Meiji Constitution were made so difficult they never occurred until 1946. Diehards might even say the old constitution was unamendable and, therefore, it has never been amended. In theory, only the emperor could assume the initiative to amend (Preamble). In fact, the Privy Council (Chap. 4, Art. 56) became the "watchdog of the Constitution" and was the only body which dared interpret the organic law. But also, in fact, the constitution was amended by parallel laws and ordinances, by custom and use. Examples include the role of extra-constitutional elder (*Genro*) and younger (*Jushin*) statesmen; the unfortunate separation of military and civil administration; and the ordinances which gave professional militarists direct access to the throne.

In 1946, the drafters of the MacArthur Constitution took elaborate precautions in the attempt to maintain legal continuity during the adoption of the MacArthur Constitution.[6] The old Privy Council was called back into session to approve the new constitution; it was put through both houses of the Diet; and it was promulgated by the emperor. Amendment of the Mac-Arthur Constitution (Chap. 9, Art. 96) has proved almost equally and, for Americans, embarrassingly difficult: the process requires a two-thirds vote by both houses and ratification by a majority of all votes cast in a special referendum among the people.

[6] The problem was exhaustively treated by Alfred Oppler, Chief, Courts and Law Division: "Powers of the Diet with regard to Constitutional Amendments under the Meiji Constitution," Appendix C:15, *Political Reorientation of Japan; September 1945 to September 1948,* Report of Government Section, Supreme Commander for the Allied Powers, Washington, 1949, pp. 662–666.

By way of summary, the Meiji Constitution sought to take account of new social and economic forces by subtly insulating them in the wrappings of modern government. To strengthen a new oligarchy, it exalted the formal powers of the emperor and made certain they were exercised by executive advisers who, being responsible to the emperor, were thus accountable only to themselves. The supreme advantages of the old constitution were that it was entirely compatible with Japanese ideology, and it was buttressed by the entire social organization of Japan.[7] The chief disadvantage was that it permitted, under its more authoritarian provisions, the hobbling of the decision-making process by militarists.

The MacArthur Constitution, as drafted by the Occupationaires, is replete with New Deal philosophy, a monument to the New Deal which had long since died a natural death in America. It was far more radical than proposals by any of the Japanese postwar political parties, save those of the communists. The conclusion of Professor Robert E. Ward was that,

The Government Section patched together an almost ideally democratic constitution, one that could scarcely have gained serious consideration if advocated for adoption in the United States. It had even less relevance to the traditional and dominant political aspirations or practices of Japan.[8]

Beyond doubt the most unusual and controversial feature of the new constitution is the renunciation of war (Chap. 2, Art. 9). By this provision, the Japanese people aspire to international peace and "forever renounce war as a sovereign right of the nation and the threat or use of force as means of settling international disputes." In order to accomplish this aim, "land, sea, and air forces, as well as other war potential *will never be maintained*." [9]

Between these two remarkable constitutions, the Japanese wrote a great deal of political history—including dominance by the oligarchy (1890–1898); the rise of semi-party, *Genro*-controlled cabinets (1898–1917); the emergence of true party cabinets (1918–

[7] See Kawai, *op. cit.,* p. 663.

[8] Robert E. Ward, "The Origins of the Present Japanese Constitution," *American Political Science Review,* L, No. 4 (December, 1956), p. 1,001.

[9] Italics added. Somewhat less unique, since it followed the American extra-constitutional tradition, is the provision (Chap. 5, Art. 66) that all cabinet members must be civilians. To be more precise, the American tradition dictates civilian control of professional military services in our Department of Defense.

1931); the re-emergence of dualism and military predominance (1931–1945); participation in two world wars; defeat punctuated by the first two atomic bombs; and occupation—history which can but scarcely be summarized here. Since the adoption of the later constitution, the Japanese have once again begun a search in their past, attempting to apply its lessons to the future. In this search, which has been accelerated since the peace treaty in 1952, Japanese political issues have revolved around the two constitutions of modern Japan. The remainder of this volume is a more detailed examination of many of these issues, but perhaps four major problems can be identified here: (1) the search for constitutional continuity; (2) the search for a modern, viable relationship between the emperor and the people; (3) the search for a means of maintaining military forces for defense, while avoiding militarism; and (4) the search for a workable administrative structure in face of the pressing social and economic problems of twentieth century Japan.

Constitutional Continuity

It should come as no surprise, in view of the capsule summary of the MacArthur Constitution already given, to learn that it has already been considerably altered in spirit and in practice, if not by formal amendment. A few examples include covert rearmament, with American encouragement; departures in practice from the spirit of local autonomy (Chap. 8); attempts toward and to some extent achievement of centralization, within limits, of police control. Moreover, outright revision of the constitution has become a major political issue.

It is not accurate to say that all socialists (who, incidentally, stand against the pro-American foreign policy of the conservatives) oppose revision of the American-sponsored constitution; nor do all conservatives (who, incidentally, have fashioned the Japanese-American alliance) favor revision of the American-inspired constitution. For example, Yoshida Shigeru, who was premier when the organic law was adopted, feels that it is well designed for modern Japan. Dr. Takayanagi Kenzo, Chairman of the Constitutional Inquiry Committee (*Kempo Chosakai*), after his return to Japan from America in 1958, admitted to the need for revision of certain provisions. He denied, however, that the constitution was a document imposed upon the vanquished by the victor.

It is safe to say, however, that most of the powerful conservative groups which have controlled contemporary Japan have argued that, while the intent of the Occupation's reform was praiseworthy, certain key provisions in the constitution are simply not in accord with Japanese traditions or practices.[10] Most often suggested as reasons for change, or even as specific alterations, have been the following: untraditional, unsatisfactory definition of the status of the emperor and failure to recognize him as the chief of state (discussed below); the need to recognize more extensive, if limited, armament (also discussed below); the need, in the words of the late Premier Hatoyama Ichiro, for "overall revision of the administrative structure;" and finally, the historic fact that the constitution represents alien authorship, in that it was imposed upon the Japanese people by SCAP.

It is also safe to say that most of the several left-wing factions, parties, labor groups, and a wide sector of the intelligentsia have agreed to oppose all efforts at revision, as endangering peace, civil liberties, and democratic rights.[11] Even opponents of revision admit the constitution was a product of the Occupation, but contend that the democratic reform of Japanese politics has occurred under it. Revision is inevitably linked to rearmament; the opposition avers that arguments for rearmament are based on American demands, so that revision once again serves only American interests. Nevertheless, it is safe to predict that public opinion will steadily mobilize behind the movement for limited revision.[12]

At the very least, Americans are now going to have to join Japanese in the rediscovery of their recent past, to face up to our

[10] In 1954, the ruling Liberal Party established its own Constitutional Investigation committee, under the chairmanship of a man later to become premier, Mr. Kishi Nobusuke. There followed a Special Diet committee, whose proceedings were at first blocked in the upper house. In June, 1955, the above-mentioned Constitutional Inquiry committee was formed with thirty Diet members, twenty scholars and experts. Its chairman, Dr. Takayanagi, has listed its objectives: (1) a study of the history of the making of the constitution; (2) a sociological study of the actual operation of the law; and (3) a study of the need for revision of the text, in light of actual operation. Occasional reports of the committee have appeared under the following heading: *Henshu, Kempo Chosakai* (Constitutional Inquiry Committee, ed.), published by *Okurasho Insatsukyoku* (Ministry of Finance), Tokyo, *Seifu Kankobutsu Sabisu Senta* (Government Publications Service Center).

[11] In January, 1954, these groups formed the National League for the Defense of the Constitution.

[12] Miyasawa, Tosiyosi, *Japan's Constitutional Problems and Her Political Chart* (Tokyo: Ministry of Foreign Affairs, The Japan's Problems Series, 1956). See also Robert E. Ward, "The Constitution and Current Japanese Politics," *Far Eastern Survey*, XXV, No. 4 (April, 1956).

moral responsibility for helping to shape that past. At most, Americans are going to have to be patient while our Japanese friends struggle with the problem of revision. We have steadily increasing historical data, uncovered by American and Japanese scholars alike, information which demonstrates why alien authorship of the constitution can be so readily exploited.

The story, which can only briefly be retold here, begins with the surrender of Japan in 1945. Most critical in that surrender was the famous Potsdam Proclamation, which came to define the "conditions" of "unconditional surrender." [13] After he had studied the terms, Baron Hiranuma Kiichiro, one of the emperor's chief advisers, sought specific assurances that Potsdam did not prejudice "the prerogatives of His Majesty as a sovereign ruler." [14] The Allies' reply [15] was deliberately ambiguous, for they wanted the emperor's help in engineering the surrender and at the same time, they wanted to leave open the future form of the Japanese government. The issue was eventually resolved by the emperor himself, who was certain his prerogatives were not endangered by the surrender. The role of the emperor in the close of the war was thus central.[16] Indeed, the surrender was apparently effected to protect the famed *kokutai*, the national polity of Japan.

Allied policy for Japan thus opened on a note of ambiguity, a basic dilemma shadowed the later constitutional reform, and this dilemma has since provided a foundation for the revision movement. The Potsdam Proclamation promised elimination of leaders of conquest (Section 6), removal of obstacles to the revival of democracy (10) but also, at the same time (12), withdrawal of occupying forces when "there has been established in accordance with the freely expressed will of the Japanese people a peacefully inclined and responsible government." Even Japanese experts now concede that, despite assurances by leaders to themselves and to the people that national polity remained unbroken, in acced-

[13] "Proclamation Defining Terms for Japanese Surrender, July 26, 1945," The Department of State, *Occupation of Japan; Policy and Progress* (Washington: Publication 2671; Far Eastern Series 17, 1946), Appendix 3, pp. 53–55.

[14] First Japanese Offer of Surrender, Aug. 10, 1945," *ibid.*, Appendix 4, pp. 56–57.

[15] "Reply to First Japanese Offer of Surrender, by Secretary of State Byrnes, Aug. 11, 1945," *ibid.*, Appendix 5, pp. 57–58.

[16] Prince Higashikuni, who had formed the surrender Cabinet in 1945, in addressing the Diet a few days after the surrender, said: "The termination of the war has been brought about solely through the benevolence of our Sovereign." *Nippon Times*, September 6, 1945.

ing to the "freely-expressed will" clause, Japan did fundamentally affect the traditional *kokutai*. On the other hand, the Allies too assumed a deep moral responsibility.

In the very first days of the Occupation, constitutional reform carried no high priority.[17] The Japanese welcomed this respite and chose a gambit of delaying tactics.[18] As late as January 30, 1946, General Douglas MacArthur assured visiting Allied representatives that constitutional reform was not within his powers. One month later, however, he had decided the best way to prod reform was to prepare a model constitution for the Japanese. Within another three weeks, an entirely new constitution was drafted by SCAP officials. Symbolically, on Washington's birthday, Japan accepted the basic principles of the constitution. By March 5, the emperor had approved the "drastic revision." By late June, the Japanese had writhed through four drafts, which were but slight revisions of the original document. By October 7, the new constitution had passed both houses of the Diet, under tremendous pressure from SCAP, and had been approved by the defunct Privy Council. On November 3, 1946, the emperor promulgated the new constitution of Japan, which went into effect May 3, 1947. As Professor Ward has put it, this awesome display of speed and efficiency represents a world record for devising and gaining acceptance of a constitution for a modern state. "For all practical purposes, then," he wrote, "the so-called 'MacArthur Draft' became the constitution of Japan." [19] American scholars, as well as Japanese students and experts, have since been rewriting the veritable detective-story explanation of

[17] The first steps were taken by George C. Atcheson, Jr., political adviser assigned by the Department of State to SCAP, in conversations with Prince Konoe Fumimaro. Atcheson did not advocate elimination of the *Tenno* system, but suggested democratic reforms. On November 1, 1945, SCAP announced pointedly that Konoe had not been chosen to revise the constitution. In December, Konoe was indicted as a war criminal and committed suicide. Theodore McNelly, "The Japanese Constitution: Child of the Cold War," *Political Science Quarterly*, LXXIV, No. 2 (June, 1959), pp. 176–195.

[18] In October, 1945, Prime Minister Shidehara Kijuro appointed a special investigation committee with Minister of State Matsumoto Joji, chairman. The Matsumoto committee continued to study reform until shocked into action by SCAP, in February, 1946. See Sato Tatsuo, "The Origin and Development of the Draft Constitution of Japan," *Contemporary Japan*, XXIV (1956), Nos. 4–6, 7–9.

[19] Ward, "The Constitution," *loc. cit.*, p. 54. Although SCAP's own official history included several of the other Japanese drafts, it omitted this most important document in *Political Reorientation, op. cit.* The draft was first published in Japan, in September, 1954; the English-language, mimeographed text was reproduced in *Contemporary Japan, XXIV* (1956), Nos. 4–6, 7–9.

why this process was used and why speed was considered so necessary.

Some observers have explained the headlong rush primarily as a product of American intra-governmental rivalry.[20] It is true that on one point the Supreme Commander and Washington policy-makers were in agreement: the "freely-expressed will" commitment could not take precedence over the need to reform basic law, altered to provide a responsible Japanese government.[21] Nevertheless, no United States government agency ever suggested permanent disarmament for Japan. Nor can there be any doubt that SCAP violated the spirit of one specific directive: "Only as a last resort should the Supreme Commander order the Japanese government to effect the above listed reforms, as the knowledge that they have been imposed by the Allies would materially reduce the possibility of their acceptance and support by the Japanese people for the future." [22] This was not, of course, the last time General MacArthur asserted the right to independent, autonomous power of a military theater commander.

Naturally, in light of these circumstances, a lively dispute has since sprung up among both Americans and Japanese concerning the degree of coercion involved. General Courtney Whitney, Chief of Government Section of SCAP, later admitted that at one critical point in the proceedings he threatened "to lay the issue before the people" and that, actually, he had no authorization by General MacArthur to say this. (The Japanese had an acute fear of drafting the constitution in the open market.) At another point in the negotiations, General Whitney excused himself for a brief stroll "in the atomic sunshine." [23] Both Minister Matsumoto, chairman of the old constitutional committee, and Profes-

[20] Professor Ward, "The Origins," *op. cit.,* p. 989, refers to the common knowledge in Washington, during the early stages of the Occupation, that relations between the Department of State and SCAP were scarcely cordial.

[21] Dr. Takayanagi himself concurred in this point: "Making of the Japanese Constitution: What Really Happened" (an address, Harvard Club, Tokyo, March 9, 1959), *The Japan Times,* March 16, 1959. See also Ward, "Origins," *op. cit.,* p. 991; and McNelly, *op. cit.,* pp. 183–184.

[22] This was the now-famous State-War-Navy Coordinating Committee (SWNCC, pronounced "Swink") directive, SWNCC-228, Jan. 7, 1946. Professor Ward, *op. cit.,* first summarized parts of the directive; the Constitutional Inquiry Committee of Japan was supplied a copy in 1958; and McNelly, *op. cit.,* pp. 183–184, summarized the important "Discussion" in his article.

[23] Courtney Whitney, *MacArthur: His Rendezvous with History* (New York: Knopf, 1956), pp. 250 *ff.* General Whitney's later letter to the Constitutional Inquiry Committee tried to make clear that he did not mean to threaten the status of the emperor. McNelly, *op. cit.,* p. 187.

sor Ward have charged that the ominous threat, "the person of
the emperor could not be guaranteed" unless the MacArthur
draft was seriously considered, was most significant. There was at
the time a danger that the Allies would indict the emperor as a
war criminal. General Whitney himself has claimed (and Professor McNelly believes it to be true) that he intended only to ad-
vise on what had to be done to save the institution of the emperor. In either case, as Dr. Takayanagi has admitted, everyone
knew the proceedings were conducted under close SCAP supervision. In this sense the cause of so-called democratization may
have been poorly served. Changes were imposed by military fiat,
as they had been in the 1930s.[24]

Other observers have come to explain the unseemly haste as
a product of Allied inter-governmental rivalry. Professor McNelly has celebrated the MacArthur Constitution as a "child of the
Cold War." Dr. Takayanagi concluded: "A complex of international factors was in play when the present constitution was
drafted." [25] In this version of the process, the critical turning
point was December, 1945, when the Big Three Foreign Ministers, meeting in Moscow, set up the eleven-nation Far Eastern
Commission. Its terms of reference, with regard to constitutional
reform, are of interest:

Any directives dealing with fundamental changes in the Japanese
Constitutional structure or in the regime of control, or dealing with
a change in the Japanese Government as a whole will be issued only
following consultation and following the attainment of agreement in
the Far Eastern Commission.[26]

General MacArthur had not been consulted with regard to
establishment of the commission and his bitterness over its appearance was ill disguised. It now seems apparent that General
Whitney persuaded the Supreme Commander that, if he desired
to avoid intervention by international bodies, reform should be
hastened and should technically be instituted by the Japanese.
The Far Eastern Commission, as well as the Department of State,
were completely surprised when they first saw the draft constitution on March 5, 1946. They faced a *fait accompli,* however, a
draft publicly approved by the Japanese Cabinet, the emperor,

[24] Kawai, *op. cit.*

[25] Takayanagi, Kenzo, "Review of the Constitution" in "Guest Column,"
The Japan Times, July 27, 1959.

[26] *Occupation of Japan, op. cit.,* Appendix 12, pp. 69–73; also The Department of State, *The Far Eastern Commission, 1945 to 1952,* Washington: Publication 5318, Far Eastern Series 60, December, 1953.

the Supreme Commander (who technically had never issued a directive to the Japanese). Both SCAP and, somewhat less enthusiastically, the American Secretary of State maintained the myth of Japanese initiative. The Russians and others represented on the Far Eastern Commission, including the Australians, expressed severe doubt that the constitution was a product of the free will of the Japanese.

Now, finally, from the Japanese point of view, why the haste in accepting a constitution of so obviously alien authorship? In Italy and West Germany, where constitution drafting was also under Allied supervision, materials were prepared from the outset by Italian and German jurists. It is now equally apparent that Japanese leaders at the time saw eye to eye with SCAP, far more than we had previously believed possible, and regarded the draft as a lightning rod constructed to ward off further damage to the state. Both the Japanese and SCAP were fearful that the U.S.S.R. and others on the Far Eastern Commission were determined to propose a republic for Japan and elimination of the emperor system.[27] General MacArthur later wrote directly and succinctly to Dr. Takayanagi to this effect:

> The choice was alien military government or autonomous civil government. . . . My fixed determination and purpose was to avoid such violent discrimination and to reconstruct Japan's sovereignty along modern and liberal lines as soon as practicable.[28]

This basic motivation has since been obscured by controversy over the unique self-renunciation of force (Art. 9). In his letter to Dr. Takayanagi, General MacArthur claimed that Premier Shidehara had first suggested the clause (Baron Shidehara repudiated this statement shortly before his death). It was inserted for the same reason Shidehara had drafted the imperial rescript of January 1, 1946, as means of mollifying the Allies and of preserving the emperor system. Therein lies the original dilemma.

Had the MacArthur Constitution been presented to the Japanese people as a sharp break with tradition, necessitated by revolutionary developments, it might possibly have been accepted and have been acceptable. Instead, the fiction was continued that the MacArthur was only an amendment of the Meiji

---

[27] Professor McNelly states that Colonel Charles L. Kades and Commander A. Rodman Hussey, SCAP aides, in strictest confidence warned Narahashi Wataru, Chief Cabinet Secretary, of the possibility of a republic and the elimination of the throne; *op. cit.*, pp. 187–188.

[28] Takayanagi address, *loc. cit.*

Constitution, adopted by the people of Japan. Yet the bill itself clearly indicated it was first drafted by American lawyers. Only two changes of primary institutional significance were made from the original SCAP draft: one, a concession to the Japanese, provided the bicameral form of Diet; the other widened the American concept of judicial review. In the House of Peers, at the last moment, Professor Nambara Shigeru officially pointed to the alien authorship and questioned the wisdom of the whole procedure.[29]

The emperor had ordered surrender in order to protect the national polity; again "enduring the unendurable," he had ordered acceptance of the alien draft; nevertheless, equally obviously the *kokutai* was fundamentally affected by adoption of this draft. In the Diet, under searching questioning, Minister of State Kanamori Tokujiro tried to rationalize the ancient sovereignty and the new democracy: the substance of sovereignty, he said, lies in the "people as an organized entity, inclusive of the emperor." Another sophistry held that the emperor's position rested on moral, not legal, foundations and thereby, the moral *kokutai* remained unchanged.[30] As a matter of fact, such fictions were entered into not to subvert the MacArthur Constitution but to get it passed by any means, for reasons we have examined. Paradoxically, as Professor Kawai has pointed out, the appearance of the MacArthur Constitution at first filled Japanese liberals with consternation. They welcomed the objective, a challenge to reactionary concepts of the *kokutai;* they were worried about the means, concepts of popular sovereignty with which reactionaries had always and easily smeared liberals in Japan. Furthermore, the constitution was imposed from the top down, just as in 1889, and by military men (this time, Americans), just as rules were imposed by militarists in the 1930s. The method made practically inevitable a political movement to revise, some day, the MacArthur Constitution.

In 1958 when Dr. Takayanagi visited the United States and, through a misunderstanding, was denied a personal interview with Generals MacArthur and Whitney, the Japanese press widely commented on the unfavorable psychological reaction among the Japanese. *The Japan Times,* usually sympathetic to the United States, assured Americans they need have no qualms about the Occupation. Under it, the United States was primarily responsible and could take credit for many fine, democratic re-

---

[29] Takayanagi address, *loc. cit.*
[30] Cited and discussed in Kawai, *op. cit.,* p. 667.

forms. "What is needed now," the newspaper continued with regard to the constitution, "is a dispassionate reassessment of the great experiment by both the former occupier and the formerly occupied." [31]

The Emperor and the People

Perhaps enough has already been said about the central role of the emperor in the surrender, in his own imperial rescript, in the adoption of the new constitution, and, from a revisionist point of view, the anomalous status accorded him in the new organic law. Later, the precise relationship of the emperor to the modern Japanese executive will be described (in Chap. 5). Here a few thoughts can be hazarded concerning the political issue and the future of the imperial institution in twentieth century Japan.

Perhaps the original Allied dilemma, which created the status of a hybrid somewhere between the traditional *kokutai* and popular sovereignty, is now only of historic interest. From the viewpoint of political science, however, it is worth noting that neither the Meiji nor the MacArthur Constitution accurately defined the position of the emperor in relation to the actual conduct of government. The *Tenno* has not usually been a source of political decision; as in the case of the United Kingdom, the monarch has not been just a symbol. The emperor has been an important part of government.[32]

From the sheer historical point of view, some restoration of theoretical authority with popular controls (as expounded in the organic theory), is almost inevitable. In a parliamentary system, since the premier represents only a party, the monarch can play an important role in representing the whole people. Advocates of revision, like former Premier Kishi, urge that the emperor be restored to the position of head of state, for example, to accredit diplomatic missions to foreign countries.[33] Proponents of this view do not argue for a return to absolutism or a rejection of popular sovereignty. Even outside, objective observers have argued that a partial restoration might serve to strengthen democratic development by re-establishing it on a sounder historical foundation.[34]

[31] *The Japan Times,* November 30, 1958.

[32] So argued the distinguished American authority, Professor Harold S. Quigley, "Modern Monarchy in Japan," *The Japan Times,* June 30, 1959.

[33] Miyasawa, *Constitutional Problems, op. cit.*

[34] Kawai, *op. cit.,* p. 672.

Even the Japanese word for symbol (*shocho,* in Chap. 1, Art. 1 of the constitution) again represents an alien concept. Americans had somehow to define a symbol, although a true symbol cannot be conveyed in legal terms and, indeed, may be out of place in a constitution. A symbol is usually inanimate, a rose, a maple leaf or a flag. Furthermore, the relationship between a symbol and that which is symbolized cannot be determined by parliamentary deliberation but by entirely subjective, emotional, and even intuitive mental processes. At this stratum, deep below surface law but slowly permeated by long-range changes in Japanese social structure and mores, the fate of the imperial family will be determined.

Militarism vs. Antimilitarism

Again, perhaps enough has been said about the inclusion in the MacArthur Constitution of the unique Article 9—the self-renunciation of force—and why it was inserted. The effect of the clause on executive functions (Chap. 5 below) and Japan's foreign relations (Chap. 11), as well as its interpretation by the Supreme Court (Chap. 8), must be further discussed. Here, the fateful rise of militarism in prewar and wartime Japan and the persistence of antimilitarism in the postwar era must be weighed as one of the dominant political themes of twentieth century Japan.

Unfortunately, the pattern of war in modern Japan cannot be compressed into the mold that reactionary politics led to militarism and militarism led to extreme reaction. In the first tentative experiments with force as an instrument of policy, the so-called liberal opposition to the oligarchy demanded military solutions as readily as did the government. In the Sino-Japanese War, 1894–95, the Russo-Japanese War, 1904–05, and World War I, most Japanese found that war solved many of Japan's internal problems, if it did not pay. After 1937, Japan was in uninterrupted conflict for almost eight years. Before and during the great Pacific War, Japan did develop several blueprints for a monolithic, war-dedicated state. Yet characteristic diffusion of power and the failure to mobilize completely not only led to defeat but also has cast doubt on the wisdom of applying the word fascism, like so many other Western political terms, even to wartime Japan. In the long and tortuous process of modernization the Japanese did, of course, become thoroughly familiar with militarism.

In other words, Japan down to 1945 could be described as

another of those thoroughly modern nations in which military factors had become dynamic shapers of policy and even of culture, rather than instruments in the hands of policy-makers. The now famous Article 9 may have been inserted on Japanese initiative for subtle reasons, to protect rather than to subvert the national polity. It was certainly subscribed to by General MacArthur himself, whose own note-directive to Government Section suggested Japan's renunciation of war "even for preserving its own security." American lawyers in SCAP were skeptical and, fortunately, deleted this clause. Seven months after the drafting of the MacArthur Constitution and four months before its promulgation, the Supreme Commander concurred in revisionist interpretations. The article was never intended to limit self-defense, he argued. These first pronouncements, not entirely straightforward in admission of mistake, laid the first stones in the foundations of antirearmament and anti-American sentiment.

It is significant that rearmament—constitutionally or extra-constitutionally—has had to proceed slowly and surreptitiously. Proponents of rearmament themselves do not like the constitutional basis and urge revision.[35] Nonetheless, the plea for openly legitimizing rearmament is the weakest argument in the revisionists' arsenal. Self-righteous Americans, whose contacts are strictly limited to Japanese officialdom in Tokyo, and timid Japanese leaders, who have not dared meet the issue head-on, assure themselves that the opposition is limited to radical left-wing elements and hare-brained students. In the far more honest and informed view of Matsumoto Shigeharu, Director of the Rockefeller-backed International House of Japan, disguised rearmament "has been brought about against the sentiment of a large segment of the Japanese population." [36]

Militarism in Japan may not be "gone forever," as Kakitsubo Masayoshi, deputy Japanese delegate to the UN, told an American audience; nonetheless, since the end of the war the demand for a pacific, civilian government in Japan has been overwhelming. If pacifist and antinuclear armament feeling in Japan is not a new religion of almost fanatical sort, it is at least a deep, emotional response which has had a powerful effect on the definition of national interest. An objective view raises the question of

[35] Dr. Takayanagi thinks the war-restrictive clause should be changed in light of current conditions. *The Japan Times,* December 5, 1958.

[36] Address to Fulbright scholars, Tokyo, October 7, 1958; see, by the author, "Ideological Issues Facing Japan Today," *SAIS Review,* Washington, School of Advanced International Studies, Summer, 1959.

whether a medium-scale power like Japan can mount a viable diplomacy in the modern world, free from inferiority complex, without military capability.[37]

Nor does the Supreme Court decision, in 1959, satisfactorily solve the dilemma. Critics like university president Ouchi Hyoe have challenged the government: either forthrightly try to amend the constitution or drop bilateral security pacts and rearmanent. A Japanese newspaper took a slightly different tack:

Pacifism and democracy, manifested in the present constitution, were foundations for building a postwar Japan and they should not be subject to change under any circumstances. However, the people's responsibility to defend their country should be clearly stipulated in the supreme law.[38]

The Geography and Economics of Sovereignty

Now there is always a danger that we shall attribute to an unbroken line of emperors eternal, to the modernizers of Meiji Japan, and to the democratizers among MacArthur's Occupationaires, the roles of supermen. No matter what any of these may have done, we should never overlook the simple facts that nature has made Japan an island country; that Japan has been endowed with great physical beauty and has been denied the elemental resources needed in a modern nation; and that, within the context of persistent tradition, Japanese society has been as much shaped by the unchanging facts of geography and pressing needs of the economy. It is now high time we turn to these less controversial aspects of the land, people and society of Japan.

3 - The Land, People, Economy and Society

Japan and its beautiful but rugged terrain are more easily described in literary fashion than in the objective terms of the

[37] See Chap. 11, below.
[38] President Ouchi's remarks were carried in *Sekai,* September, 1959; the quotation is from *Mainichi,* May 4, 1959.

earth sciences. The physical structure resultant from awesome volcanic disturbances is something like Japan's social fabric, a sort of fault line between East Asian and Western cultures. For sheer grandeur of scenery Japan is a tourist's paradise. The neighborliness of mountain and sea, celebrated in art and in a Japanese word (*sansui*), makes for fascinating vistas. Nature has blessed the Japanese islands in several ways: a significant location, magnificent landscapes and many Japanese people. On balance, however, these assets are weighed against heavy liabilities.

Geography

Persistent tradition refers to Japan as an island-nation located in the Far East. Even today, to the extent that it is at the very eastern terminus of a traditional sea-route—Western Europe, Mediterranean, Suez, Ceylon, Malacca, Hongkong, Taiwan, Kobe —it is indeed the "Farther East." Express service on French steamships of Messageries Maritimes still requires thirty-two days from Marseilles to Kobe. As viewed from the continent of Asia, historically and culturally Japan has been Eastern Asia, out on the rim of the famous Sinic node of civilization near the "root of the sun" (*Nihon*).

During World War II Americans tended to think of Japan as the western rim of the Pacific Ocean areas, reached by island hopping via Hawaii and Wake toward the Far West. Japan Air Lines still uses this relatively slow route. Pan American Airways jet aircraft have recently cut the flight time, Tokyo-San Francisco, to 12 hours 50 minutes.

Both Japanese and Americans think of the route used by Northwest-Orient Airlines—Tokyo, Anchorage, New York— whereby Japan has become the Far North or even the Near West. Japanese now advertise one-day delivery on high quality cameras, via this new, great circle polar route. Even by new, fast S-class NYK freighters, however, ordinary freight takes ten days across the North Pacific to San Francisco, and an additional thirteen days via the Panama Canal to New York.

Looking out from Japan, from a strategic point of view, the physical proximity northwest to the Soviet Union, west to the peninsula of Korea and continental China, and southwest to Southeast Asia is the significant geographic relationship. Nevertheless, geographers call Japan a natural region, with distinct boundaries and a uniform way of life.

In tectonic structure, the Japanese islands are part of the

family of grand mountain ranges which rim the Pacific Basin. Measured from sea bottom, the peaks rise from 18,000 to 27,000 feet in height, but in fact only the upper slopes and peaks are above sea level. On each side of the islands are vast trenches, 11,000 feet deep in the Sea of Japan to the west and 34,000 feet deep off Tokyo Bay to the east. When one realizes that beautiful Mt. Fuji rises symmetrically to 12,800 feet above sea level, within sight of Tokyo, he can understand the tremendous stresses and strains inherent in the vertical differential of 7–8 miles within about one degree of latitude. Most of Japan, then, has relatively steep slopes, over two-thirds of the land area being mountainous.[1]

This festoon of volcanic islands lies in four great arcs, convex toward the Pacific Ocean. Each intersection of arcs is marked by a knot of highlands with associated clusters of volcanoes (there are a total of 500 in Japan, fifty active). The four principal islands— Hokkaido, Honshu, Shikoku, Kyushu—form one bow (under Japan's jurisdiction). This is crossed in the north by the sweeping Kuril Islands arc (still under Soviet occupation); at the Tokyo Bay area by the Mariana-Ogasawara (Bonins)-Izu arc (part still under American occupation); and in the southwest by the Ryukyu Islands arc (Okinawa, still under American occupation).

Topography offers spectacular indentations, suitable for fishing, along the 17,000-mile coastline. Japan's mountains have deeply influenced the culture, social life and economy of the people. Even today Japanese in the remote valleys of Shikoku and Kyushu have retained their ancient customs, cut off from modern currents of life.

The size of the main islands can easily be underestimated. It is true that Japan is now smaller than France or prewar Germany, but it is larger than either Italy or Great Britain. The four main, together with smaller adjacent, islands total 142,000 square miles (the state of Montana, 147,000 square miles). Since mountains cover about six-sevenths of the total area, however, Japanese occupy and cultivate only about 25,000 square miles of lowlands (about half the area of Ohio). These plains are scattered and discontinuous: the Kanto, around Tokyo; the Ishikari, around Sapporo; the Echigo, around Niigata; the Nobi, around Nagoya; the Sendai, around the city of the same name; the Settsu, around Osaka; and the Tsukushi, in North Kyushu.

It is perhaps better to think of landform regions, made up of

[1] *Japan: Its Land, People and Culture*, compiled by Japanese National Commission for UNESCO (Tokyo: Ministry of Finance, 1958), Chap. 2, "Natural Features," pp. 91–96.

plains between mountains.[2] First, there is Hokkaido, excepting
the southwest peninsula, extending from Sapporo to Hakodate;
Hokkaido is mountainous but rounded. The peninsula regionally
belongs to northeast Japan, which extends through northern
Honshu and consists of plains woven between mountains. Central
Japan is a complex which includes the photogenic Japan Alps
and two great plains. Southwest Japan includes southern Honshu,
Shikoku and Kyushu.

Japanese soils are most influenced by topography and climate. Since three-fourths of the country is mountainous or
ruggedly hilly with slopes exceeding 15°, much of the area is
unfit for cultivation. Even the plains are mixed, diluvial uplands
with deep water tables (as in the case of the Kanto Plain around
Tokyo) and alluvial lowlands on which agriculture is carried out.
Urban settlement, industry and transportation, however, compete
for the use of choice land, so that less than 16 per cent of Japan's
total area is under cultivation.

One other meaningful classification of regions sorts out four
major nodes of industry, which lie in an urbanized belt between
Tokyo and northern Kyushu and account for 80 per cent of all
manufacturing output. The *Kei-Hin* (Tokyo-Yokohama) includes
the capital, industrial Kawasaki, the port of Yokohama and naval
facilities at Yokosuka. This great complex is diversified in iron
and steel, optics, beer, printing, banking and commercial activities, and accounts for over 30 per cent of Japanese production.
The *Han-Shin* (Osaka-Kobe) embraces a triangle at the eastern
end of the inland sea from Wakayama and the port of Sakai to
Osaka and the port of Kobe, out to the western edge at Himeji;
and it reaches north to the *Kei-Han* (Kyoto-Osaka), including the
dormitory, craft and tourist center of Kyoto. Industry in *Han-
Shin* is heavy and diversified: steel, shipbuilding, commerce,
finance and newspapers. Kobe handles 35 per cent of Japan's foreign trade. *Nagoya*, with its port of Yokkaichi, is an automotive,
textile and pottery center. *Yawata* in northern Kyushu is at the
core of the most intense concentration of heavy industries, including iron and steel. The complex stretches from Fukuoka
through Yawata-Kokura-Tobata-Wakamatsu to Moji, and even

[2] A. Watanabe, "Landform Divisions of Japan," *Bulletin of the Geographical Survey Institute,* II, Part 1 (Tokyo, 1950), pp. 81–94, cited and ably summarized in Norton Ginsburg, ed., *The Pattern of Asia* (Englewood Cliffs,
N.J.: Prentice-Hall, 1958), p. 67. For a more detailed breakdown, see Glenn
Thomas Trewartha, *Japan: a Physical, Cultural & Regional Geography* (Madi-
son: University of Wisconsin, 1945), Part 3.

across the straits to Shimonoseki. Ports and rails handle metals, cement, chemicals, glass and even coal for export.[3]

As we shall see (Chapter 10), Japan is politically subdivided into forty-six units, including one capital prefecture (*to*), two metropolitan prefectures (*fu*), and forty-three rural prefectures (*ken*). Traveling on the main railway lines in Japan even today, one can sense the geographic outlines of older feudal domains. The train departs from a former castle town, like Himeji in Hyogo Prefecture; it chugs across a broad rice plain, which formerly measured the economic power of a feudal lord in kind, and climbs painfully up a winding mountain pass; the train emerges from a tunnel, which short-cuts the top of the pass, and rapidly descends into another fertile rice plain, in the center of which is the next former castle-town, Okayama. From Okayama one ascends over another pass and descends into Hiroshima, and so on. When the modern prefectures were created in 1871, an attempt was made to amalgamate the former provinces, as far as tradition and natural boundaries allowed. Agrarian, industrial and tax-rich coastal plains match the inner, tax-poor plateaus and mountains. In some cases, prefectural tax revenues exceed the national subsides to the prefecture; in others the reverse is true.

Climate

Japan is a middle-latitude country marked by great variations of rainfall and extreme temperatures. The relatively wide variety of climate has had a great influence on the manners, customs and productivity of the Japanese people. There are four major influences on Japan's weather.

The wide latitudinal spread of Japan obviously is the major influence. Its extremes are something like the climate of Jacksonville, Florida, and that of Quebec, Canada. For agricultural purposes, Hokkaido has 140 frostless days in a year; Kyushu ranges up to 300 days.

Japanese climate is monsoonal, with cold, dry, continental air in winter, and humid, tropical, maritime air in summer. During winter months, the railways wage a constant battle to keep main lines into the Japan Sea coastal area free from snow drifts. In mid-August, civil servants in Tokyo suffer as much as Washington bureaucrats did on the banks of the Potomac before the advent of air-conditioning.

Since Japan is an island-nation, it constantly feels the effects

[3] Ginsburg, *op. cit.*, Chap. 6, pp. 115–119.

of the sea on climate. The Black Current (*Kuro Shio*) warms southern and central coasts clear up to Tokyo. Out of the Bering Sea flows the *Oyashio* Current, which cools all the northeast coasts. And out of the south, six or seven times a year, roar typhoons (*tai-fu:* literally, big wind) which destroy people, houses and crops, and call the Japanese Diet back into special session to pass emergency and relief measures.[4]

Finally, the rugged topography also governs climate along the peninsulas, in deep mountain basins and in the Japan Alps.

Resources

"Japan is land-poor, resource-poor and over-populated." In these words, an American expert described the foundations for the Japanese economy.[5]

Despite the fact that Japan's rice yield, a result of a fearful outlay of labor, a complex irrigation system, and an intensive use of fertilizers, is among the highest in the world, the country must still import more than a fifth of the food it consumes. Professor Cohen estimates the dependence on imports of staples rose from about 10 per cent in 1934–36 to almost 23 per cent in 1955.

Furthermore, most of the raw materials required for Japan's growing industry must be bought abroad. The position in non-fuel minerals is especially weak. There is only one major iron ore mine, and Japan must import about two-thirds of its total needs. There is enough copper to meet demand. Limestone, fortunately found near Kyushu coal, is abundant; there is an exportable surplus of sulfur. In the face of Asia's largest demand, however, there is a critical lack of fertilizer material in Japan. Despite widespread manufacture, Japan produces only about one-fifth of the salt consumed.

In the field of fuel and energy, despite key weaknesses in natural gas and petroleum, Japan's posture is favorable. In terms of heat values, coal accounts for two-thirds of total fuel and energy. It is, nevertheless, low-quality, uneconomic to mine, and poor in coking quality.

[4] According to the Police agency, the fifteenth typhoon (Vera, or Typhoon Ise Bay as the Japanese named it) in 1959 killed 4,500 and injured 30,000 persons. Premier Kishi Nobusuke converted an extraordinary session of the Diet in October, to pass a supplementary budget totaling 20,000 million yen (360 yen = $1.00). *The Japan Times*, October 7, 1959.

[5] Jerome B. Cohen, "International Aspects of Japan's Economic Situation," *Japan Between East and West*, published for the Council on Foreign Relations (New York: Harper, 1957), Chap. 3, p. 108.

Fortunately, about two-thirds of Japan's surface area is in productive forest. About one-fifth the total thermal energy produced in Japan is derived from wood. This resource and its by-products also provide materials for most buildings and the cellulose, rayon and paper industries.[6]

Japanese rivers are short, swift and spasmodic. They do provide water for irrigation and hydroelectric facilities, in which in 1959 Japan held an installed capacity of 9,400,000 kilowatts (thermoelectric plants make up the deficit of 4,900,000 kilowatts).[7] In 1958, Japan became the largest borrower from the International Bank for Reconstruction and Development: of total loans of $164 millions, $91 million went into expansion of electric power facilities.

Undoubtedly, Japan's future energy requirements will be increasingly met by pacific uses of atomic power. Its first atomic reactor went into operation in September, 1957, at the Japan Atomic Energy Research institute, Tokai-*mura*, Ibaraki-*ken*. The government had encouraged atomic development by passage of relevant legislation and by agreements with the United States and Great Britain. Meanwhile, there had been a flurry of activity among five major industrial groups in the field of atomic research.[8]

Population: Ethnology, Age, Trends

Despite a high degree of uniformity in physical appearance, it is as difficult to relate the Japanese people to a so-called pure race as it is in the case of any other group. Ethnically, the Japanese belong to the Mongoloid family with straight, dark brown

[6] Extremely detailed and voluminous were the *Reports* of the Natural Resources Section, Supreme Commander for the Allied Powers (SCAP). These have been ably collated and analyzed in Edward A. Ackerman, *Japanese Natural Resources* (Chicago: University of Chicago, 1953). For a briefer summary, see Ginsburg, *op. cit.*, Chap. 4, pp. 72–83.

[7] "Japan's Electric Power Industry," *Japan Report*, V, No. 9 (May 1, 1959), pp. 7–9.

[8] (a) Nippon Atomic Industry group (NAIG), joint investment of forty Mitsui-affiliated firms; (b) Mitsubishi Atomic Power industries (MAPI), joint enterprise of Mitsubishi concerns; (c) Sumitomo Atomic Energy commission (SAEC), the Sumitomo group; (d) The First Atomic Power industry group (FAPIG), with Fuji Electric Manufacturing Co. in the leading role; and (e) Tokyo Atomic Energy Research group, the oldest consortium, nineteen companies formerly affiliated with Hitachi and Mori concerns. The first three descend from the former, giant *zaibatsu*—cliques or *konzerns*—and the other two are newly organized firms.

hair, sand brown skin (it is actually not yellow), olive brown iris, and shallow facial relief. The inner edge of the eyelid very often shows the characteristic Mongolian fold (the eyes are not slanted).

The average Japanese is a little shorter than the world average. Japanese college males have, however, gained almost an inch and a half in the forty years 1910–1950.[9] The body weight of the average Japanese is comparatively light, as against height.

Japanese consciousness of population pressure is not entirely a modern cultural phenomenon. It is often stated that Japan's population during the Tokugawa era (1600–1868) remained stable; nevertheless it is recognized that population pressure was intense, and indeed it is now believed that isolated Japan had to support an increasing population for no less than 200 years.[10]

Japan's modern population problem may be simply and grimly stated. In 1872, with the adoption of the first modern registration system, Japan's population stood at about 35,000,000. At the turn of the century it approached 45,000,000, an increase of 10,000,000 in three decades. By 1911 it had risen to 50,000,000; by 1920, 56,000,000, an increase of 65 per cent in fifty years; by 1925, 60,000,000; by 1936, 70,000,000. The population had doubled in sixty-four years!

During World War II, of course, there were setbacks in population growth, but immediately thereafter occurred the postwar marriage boom. The birth rate zoomed higher than that of prewar Japan and between 1945 and 1955, Japan added 17,300,000 to its population. This increase exceeded the total (1950) population of Argentina, and amounted to more than three times the population of Switzerland.[11] By July 1, 1957, with 91,000,000 Japan had the fifth largest population in the world, supported on about 46 per cent of its prewar territories. The density was 619 per square mile (Montana, 4; Korea, 346; United Kingdom, 527; Netherlands, 850); even this figure is misleading, however, for in density

[9] The average Japanese male is 62.6 inches tall; female, 58.1 inches (world average, 64.3 inches). It is interesting to compare second-generation immigrants from Japan in Hawaii, male: 162.83 cm.; with residents of their ancestor's villages in Japan, male: 158.39 cm. Japanese UNESCO, *op. cit.*, p. 108.

[10] Nomura Kanetaro, *On Cultural Conditions Affecting Population Trends in Japan*, Tokyo, Science Council of Japan, Econ. Ser. No. 2, October, 1953, p. 3.

[11] Okasaki Ayanori, *Japan's Population Problem* (Tokyo: Ministry of Foreign Affairs, 1956), p. 1.

per unit of cultivated land—4,220 per square mile—Japan is among the first in the world.

Since about 1950, the birth rate has fallen sharply from 25.6 per thousand (1950–52) to 18.5 (1956; about half the rate of the 1920s) and further to 17.9 (1958).[12] It is now about the same as those of France and Italy. Yet no matter how quickly the birth rate has fallen, the death rate fell even faster because of steps to strengthen public health. Indeed, Japan's population problem is now qualitative, not quantitative, and centers about familiar Western issues of structure, age, and the productive age group with attendant problems of employment.

In October, 1959, Japan had an estimated population of 92,970,000. Welfare Ministry forecasts for the period 1950–1965 allowed for an increase of 13,200,000, or an annual average of almost 900,000 (1930–40 annual increase, 750,000). About 1970 the disturbing effects of the postwar boom will begin to decrease and Japan's population will stabilize around 100 millions.[13]

Meanwhile, a definite trend toward an aging population has begun. Before the war, the proportion of children under the age of fifteen was steadily growing; the proportion of old people over sixty-five, decreasing; the average age also decreasing. Since 1950 these trends have been reversed and, most significantly, those in the productive age (14–59) have increased 2.2 times the prewar rate. Between 1955 and 1959 this group rose at the rate of 1,100,000 annually. After careful calculation of death rate, employment and retirement trends, experts estimate that the Japanese economy must absorb a new working population of around 900,000 per year until 1965. Although the rate of unemployment has remained at only about 1 per cent, the semi- or under-employed may well number from 5 to 10 millions. Despite recent increases in cultivated areas, there may be an overpopulation in agriculture of some 5,000,000.[14]

The population structure is significant in one other sense and provides a useful bridge to consideration of the Japanese economy and its effects in turn upon political behavior. The modern population explosion in Japan since the Meiji era (1868–

[12] The number of Japanese who practice contraception has doubled in ten years. A majority of Japanese couples questioned approved the small, well-planned family. *Mainichi,* May 26, 1959.

[13] Population Problems Research Institute statistics, cited by *The New York Times,* November 1, 1959.

[14] Okasaki, *op. cit.,* pp. 9–11; Tobata Seiichi, *Japan's Agriculture: Farming Population* (Tokyo: Ministry of Foreign Affairs, Japan's Problems Series, 1956), pp. 1–5.

1911) has been accompanied by a social revolution. One detects it first in data on population distribution by employment. In 1872, 85 per cent of the Japanese were engaged in primary industries (agriculture, fishing, forestry, and such); by 1920, the ratio was down to 54 per cent and by 1940, to 44 per cent. Nevertheless, even in 1950, 45 per cent (38.8 millions) were still engaged in agriculture. Almost three-fourths of these were petty farmers tilling less than 1 hectare (2.5 acres) each. This means that Japan's population in rural *agraria* has remained relatively stable over the years of modernization, and the vast increase in population has flowed into urban *industria*.

Japanese city life, as a matter of fact, can be traced back to the seventh century (when Nara, the oldest capital, was founded) or at least to the eighth (when Kyoto, the former capital, was first built on the model of a Chinese metropolis). Medieval cities emerged from fairs in front of temples or shopping centers around castles in the domains. Professor John Hall wrote:

> During roughly three centuries, from the 1570's to the 1870's, the castle town, *jokamachi,* assumed an importance out of all proportion to other types of urban communities. The story of the rise of the castle town and its eventual modification under the forces of internal decay and Western influence may be taken as the central theme of Japan's modern urbanization.[15]

After the Restoration (1868), post, transport and port cities began to spring up and eventually formed the foundation for the urbanized belt already described above. As of January 1, 1956, Japan had ninety-seven cities of more than 100,000 population each, one in every prefecture except southwestern Shimane.

Today all labor and crafts not connected with agriculture account for about 23 per cent of the Japanese labor force (in the United States, about 30 per cent). Over 40 per cent of the Japanese people, the highest proportion in Asia, now live in urban areas or in cities of over 30,000 population; one in four Japanese lives in cities of 100,000 or over; and 15 per cent live in the very largest cities of 1,000,000 population or over.[16] Obviously, this shift of population from rural to urban Japan has had profound implications for political behavior.[17]

[15] John Whitney Hall, "The Castle Town and Japan's Modern Urbanization," *The Far Eastern Quarterly*, XV, 1 (November, 1955), p. 38.

[16] Ginsburg, *op. cit.*, pp. 109-111.

[17] Jun-ichi Kyogoku & Nobutaka Ike, "Urban-Rural Differences in Voting Behavior in Postwar Japan," *Proceedings* of the Department of Social Sciences, College of General Education, University of Tokyo, 1959 (reprint, Stanford University, Political Science Series, No. 66).

The foreign observer, looking in on Japan of the 1950s, was often tempted to concentrate on the changing cultural attitudes previously described. Exclusive and receptive tendencies seemed to shape in complex fashion the structure of government and to point to the paths of politics. The boundaries of modern Japanese political behavior have also been set by more fundamental factors: the geography, natural resources, size and structure of population, and the dynamic economy.

Not one postwar cabinet, for example, has dared to ignore the perils and promise inherent in economic reconstruction and development. Dramatic issues concerning the status of the emperor, rearmament and security policy have made the front pages of the world. Day-to-day Japanese government concern has concentrated more on the overwhelming, absolute size of the population; on the implications for social security of an aging population and a bulging labor force; on the problems inherent in a tradition-centered, rural Japan existing alongside a modern, urban Japan; and on the growing pains inevitable in the conversion from an underdeveloped to a developed nation.

Nor is the problem significant to Japanese alone: all Asia has watched the remarkable progress of Japan, with some faltering steps, as a model of what to copy and what to avoid. Here is a case study in what happens, particularly to political behavior, when a previously underdeveloped country emerges into a dual economy. Not the least significant development (to be explored in Chap. 4) is the sudden, heady break-through into a consumer-centered way of life. The effects on popular culture, on mass media, on interest groups, on political parties, on government, are often unforeseen. They may indeed add up to the costs of modernization.

The Economy: Developed Japan

If the traveler to Japan approaches from the Middle East and South Asia—from Egypt, Iran, Pakistan, or even India—then most certainly, his first impressions will add up to the belief that he has come to a developed country. Indeed, Japan accounts for much of the industrial output in the area covered by the United Nations Economic Commission for Asia and the Far East (ECAFE): almost three-fourths of the electric power, two-thirds of the steel, half of the coal, pig iron, and cement, and a third of the cotton yarn and fabrics.[18]

[18] Jerome B. Cohen, *Japan's Postwar Economy* (Bloomington: Indiana University, 1958), p. 7.

If, as is most likely, our traveler first sees the Tokyo area, he will immediately be struck by the fact that Japan is on the edge of, if it has not already entered upon, one of the world's greatest consumer booms. Small cars like the Datsun and Toyopet scurry around the great city and cause hopeless traffic jams. In the center of the world's largest metropolis stands the Tokyo Tower, one of the world's tallest free-standing structures, from which emanate television programs ranging from quiz shows, musical reviews, *sumo* wrestling, and baseball to news, political commentary, and great public events like the marriage of Crown Prince Akihito, in 1959. TV sets have spread out since the days when they were curiosities confined to public bars and radio stores, until now thousands of tiny shops and millions of homes enjoy the modern miracle. From the city come durable consumer goods too, like the tiny electric refrigerators and the electric rice warmers to be found in many of the farm households.

Japan, in this sense, is a unique case study. A non-Western nation which may properly be described as industrial, it nevertheless remains clearly and consistently Asian. The Japanese economy has of course changed greatly in the last century, yet it cannot be described in terms used for a Western economy. As we have seen, decisive factors governing the type of economy include the limited area, scarce natural resources, the mild climate and abundant rainfall. These account for the persistence of rice culture, reliance upon hydroelectric power, processing industries producing for export, and a developing foreign trade. Furthermore, in critical areas of interpersonal relations and group interaction—in defining the relations between labor and management, for example—and in the manner in which skills and energies are mobilized, Japanese industrial development is definitely a variant from industrialization on the Western model. As one observer has put it, "The moral is that the interpersonal relationships which will be effective in economic activity in a given country depend on the country's culture. Principles of business administration are not absolute; they are relative to the culture of the society." [19]

The historic problem, "why and how could Japan emerge as a modernized and an industrialized country, alone among the underdeveloped countries of East Asia, when they came into con-

[19] Later, further reference will be made to the pioneering study by James C. Abegglen, *The Japanese Factory; Aspects of its Social Organization* (Glencoe, Illinois: Free Press, 1958). See the foreword by Everett E. Hagan, found on p. vii.

tact with western civilized countries in the middle of the nine-teenth century," is still a puzzle to Japanese experts.[20]

In some Japanese academic circles there is a theory which attempts to explain modernization from the viewpoint of class differentiation and struggle. This implies, of course, economic determinism. The problem is by no means so simple however and involves, as Professor Horie Yasuzo put it, interdependence on many fields of life. Economic development does not occur automatically: the master of the economy is the human being.

The emergence of Japan from feudal seclusion was partly the internal process of shifting from a static to a dynamic society, from a conventional to an unconventional way of thought. It was a revolution, not of the bourgeoisie so familiar to the West, but of lower-class *samurai*. This process coincided with intense pres-sure from abroad.

Japan's economic modernization followed a path quite dif-ferent from that taken by Great Britain, France or Germany, where cottage and pre-capitalist crafts came to be dominated by the factory system representing large-scale production. Manufac-tures were fairly widespread in the Tokugawa era, but did not provide the foundations for industrialization. Rather, large-scale production was imported from abroad. The Japanese economy came to rest on two pillars: native crafts, producing exports, with which to finance imports of new equipment, and consumers' goods turned out by cheap labor; and basic, imported industries like munitions, shipbuilding, spinning, iron and steel. "Capital-ism in Japan was characterized by the fact that it had a strong military coloring and developed with the big *zaibatsu* as its center." [21]

Japan's participation in the Sino-Japanese War, Russo-Jap-anese War and World War I, coupled with the panics of the 1920s and 1930s, tended to increase industrial concentration and to hold down the standard of living. During the period of indus-

[20] *Kinsei Nihon no keizai to shakai* (The economy and society of Japan in the early modern period), 1958, an essay by Horie Yasuzo, summarized in "The Feudal States and the Commercial Society in the Tokugawa Period," *Kyoto University Economic Review,* XXVIII, No. 2 (October, 1958).

[21] Japanese UNESCO, *op. cit.,* p. 297. The *zaibatsu* (literally: finance cliques) were huge firms, like the German *konzern,* dominated by persons with family or capital lineage. Through holding companies (*honsha*) they controlled banks, concerns and companies. *Kyoto daigaku bungakubu, Ko-kushi kenkyu shitsu* (Kyoto University National History Research Institute, ed.), *Nihon kindai shi jiten* (Dictionary of Modern Japanese History) (Tokyo: Toyo Keizai Shimpo Sha, 1958), pp. 217–218.

trial rationalization (1920–World War II), four main types of production emerged: (1) small, independent factories in specialized local industries; (2) cottage industry, subordinate to commercial capitalists (for example, in silk weaving); (3) a true factory system, also subordinate to commercial capital (for example, ceramics, rubber goods); and (4) a subcontract system, under domination of large industry (for example, metals, machines).[22]

Meanwhile, the growth in size of the giant *zaibatsu* combines —Mitsui, Mitsubishi, Sumitomo, Yasuda and the like—and concentration of economic power in their hands, is perhaps all too familiar a story to be repeated here.[23] The working force employed in the biggest concerns (Mitsui, 1,800,000 in Japan and 1,000,000 overseas; Mitsubishi, 1,000,000 employees) dwarfed those of any American company. In markets where single *zaibatsu* dominated, sales ran as high as 50 to 60 per cent of the total. Through stock ownership the *zaibatsu* directly controlled one-sixth of the commercial banks, though they were also able to exercise indirect influence over many others. At the end of 1945 the main *zaibatsu* banks accounted for 57 per cent of total assets of all ordinary banks and almost 80 per cent of all loans and advances. Personal ties at the highest level of the *zaibatsu*, between the combines and the government and especially with the rising military bureaucracy, led to the formation of all kinds of special and national policy companies. Examples included the Bank of Japan, South Manchurian Railway Company, North China Development and the Southern Development Bank. As the war in China merged into World War II, the Japanese economy felt the force of *tengyo* (forced conversion), further concentration of industry and contraction of the domestic market.

In the late stages of the war, heavy industry was the hardest hit; small and medium factories were the first to recover from the damage. Furthermore, General MacArthur's trust-busting of the *zaibatsu* also added to the confusion.

Occupation policy on dissolution of the combines, when it hit the Japanese economy, was more far-reaching and thoroughgoing than Japanese business leaders had ever anticipated. Occu-

---

[22] Yamanaka Tokutaro & Kobayashi Yoshio, *The History and Structure of Japan's Small and Medium Industries—with Two Specific Surveys* (Tokyo: Science Council of Japan, March, 1957), pp. 40–41.

[23] U.S. Department of State, *Report of the Mission on Japanese Combines* [Edwards Mission], Washington, Far Eastern Series 14, Publication 2628, 1946, Part 1. See also Jerome B. Cohen, *Japan's Economy in War and Reconstruction* (Minneapolis: University of Minnesota, 1949), especially Chap. 1, "A Decade of Preparation."

pationaires proceeded to dismantle the top fifteen corporate communities, attacking concentration of economic power, centralized stock ownership, oligarchical control and market power. The policy left completely intact, however, Japanese banks developed by the former *zaibatsu*.[24] Finally, in the spring of 1948, the so-called Johnston Report marked a turning point in American Occupation policy on the economic reorganization of Japan. In essence, the report called a halt to the disintegration of the *zaibatsu*. One factor was the American taxpayer's restiveness in supporting the Japanese economy. Another was the fact that economic reform had become a victim of the cold war and necessarily gave way before economic reconstruction.

A mere listing of the problems inherent in postwar economic revival is impressive: rationalization of the economy without revival of extreme *zaibatsu* control; replacement of agriculture as the blotter to absorb surplus population; armament within limits of livelihood; expansion of foreign trade; a shift from export trade built around light, over to heavy industry. It is no wonder that national income in 1946 was only about half that of the 1934–36 average. By 1948 the economy had reached a sound footing, and in 1950 entered the unusual Korean war boom. By 1951 national income topped pre-World War II levels by 8 per cent; by 1954 it stood at 137 per cent of prewar figures. Per capita income did not reach prewar levels until 1953, however, because of the immense increase in population. It is still inferior to that of the United States, the Soviet Union, Great Britain or West Germany. In the mid-1950s Japan's consumption level was about twice that of the average Asian nation, about one-half that of West Germany, and about one-eighth that of the United States.

Businessmen and economists in Japan agree that cartels had consolidated their positions by 1954–55. Three of the old combines—Mitsubishi, Mitsui, Sumitomo—reappeared but were still unable to recapture their prewar positions in four sectors: paper, calcined soda, shipbuilding and shipping. They far surpassed the prewar degree of control in electrolytic copper, automobiles, plate glass and staple fibers. Nevertheless, the common question even in Japan, Have the *zaibatsu* made their comeback? is strictly an academic one. Unlike the old days, no single family or holding company is at the top directing the whole structure. The percentage of intra-combine stock holdings runs unspectacularly low. Groups are little more than loose federations of companies

[24] T. A. Bisson, *Zaibatsu Dissolution in Japan* (Berkeley: University of California, 1954).

which prefer to do business with one another. Competition in new industrial fields is fierce and the cartel (not, in fact, the *zaibatsu*) satisfies the compelling need of businessmen to be shielded from the cold winds of unrestrained competition.

The new Mitsui Bussan Company, which made its comeback in February, 1959, will serve as an illustration. For this group, a nonmember bank (Fuji) is the leading money lender and a member (the Mitsui Bank) second in line. Mitsui deals chiefly in foods, oils, fats and fertilizers. Its capital runs up to almost 6 billion yen and it does about 500,000 million yen in value annually. It has a cluster of forty branches in Japan, and an equal number abroad. It has 5,300 workers on its payroll, plus 350 foreign employees. Stocks of Mitsui Bussan are open to public investment.[25]

Organized labor, as a matter of fact, represents a degree of concentration even greater than that of capital, in the industrialized sector of the Japanese economy. According to a union census of June 30, 1959, made by the Labor Statistics Bureau of the Ministry of Labor, some 7,077,510 workers were organized into 39,303 local unions. Local unions were more or less consolidated into three major federations: the General Council of Trade Unions (*Sohyo*), with 3,670,000 membership; the Congress of Industrial Unions (*Zenro*), with 830,000; and the National Federation of Industrial Organizations (*Shinsambetsu*), with 430,000.[26] Despite the annual numerical increase in the unionized sector, the rate of union growth is not keeping pace with the expanding labor force. From a peak of 53 per cent in 1948, it has actually declined to 34.5 per cent in 1959.

The Economy: Underdeveloped Japan

The Japanese economy thus can be called a developed one, in the manner so far described. Nevertheless, even today it is not

[25] Even an outline of companies affiliated in the Mistui group fills a newspaper page. Here are a few examples: Mitsui Mining, Mitsui Shipbuilding & Engineering, Showa Aircraft, Mitsui Chemical, Toyo Rayon, Mitsui Bank, Mitsui Mutual Life Insurance, General Warehouse (in turn affiliated with Standard Vacuum Oil Company), Mitsui Petrochemical and Japan Steel. "Outline of Affiliated Companies," *The Japan Times,* February 16, 1959.

[26] "Organized Labor in Japan," *Japan Report,* VI, No. 6 (March 15, 1960). In 1958, mining had become the most highly unionized (83 per cent); agriculture and forestry, the least organized (14 per cent) sector. See Benjamin Martin, "The Labor Scene: Union Census—1958," *The Japan Times,* December 8, 1958; also Okichi Kazuo, *Labor in Modern Japan* (Tokyo: Science Council of Japan, March, 1958).

free from underdeveloped sectors. The predominance in sheer number of small and medium industries is neither a phenomenon of the past nor something transitional, but is still inseparably related to the economy. There are still 6,000,000 small farm families in Japan. The economy is reaching for full employment, but underemployment remains high. This is because increases in the population of labor force age will continue until at least 1965. The annual per capita income remains low, despite steadily increasing production. The proportion of selfemployed (26 per cent) and unpaid family workers (35 per cent) is exceptionally high. Thus although the unemployed sector (less than 2 per cent) remains low, as compared with countries of Europe or America, the number of underemployed remains high.

The number of small and medium businesses—those which employ fifty or less—is proportionately greater (97 per cent) in Japan than in many industrialized countries (Great Britain, 90 per cent; the United States, 80 per cent). Over half of the total number of Japanese employees work in such small firms. The average wage of such workers is less than half that of employees in the large factories. Unionization in small plants is extremely low and working conditions often deplorable. Furthermore, whereas the larger industries can act independently, the small and medium plants are controlled against their will and limited in financing, management, techniques and even sales by their elder brothers. It is quite clear that the persistence of small and medium industries is not an isolated, but a deep-seated characteristic, related to the entire economic structure. The scale of the Japanese economy cannot, therefore, be enlarged in a single coup.

Despite the remarkable industrialization of Japan, agriculture remains the chief occupation of the islands. The agricultural labor force varies from about 13,000,000 (in February) to about 19,000,000 (during June planting), at least 40 per cent of the total employed. Yet in 1951 less than half of the farm families supported themselves by farming alone. Many family members had to seek supplementary income in the cities.[27]

The Japanese engage in what is often called garden agriculture. This simply means it is extremely localized and concentrated; it is also land-intensive and labor-intensive. A fearful

[27] In over 100 sample farm households chosen for study in the *Tohoku* (N. E. Honshu) region, 2,055 hours per year per household were spent strictly on agriculture, as against 1,166 hours on employment outside farming. Tobata, *op. cit.*, p. 16.

amount of human labor goes into irrigation, transplantation, terracing and intensive fertilization.

Well over half of the total agricultural land lies in paddy fields, and thus rice provides the mainstay of farm income and the national diet. Rice is seldom the second crop, but is rotated with wheat, barley, millet, soy beans and industrial fiber crops. Average yields of 79 bushels of rough rice per crop per acre are among the highest in the world. If exceptionally good and bad crop years are eliminated, the average annual yield of rice is 291,600,000 bushels; of wheat and barley, 87,800,000 bushels. Since the annual grain requirement is 477,400,000 bushels, Japan has an annual shortage of 98,000,000 bushels.[28]

It is still too early to estimate the far-reaching effects of the earth-shaking land reform carried out during the occupation of Japan. In fact, it may take years for Japanese experts themselves to measure the impact on crop yield, for example. Tenant families, who had comprised one-fourth of the total farming households in Japan in prewar days, fell below 4 per cent of the total, in June, 1957. Owner-cultivators more than doubled in percentage by 1950, and reached 70 per cent of the total number of households in 1957. If the semi-owner, semi-tenant group is added, the total almost reaches an astounding 97 per cent. The results[29] are, as far as social structure and political behavior are concerned, of course significant. But there is no doubt that the reform furthered fragmentation of holdings. Farms remain tiny (two and a half acres on the average) and plots separated (anywhere from six to twenty fields scattered about the village). Farmsteads have retained their communal orientation out of necessity, clustered in the *buraku* (hamlet).

Society, Way of Life

Although there have been numerous attempts during and after the war, by Japanese and outsiders alike, a picture of the total national character of the Japanese has never really been drawn. For all its apparent homogeneity, Japanese society is rich and diverse. Within a great metropolis, like Tokyo, the pattern of life of *Yamanote*—the suburb—varies from that of the more

[28] A survey listed twenty-five major varieties of vegetables; fifteen kinds of fruits; a variety of flowers, seeds, seedlings; among industrial crops, leaf tobacco (national monopoly), sugar beet, rape seed, flax, hemp, tea and mulberry (for silk). Japanese UNESCO, *op. cit.*, pp. 354–361.

[29] The most careful estimation, in Western languages, is the study of R. P. Dore, *Land Reform in Japan* (New York: Oxford, 1959).

traditional *Shitamachi*—downtown. The pace of Kyoto, which jealously guards its urban tradition running back over 1,000 years, is quite different from that of frantic Tokyo.[30] There is an even wider gap between the city and the village. Indeed the dual nature of the Japanese economy described above—the developed, industrial, urban Japan atop the underdeveloped, agrarian, rural Japan—has had a profound influence on the way or, better, two ways of Japanese life.

In the block or precinct (*cho*) of the large city, the curious tourist is apt to be disappointed, for he will find little to illustrate the fine esthetic sense for which the Japanese have become world famous. The streets are narrow and twisting and, even where paved, barely provide room for the passage of an automobile. Most urban districts, thoroughly bombed and burned out during the wartime fire-raids, have been jammed once again with ramshackle houses. In the outskirts are springing up the postwar *apāto*, the multiple-unit future slums of the voracious city. Children play and mothers gossip in the streets, defying the traffic. Bicycles zip along the lanes, punctuating their sudden stops with the screech of hand-operated brakes. The *kamikaze* taxi spins around the blind corner, relying on fate to decide whether it will meet an onrushing *bata-bata*, an overladen three-wheeled truck. The city block, in the words of one careful observer, represents one end of the continuum of Japanese development:

. . . An open competitive society in which the family plays no part in the economic productive activities of large sections of the population, in which codified law is a major element in social control and educational institutions outside the family play a major part in the training of new members of the society, in which a wide range of man's daily contacts are of an impersonal kind, and in which a rising standard of material well-being produces a constantly changing set of material values and has created an expectation of continuing change and continuing progress.[31]

This same writer, the British sociologist R. P. Dore, made a detailed survey of an average Tokyo block, "Shitayama-cho." There were about 310 households in the precinct, with a total population of 1,225 persons. Average household size (3.8) was

---

[30] In a simplified but knowledgeable treatment, this contrast—between newer, brash Tokyo and older, staid Kyoto—is sharply drawn in Chap. 7 and 8 of Donald Richie, *The Land and People of Japan* (London: A. & C. Black, 1958).

[31] R. P. Dore, *City Life in Japan; A Study of a Tokyo Ward* (Berkeley: University of California, 1958), p. 5.

smaller than in most Tokyo wards (4.2), in turn smaller than in all urban areas of Japan (4.5) and, of course, smaller than households in rural areas (5.3). About nine of every ten males in "Shitayama-cho" had been born elsewhere; the figure for women was even higher.

There is a pleasant myth, enjoyed mostly by those who reside permanently outside the country, that Japanese living costs are low. Symposia in Japanese magazines testify otherwise and are widely devoted to the problem of making ends meet. One estimate, based on the average, scrimped diet of an urban family, found that about 23 cents is spent on each person per day, or about $35 for a family of five per month. The average daily protein intake per person is about 25 grams, most of which is from fish and marine products. The average rent consumes about one-third the monthly income and for this the tenant gets little more than a frame tenement with no sidewalk, no modern sewage, no running water, no central heat. A suit of clothes is relatively expensive and is usually managed out of the universal year-end bonus. The urban Japanese does save on his transportation: streetcar, subway, bus and train fares are comparatively cheaper than in America.

Recreation is still of the simple variety, but nonetheless thoroughly enjoyed. The newspaper, magazines, rented books, radio and now, TV, make the Japanese among the best informed citizens of the world. Almost everyone recalls the tour to a national park or historic monument during his student days. The wealthier businessman or influential politician goes to the hot-spring resort; the ordinary person, to the local, public bath. These and the parlor for *pachinko* (the tinkling name is for an upright pinball machine) provide gossip. Almost everyone is interested in sports: *besuboru, sumo* wrestling, track and swimming. The élite endanger life and limb on crowded golf courses in summer, on packed ski runs in winter.

Even in this new, strange, urban way of life, nevertheless, there are clues to the fact that many social norms have been carried over from rural antecedents. Except in Japan's exurbia, which is subdivided by high, hostile walls, there are close relationships among neighbors in a block, and local festivals are joined with tremendous enthusiasm.

Furthermore, even the Japanese worker in a factory is a member of the firm in a manner like that in which his American counterpart would be a member of a family, a fraternal lodge or some other close-knit group. At whatever level, the worker commits himself, on entrance, for the remainder of his career. The company in turn will never discharge him, save in an extreme crisis. In addition to his salary, admittedly low, there are all the fringe benefits of one of the world's most subtle built-in social security systems: food at cost, a complex system of allowances, bonus, housing subsidy, health and recreation services. Our system, in the West, is supposed to provide an impersonal exchange of services for cash rewards, theoretically geared to incentive and skill.

The Japanese employee is part of a much more personal system, a system in which his total functioning as a person is seen as management's responsibility, and in which his group membership transcends his individual privileges and responsibilites.[32]

One thing is clear: if life in urban Japan is not exactly like that in city America, it is also definitely not like that in rural Japan. And although year by year Japan becomes more urban, village Japan still represents a significant societal segment. Many of the Japanese now in cities were born in rural communities and subsequently migrated. To this day, almost half of all Japan remains rural, residing and working in the tiny rice-cultivating villages. Until only yesterday, Japan was predominantly premodern in economic and social structure. Like the American frontier and its continuing effect on American character, the Japanese village marks the base line from which to survey the cultural change to modern Japan.

. . . Life in the countryside is much less distorted by the strains of accommodation. The rural culture is a full, traditional, stable way of life. If is founded on the requirements of intensive agricultural technology and agrarian economy, which were dominant through centuries of Japanese history. The continuing importance of intensive agriculture gives this cultural tradition great durability today and makes it a living reservoir of traditional norms that are distinctively Japanese.[33]

Translated into terms significant for political behavior, this means that in much of Japan, the real as compared with the formal social and political leadership is still chosen according to traditional qualifications: ancestral status, age and family connections. A mathematical division through a vote may be formally necessary for the record, but agreement through consensus is far less dangerous to the tightly knit communal social structure.

[32] Abegglen, *op. cit.*, p. 66.
[33] Richard K. Beardsley, John W. Hall and Robert E. Ward, *Village Japan* (Chicago: University of Chicago, 1959), p. 3.

Settlement of disputes has little to do with the formally constituted judiciary and even less with law as we know it. In the
yakuba, or township hall, taxes are dutifully recorded as assessed
against individuals: in most villages, they are spread over the
communities and among the families, according to ability to pay,
and so as to confound the statistician.[34]

Technically, all of Japan outside the cities and towns is
covered with a net of *mura* (township or administrative village),
But it is the *buraku,* or hamlet, wherein one finds the constant,
face-to-face, social and economic identity. The government of the
buraku is entirely unofficial, but it is real. The life of each *ie*
(household) is in turn dependent on the hamlet. Individuality is
suppressed for the sake of both. Cooperation does exist with local
—which may or may not be legal—authority, but submission to
any abstract prefectural or national welfare means sacrifice for
the welfare of outsiders.

University of Michigan field studies of over 1,000 households
(in townships with less than 5,000 population), in ten prefectures
around the Inland Sea, revealed an average household of six
persons. All but a sprinkling of household heads were male. Over
three-fourths of the respondents lived in the same community in
which they were born. About 70 per cent of the households were
engaged primarily in agriculture.[35] More recent studies by a
Kyoto University team among fifty family farms in the *Kinki*
(Kyoto, Shiga, Nara prefectures) region, found that family members averaged 5.5 (2.9 male, 2.6 female). Arable land holdings
averaged about three acres. (The national average is about 2.45
acres of cultivated land.)[36]

The Japan FAO association has succinctly summed up rural
living standards: "An ordinary farmer's agricultural income is
relatively small to cost of farm management, which together with
taxes and public imposts and living expenditures exceeds that
small income, leaving deficits behind." In 1956 the annual cash

[34] See Robert E. Ward, "Village Government in Eastern and Southern
Asia: A Symposium," *The Far Eastern Quarterly,* XV, No. 2 (February, 1956),
p. 175. Professor Ward himself has contributed much to an understanding of
rural Japanese politics; see "Patterns of Stability and Change in Rural Japanese Politics," *Occasional Papers,* No. 1 (Ann Arbor: University of Michigan,
Center for Japanese Studies, 1951). See also Chap. 10, below.

[35] University of Michigan, Center for Japanese Studies, "Inland Sea Survey" (mimeographed), *passim.*

[36] Kyoto University, Faculty of Agriculture, Research Institute of Farm
Accounting, *Nogyo-boki kenkyu chosa-jo,* "*Showa 31 nendo, Noka keizai chosa
hokoku sho; kinki chiku ni okeru*" (Report of investigation of family farm
economy in 1956, Kinki district, Japan), No. 1, Kyoto, February, 1959.

receipts, gross, per farm household amounted to $975; net cash income, before taxes, came to $706 per household; and, with $87 in taxes deducted, a balance of $619 was left in disposable cash income.[37] Of course, expenses seldom include payment for farm labor but, as one Japanese expert put it, "There is nothing so cheap as the labor of family members." [38]

Indeed, this brief sketch of underdeveloped, rural Japan will serve to explain the comments, made above, that the country suffers under conditions of imperfect employment or disguised unemployment. The surplus population, as it is referred to, is never completely discharged from the farms; city labor, furthermore, often leaves one foot in the farm household and gingerly puts the other in small-scale industry. This is why it is often said that Japan still has a landed proletariat.

Culture, Education

In modern Japan, education has never quite attained the ideal plateau of apolitical instruction and training. Even today, government, teachers, and students alike are struggling to adjust the postwar educational system to Japan's culture, science and industry.

Educational reform under the Occupation was the resultant of two powerful forces often moving in different directions. First, there was a genuine revulsion among the Japanese to the use of education for indoctrination of chauvinism, imperialism and military adventurism. Second, there was the deep faith held by alien reformers, chiefly Americans, that a people might quickly be reoriented by well intentioned reconstruction of the educational system.[39] Overlooked in the enthusiasm of the moment was the elemental truth that education, like government or any other institution, can be effective only when it taps the deep roots of native culture.

Even the Japanese admit that the postwar school system has proved its worth in several ways. Primary and secondary education were divorced from central control. In theory, greater emphasis was placed upon the individual initiative of the teacher. The objectives of lower level education were better coordinated

[37] Japan FAO Association, *Agriculture in Japan* (Tokyo, 1958), pp. 12–15.
[38] Tobata, *op. cit.*, p. 17.
[39] Department of State, *Report of the Education Mission to Japan* (Washington: U.S. GPO, 1946); see also Robert K. Hall, *Shūshin; the Ethics of a Defeated Nation* (New York: Columbia, Teachers College, 1949).

with the livelihood of children. On the other hand, local control
and financing proved to be an enormous burden—as it has even
in the United States—on the skill and resources of Japanese who
had little knowledge of educational administration. Increased
school facilities, permitting more students to go to school and
stay in school longer, have led to worrisome decline of basic
academic ability. At the upper levels, business formally and
government agencies informally, still limit their recruitment for
potential management jobs to a small number of graduates, not
of the universities at large but of selected high-ranking institutions. This has meant an even more furious competition to enter
the famous universities. And it has meant a steadily growing
backlog of unemployed college graduates, whose opportunities
do not match their rising level of expectations.

The postwar system, as modified under the Occupation,
provides nine years' free, compulsory, coeducational training in
primary and lower secondary schools. On May 1, 1958, Japan had
over 22,000 primary schools (364,000 teachers, 13,500,000 students). Competitive examinations determine who shall enter the
three-year upper secondary course. Altogether, Japan had 16,000
secondary schools (300,000 teachers, 8,000,000 students), in 1958.
That same year Japan had over 500 colleges and universities
(48,000 professors, 650,000 students). A recent innovation is the
graduate school, in some universities.[40]

Post-treaty discussions of the Japanese educational system
have revolved around a number of thorny issues: (1) continuation
of higher-level coeducation (the Ministry of Education itself is
still a firm opponent);[41] (2) the replacement of self-activating
courses, imported from America, with modern, Japanese morals
training; (3) efficiency rating of teachers, widely regarded by the
latter as a hedging of civil rights, specifically the constitutional
right of academic freedom; and (4) the reintroduction of Japanese culture-rooted texts.[42]

[40] Tokyo Kyoiku Kenkyusho, *Zenkoku gakko soran, Showa 34* (Tokyo
Education Research Institute, Survey of National Schools, 1959) (Tokyo:
Ministry of Education [Harashobo], 1959), pp. 1256–1263.

[41] An interesting symposium, "Are Women's Colleges Needed?," recently
appeared in *The Japan Times* (March 12, 1959), illuminating this controversy.
The article titles are revealing: Koichi Shiraishi (Assistant Professor, Showa
Women's College), "Yes, They Contribute to Society by Developing Special
Traits"; and Kenichi Nakaya (Chairman, American Studies, Tokyo Univer-
sity), "Girls Only Pampered by Giving Education of Lower Standard."

[42] Lecture by Dean Kaigo Tokiomi, Tokyo University School of Education, to American Fulbright professors, International House, Tokyo, October
6, 1958 (from notes by the author).

Never imagine that such problems have been discussed in the detached calm of the academic ivory tower. The Japan Teachers Union's campaign against efficiency ratings, which themselves were of doubtful validity, approached violence. The radical Hiragaki Faction of the JTU, affiliated with the Left-wing Socialists and reportedly manipulated by Japan Communist Party cells,[43] swung the union into the mass movement not only against educational re-reform but also against the government's new police reform bill (in 1958) and revision of the United States-Japanese security treaty (in 1959 and 1960). Many teachers began to defect and to join the new Federation of Teachers organizations.

Zengakuren (National Federation of Students associations) is even more militant than the teachers' union. At its fourteenth national convention in Tokyo in 1959, for example, it rejected the coexistence line followed by the Japan Communist Party as too weak, and pledged continuation of a true class struggle by means of strikes and zigzag demonstrations, to overthrow the Kishi government "supported by imperialistic capitalists." [44] The political implications of the student movement, particularly its role in foreign policy issues, are discussed below.

Science, Technology and Government

Until the end of World War II, modern pure and applied sciences in Japan were mainly linked to the drive for military development. After military devastation and defeat scientists organized the new Science Council of Japan in the hope of making peaceful contributions to the world of science. Today the Chemical Society of Japan, with 16,400 members, is the largest natural science society in Japan (in 1953, it celebrated its 75th anniversary).

The Science Council's "White Paper on Scientific Studies," published in April, 1959, revealed that Japanese scientists have grown quite restive in face of old and obsolete research facilities available to them. The report pointed to an inadequate government budget for research in the natural sciences (about half that spent by West Germany), ill treatment of scientists and the miserable state of research institutes.[45]

In 1959 such criticism led Nakasone Yasuhiro, Director of

[43] *Nippon Shuho,* November 5, 1959.
[44] *Mainichi,* June 10, 1959.
[45] Summarized in *Mainichi,* April 24, 1959.

the Science & Technics Agency, to propose a long-range plan to explore pacific uses of space. This Nakasone plan fired the imagination of Japanese and immediately received wide press comment. It aimed to by-pass orthodox methods for reconstruction of Japanese industry, in favor of gearing scientific and technical efforts toward capturing a leading role in the space universe of tomorrow.[46]

Within the more modest realm of today steps were taken in March, 1960, to strengthen government and private cooperation in scientific and technological research. The Japan Science and Technology Foundation, with a planned capital of 2,300 million yen ($6,389,000), was inaugurated to assist liaison among institutions and agencies, to bring industrial research into closer contact with public laboratories and to carry out research and planning. The foundation was also designed to publicize scientific advances.[47]

4 - The Political Public

With the possible exception of the Hollywood movie and the television crime series exported from America, rarely do the popular cultural products of a country—those most widely diffused among the people and most characteristic at home—become the ones by which foreigners come to know that country. Later (in Chap. 11), certain aspects of the remarkable Japan boom in the United States are touched on, perhaps all too lightly. Here it is sufficient to say that there is a real danger that outsiders (encouraged by well-meaning Japanese) will continue to judge Japan by Mt. Fuji, cherry blossoms, and the rightly world-famous Grand *Kabuki* dance-theatre; by the *maiko,* apprentice entertainers of Kyoto; by hostesses in kimono on the Japan Air Lines; and by the motion picture *Rashomon*. In doing so, they will see

[46] For a sampling of such discussion: *Shukan Yomiuri*, Aug. 30, 1959; *Diamond*, Aug. 22, 1959; *Sekai Shuho*, Aug. 4, 1959; and *Nippon Shuho*, July 25, 1959.

[47] The Japanese government granted a subsidy of 70 million yen ($194,000) for the initial fiscal year. "Japan Science and Technology Foundation," *Japan Report*, VI, No. 8 (April 15, 1960), p. 8.

Japan only through the eyes of traditionalists who strive earnestly to conserve high culture.

On the other hand, outsiders may suddenly be shocked by the radical image of Japan projected by the workers, the Left Socialists, or the militant student organization, *Zengakuren*.

Popular Culture of Japan

To understand the Japanese and their political behavior, as one does who lives among the Japanese, he must also know something about advice columns in the daily press; about comparative social symbols in the comic strips (for example, Sazae *san* in Japan as compared with Blondie in America); he must hear the language of improvised *manzai* comic dialogue, performed in vaudeville since the Tokugawa era and now incorporated in TV programs; he must sense the slightly deviant undertones of the Takarazuka all-girl opera and understand why the average self-respecting Japanese male resists attending this Far Eastern version of a Radio City Music Hall review.[1]

The fact is, in the field of everyday culture and public opinion, Japan has already entered upon a second revolution, which is bringing about a profound change in traditional outlook and values. For Americans, it would be pleasant to think these changes began under the Occupation. Actually, the seeds were earlier sown in the truly remarkable soil of mass media in Japan; their growth was accelerated by influences during the last war and under the Occupation; and their strength has been drawn from the steady movement of Japan into urbanization and modernization. As the distinguished Japanese political scientist, Professor Royama Masamichi, put it, ". . . In Japan the major development of modern ideology is seen in nationalism and industrialism."[2]

The growth of popular culture does not necessarily mean, of course, a parallel growth of popular sovereignty. Japan's premodern situation made it possible to establish the emperor system in place of local clans, establish big and small enterprises in place of manual industry based on family workers. Modernization was thus coupled with indigenous elements, but this has not been the case with democracy.

[1] Kato Hidetoshi, ed. and trans., *Japanese Popular Culture* (Tokyo: Tuttle, 1959).

[2] See the article by Royama Masamichi on the new Democratic Socialist Party's obligation to adjust to international and domestic change, in *Toyo Keizai Shimpo,* January 2, 1960.

Japan is now on the edge of, if it has not already entered, one of the world's most remarkable commercial and consumer booms. Some day soon, one of Japan's brilliant, cynical, young novelists is going to write a devastating piece about the new, emerging middle-class Japanese, equivalent to the 1920-style American Babbitt. Among such Japanese lie the strengths and weaknesses of Japanese popular culture in the 1960s and the fate of democratic political behavior.

Japanese political parties, which like parties anywhere have acutely tuned antennae, have picked up the vibrations of this social revolution. Thus some Liberal-Democrats on the right, who prate about conserving traditional Japanese culture, are talking patent nonsense. When they promise that every Japanese can look forward to becoming a member of the great middle class—in place of the chicken in every pot, the Japanese will have a duck on every *hibachi*—they strike responsive chords. Similarly, as Professor Royama warned, ". . . economic stability and the consumer spending boom have fostered a peaceful and conservative mood among the masses far from a crisis and tension pictured by the reformists." Thus Socialists who stubbornly insist upon picturing Japan in terms of a nineteenth-century, European class struggle between feudal nobility and the militant proletariat are also talking patent nonsense. As we shall see, the political platforms of almost all Japanese parties have felt the impact of these social earthquakes. First, however, it will be wise to measure the tremors in public opinion, in the long- and well-established organs of mass media and, particularly, in the phenomenal growth of new, slick weekly magazines. They are wreaking a revolution in Japanese public attitudes and playing havoc with the assumptions of old-fashioned political party leaders.

Mass Media, Public Opinion

Japan's first newspapers were actually either translations of Dutch and English sheets or publications by foreigners living in Yokohama and Nagasaki, in the 1860s. The very first Japanese newspaper was the *Kaigai Shimbun* (Foreign News), which appeared in 1864 and illustrated the tendency of Japanese readers ever since to demand up-to-date world news.

Limitations on the supply of news were symbolized by Japan's first press law, February, 1869. The following year, the *Yokohama Mainichi Shimbun* (Yokohama Daily Newspaper) appeared as Japan's first daily. The *Yomiuri Shimbun* started in Tokyo in 1875 and the *Asahi Shimbun* was launched in Osaka in 1879. These great newspapers also initiated the tradition of links with political parties (a custom which has largely died out), and the custom of carrying political news. Meanwhile, the newspapers soon grew to the huge size so characteristic of the Japanese press today. Even by the end of the Meiji era (1868–1912), the *Osaka Mainichi Shimbun* and the *Osaka Asahi Shimbun* already boasted circulations of 300,000 and 350,000 respectively. It was during the China Incident in the 1930s that the Japanese government began to assume control over news services through the agency of the *Domei Tsushinsha,* and to mobilize the press over its objections. During World War II there was rigid censorship exercised by the Cabinet Information Bureau. In addition, there were severe difficulties faced by the publishers. At one point, damage from air raids became so great that "The Big Three," *Asahi, Mainichi,* and *Yomiuri,* published a single, joint newspaper. During the Occupation, the only limitation imposed was on handling of news in such a way as to be detrimental to the mission of the Allied Forces, who supervised the press by means of a press code. By 1952 and the regaining of independence, Japanese newspapers cast off all shackles.[3]

Today, as has been true for a number of years, Japan's newspaper business is dominated by "The Big Three." *Asahi Shimbun* is published at Tokyo, Osaka, Nagoya and Kokura. Under contract with worldwide news services, this newspaper employs 6,000 and enjoys a daily circulation of 2,953,000. *Mainichi Shimbun* is published at Tokyo, Osaka and Nagoya; it also employs about 6,000 and has a circulation of 3,857,000. The third great paper, *Yomiuri Shimbun,* has about 3,000 employees and a daily circulation of 3,928,000. One other so-called central newspaper is worthy of mention: *Nippon Keizai Shimbun,* a daily, is an equivalent to the *Wall Street Journal* in the United States. It employs about 1,500 and has a circulation of about 755,000. Each of these four newspapers publishes, in addition, some fifty local editions spread throughout Japan.[4]

[3] *Japan:Its Land, People and Culture,* comp. by Japanese National Commission for UNESCO (Tokyo: Ministry of Finance, 1958), pp. 443–446; see also "Short History of Japanese Journalism," in Nakamura Kikuo and Matsumura Yutaka, *Political Handbook of Japan 1958* (Tokyo: Tokyo News Service, 1958), pp. 85–92.

[4] As of January, 1960, daily Japanese newspaper circulation totaled 36,356,000, with approximately 45 per cent accounted for by papers with nation-wide readership. *Japan Report,* VI, No. 2 (January 15, 1960), p. 4.

There are also of course many local newspapers, at least one in most of the prefectures of Japan. Among the foreign language newspapers, *The Japan Times* is the oldest (dating from 1897, it became the *Nippon Times* in 1943 but reverted to its original name in 1956). Many of the other large newspapers also publish English-language editions. The only important news service in Japan is Kyodo, which employs 1,500 and supplies features to the local newspapers.

By way of summary, in 1958 there were 255 dailies in Japan, including those morning and evening editions published by the same firm. If these were counted as separate papers, the grand total circulation of the dailies reached the staggering total of over 36 million. This meant that, on the average, each household in Japan read nearly two dailies.[5]

Let us now glance briefly over the typical Japanese newspaper. The daily usually consists of eight pages (morning) and four pages (evening). Page one ordinarily covers political affairs, both domestic and foreign (*Mainichi* and *Yomiuri* carry editorials here; *Asahi* can be distinguished by its column of comment, entitled *"Tensei Jingo"* (Voice of Heaven—Voice of the People). Page two presents other foreign news, including dispatches from abroad, and less important domestic and political affairs. Page three offers news analysis, opinions of various people on issues, letters to the editor and, characteristic of Japanese dailies, an installment of a novel (with illustration). Page four carries economic and financial news, with market quotations. Page five holds news of science, literature, and the arts (including radio and television programs). Page six is the sports page. Page seven contains the social column as it is called, containing news pertaining to common people and human interest stories, and comic strips for women and children. Page eight concentrates on local news, edited at the local branch in the prefecture.

Turning from specific characteristics to generalizations of political importance, what are the characteristics of Japanese newspapers? Of primary significance is the fact that circulation of morning and evening newspapers rests, not so much on sales at news stands, but upon delivery direct to the households of

[5] The grand total circulation of Japan's dailies compared with 55 million for the United States, 49 million for Russia, 29 million for Great Britain, 12 million for West Germany, 10 million for France and 2.5 million for India, according to United Nations statistics. Nakamura & Matsumura, *op. cit.*, p. 80.

Japan. Newsprint literally blankets the country. On the one hand, newspapers have become a powerfully intrenched, independent force of democratic free expression. They report news largely collected by their own reporters (especially the big three, which have broken away from Kyodo news service). Their position in popular culture is reinforced by their intense activity in charitable, sports and cultural activities.

On the other hand, the Japanese newspaper world is beginning to suffer from the same concentration of power experienced in other sectors of Japanese business. The big, metropolitan papers have branches in every prefecture and publish local editions. By 1960, comment on the status of the Japanese press expressed concern that facsimile reproduction of the big three threatened to drive local newspapers (particularly in Hokkaido) out of business. The smaller papers, it has been charged, had political links which were too close to local strong men. Their content gave the impression that they were still operating in the Meiji era. Even Abe Shinnosuke, adviser to the *Mainichi,* said that press management was amazingly old-fashioned and delivery agencies were ridden with "feudal practices." [6]

Probably no other modern government is attacked by its people as severely as is that of Japan, and this characteristic is faithfully mirrored in the Japanese press. Indeed, it has been noted that a newspaper or magazine suffers an immediate drop in circulation if it praises the government. Two basic reasons have been offered for this interesting tendency, the increasing competition in the journalistic world and the degradation of the politician in mass democracy. In any case, there are only two frankly partisan newspapers—the Japan Communist Party's *Akahata* (Red Flag, daily) and the Socialist Party's *Shakai Shimpo* (Social Journal, tri-monthly)—and they have only limited readerships. Otherwise, Japanese newspapers are strictly neutral and take an impartial stand amidst political parties and candidates, even at the time of elections. [7]

[6] Discussion of radio, television, and newspapers with Abe Shinnosuke, in *Toyo Keizai Shimpo,* July 18, 1959; see also the extremely searching analysis of the status of the press by a panel of staff writers, in *Bungei Shunju,* November, 1959.

[7] On Japanese newspapers' attitudes toward the government, see the analysis by Yasuda Keiji, in *Sekai Orai,* May, 1960; also, on the occasion of Japan's 11th Newspaper Week, Hessell Tiltman, " 'Fourth Estate' in Japan; Nation of Newspaper Readers," *Asahi Evening News,* October 4, 1958; and "Japanese Press Today," *The Japan Times,* November 1, 1958.

On one issue, however, the Japanese press is certainly not neutral. To meet the growing popular interest in scientific matters, some papers have established science sections in their editorial departments. This trend has become manifest since the Fukuryu Maru incident, in which Japanese fishermen were dusted with atomic fallout near the American nuclear test grounds in the Western Pacific. The Japanese press has taken a strong stand against thermonuclear experiments, reflecting the Japanese people's extreme sensitivity toward the problem of nuclear armament.

If the Japanese press is characterized by its tone of extreme criticism, at least it would be difficult to challenge it for lack of independence. Prime Minister Kishi once said he met defeat in 1958, in his proposed revision of the police duties law, not by the force of public opinion but by the organized press. *Zenei,* an organ of the Japan Communist Party, has charged the big three with reactionary attitudes, chiming in with the ruling Liberal-Democratic Party, and denunciation of the activities of *Gensuikyo* (Council against Atomic and Hydrogen Bombs). The magazine also claimed the Japanese press contained no articles for the people, in opposition to the proposed revision of the Japan-United States security treaty. On the other hand, a magazine publisher has denounced Japanese mass media for being almost entirely dominated by leftist editors and writers, who present a distorted view of the world. The situation, he said, has approached that of twenty-five years ago, when Japan overestimated the power of Germany and Italy. A glance at the Japanese press would lead the reader to believe that the Soviet Union and mainland China ruled the world.[8]

It is perhaps safest to say that the present condition of absolute freedom and the existence of keen competition for news is a reaction to the still-lively memories of government restrictions on the press, controlled news during the militaristic era, and the subtle censorship of the Occupation period. A few years ago, this attitude caused a storm of protest and shelving of a proposal to revive a government information agency.

Japanese public opinion is also shaped, to a very significant extent, by the some 370 million copies of magazines and 148 million copies of books published annually (not including government publications). In 1958, a check by the *Shuppan News Sha* (Publications News Company) revealed that at least 1,441 different magazines were published.[9] It is obvious the range of

[8] Masu Komihei, *Jimbutsu Orai,* September, 1959; *Zenei,* October, 1959; and interview with Tamura Kosaku, Director of *Seiji Keizai,* February, 1960.

style was wide, from the journal curiously entitled *Heibon* (Mediocrity), through the ladies' home companion-type magazine, to the *sogo zasshi* (journal for general reading), unique to Japan. Space permits only an indication of broad trends in the magazine world.

Women's magazines, although they deal with politics only obliquely, nevertheless are important in the shaping of popular culture. Certainly *Ie no Hikari* (The Light of the Home) is the most unusual of all magazines published in Japan. This journal was started in 1924 as an organ of the Central Association of Industrial Cooperative Unions, predecessor of the present agricultural cooperative federation. Before long, it became the only solid mass communication medium in Japan's rural area. The secret of this best-seller's success lies in the nationwide organization of cooperatives, through whose 13,000 chapters the magazine is distributed to farmers. In 1959, *Ie no Hikari* had a circulation of 1,510,000, which meant that every 3.1 farm households of the nation read the monthly. By and large it has exercised slight and altogether conservative influence in politics, even though it has played an important role in the cultural education of Japan's farmers.[10]

One might say that magazines like *Chuo Koron* (The Central Review) and *Sekai* (World) occupy the other end of the spectrum. Marked by a spirit of liberalism—radicalism, their critics claim— they continue a long tradition begun in the nineteenth century. Such journals provide the chief vehicle for the peculiar Japanese phenomenon, the professor-political critic. Relatively smaller in circulation, these magazines nevertheless wield such powerful political influence, especially among intellectuals, that they have alarmed financial and business circles. After a number of false starts in trying to offset the influence of *Sekai,* thirty Kansai businessmen backed Mizuno Shigeo in his take-over of the journal *Sankei,* which now represents the conservative wing of the magazine world.[11] A little broader in subject matter, the *Bungei*

[9] Classified roughly by type, the news weeklies accounted for 25 per cent of the volume; children's magazines, 23 per cent; general amusement, 15 per cent; women's magazines, 10 per cent; composite all-around monthlies, 5 per cent; economic magazines, 3 per cent; and miscellaneous, including picture and movie magazines, 16 per cent.

[10] Ishikawa Hideo, "Fabulous Monthly," *The Japan Times,* June 7, 1959. The circulation of three American magazines in 1960 was as follows: *Ladies' Home Journal,* 6,279,365; *McCall's,* 6,212,250; *Good Housekeeping,* 4,673,416.

[11] Masu Komihei, article on the new journal in *Jimbutsu Orai,* September, 1959.

Shunju review has more literary taste but also carries panel discussions on political affairs.

Between the political extremes and most significant in their subtle political influence are the new Japanese weekly magazines. Mainly for commuters' consumption, these little easy-to-read journals have reached the astounding total of 7,000,000 copies, representing some twenty titles, in circulation each week. This means that one of every three Japanese families reads a weekly. Here, indeed, is the heart of the new, middle-class, audio-visual, popular Japanese culture. Why are the weeklies so popular? First, they are cheap; they bring a wide variety of information in highly digestible form for only 30 yen (about 8 cents) per copy. Second, they contain popularized accounts of domestic and international news, mixed with a regular fare of gossip, screen and television reviews, crossword puzzles, cartoons and excellent photographs. Third, they are easy to understand. "We are trying to get readers who have an educational level of senior high school graduates," said one editor. The number of senior high school graduates has been increasing by about 700,000 every year.[12]

The other major source of news, political and otherwise, are the 14,300,000 (registered) radio sets and more lately, the some 600,000 television sets in Japan. In 1925 Tokyo Radio Station broadcast the first program in Japan. This station became the nucleus of *Nippon Hoso Kyoku* (NHK, with 85 stations in 1958) which, until 1950, held a monopoly on broadcasting.[13] Under a new radio law, wavelengths were opened to commercial companies, which operate eighty additional stations throughout Japan. Television began in Japan on February 1, 1953, and soon spread, by the end of 1959, to sixty stations operated by both NHK and private companies. By 1960, alert social critics were already estimating the formidable influence of TV on popular culture and of commercialism on Japanese attitudes.[14]

The question is, what influence does this formidable system of mass media exert on public opinion and how, if at all, does

[12] Takahashi Yoshitaka, "Weekly Magazines Boom," *Mainichi*, March 11, 1959; Staff Writer, "Weeklies Flood Japan in Tide of Popularity," *The Japan Times*, March 7, 1959; and American Embassy, Tokyo, *Survey of Leading Japanese Magazines*, May 1, 1959.

[13] Japanese UNESCO, *op. cit.*, pp. 450ff.

[14] A friend of the author's, Professor Nagai Michio of Tokyo Institute of Technology (visiting at Columbia University, 1958–59), sent back to Japan shrewd comments on the impact of the Van Doren case on American society in 1959 and attempted to forecast the effects of television on Japan. *Chuo Koron*, March, 1960.

opinion influence political behavior? Japanese experts have identified three elements in public opinion: (1) the line of the media;
(2) what people report they think; and (3) what they really think.
The first element can be described by fairly regular content
analysis; the second, by statistical surveys of opinion; the third,
by indirect methods which, so far, have been hampered by numerous difficulties. Newspapers are characteristically urban in outlook, mirror the new consumer boom and therefore range from
apolitical to conservative in impact.[15]

Surveys of public opinion themselves have of course come
to bounce back on mass attitudes and thus to affect political
behavior. Almost since the beginning of the Occupation, Japanese newspapers, government agencies and scholars have made
use of the opinion survey. When preelection polls were first
attempted (in the national elections of 1946), most proved to be
wide of the mark and the public tended to discount opinion polls.
Since then they have improved appreciably. The three large newspapers, as well as the specialized news service *Jiji Tsushin,* have
conducted national surveys on issues for years. For a time, there
was a National Public Opinion Survey institute (*Kokuritsu Yoron
Chosa Jo*) in the office of the prime minister, conducting monthly
surveys on a national basis. Scholars, inspired by the example
of Professor Royama Masamichi, have also used the survey technique.[16]

It is apparent from Professor Royama's studies that elections
are one area of political activity in which mass media significantly
make their influence felt. And this influence is not necessarily in
the direction of this or that party, this or that leader—for, as we
have seen, the press is largely skeptical and neutral—but rather
in the day-to-day projection of an image of the political situation.
If, then, the mass media often appear hypercritical and even
cynical, at least they are so far completely independent and
engaged in democratic competition in the free market of ideas.

Similarly, there is one area in which the force of public opin-

[15] *Chuo Koron* (Extra), May, 1959; Nobutaka Ike, *Japanese Politics:
An Introductory Survey* (New York: Knopf, 1957), Chap. 11.

[16] Royama Masamichi, ed., *Seiji ishiki no kaibo* (An analysis of political
consciousness) (Tokyo: Asahi, 1949). Professor Royama followed this basic
guide in his later analysis of the 1952 general election. For a complete analysis and critique of the survey method, plus data obtained from its use, the
author was fortunate in having at hand the basic study by Douglas H. Mendel, Jr., *Political Behavior in Post-Treaty Japan: Survey of Constituents and
Leaders in Two Selected Areas* (unpublished Ph.D. dissertation, University of
Michigan, 1954), especially introduction, pp. 1–18.

ion, reflected clearly in the otherwise conservative mass media, has directly limited the definition of public policy. This is the area which encompasses thorny issues of rearmament (and Art. 9 of the new constitution), American bases on Japanese soil (and administrative agreements), and mutual security arrangements (especially the revision of the American-Japanese security treaty). These issues are discussed more fully below (in Chap. 11), but suffice it to say here that no government has been able to afford the luxury of ignoring opinion on these sensitive issues. The fact that outright rearmament has not occurred is largely a result of hostile public opinion. Both the Japanese and the American government might well have tread much more softly, in 1959 and 1960, had they paid closer attention to the uneasiness in public opinion generally—and not just on the left wing—with regard to Japanese-American security arrangements.[17]

Interest and Pressure Groups

In a country so deceptively homogeneous and yet so subtly complex as Japan, it is not easy to describe the area of informal government. Most of the rest of this book purports to describe the more formal structure of the state, while assuming that it is shot through with political behavior which emanates from outside government proper and even outside the political parties. This is the area Charles Merriam called private government, in which operate individuals identified as *yuryokusha* (men of influence) by Nobutaka Ike.[18]

As has already been indicated (Chap. 1), the techniques and myths of Japanese politics can be understood only within the context of the society. Traditionally predominant—in political parties, business, labor, and even antisocial activities like crime— have been personal relationships. These in turn have been linked to more or less degree to the family as a model for social groups, from the smallest (party factions) to the largest (the nation-family). Many groups are still dominated by traditional social norms of cohesiveness and cooperation and still distinguished for their hierarchical structure. These characteristics may best be illustrated, in Japanese style, by the persistence of celebrated *oyabun-kobun* or parent-like-child-like relationships. Naturally these

---

[17] Douglas H. Mendel, Jr., "Revisionist Opinion in Post-treaty Japan," *American Political Science Review*, XLVIII, No. 3 (September, 1954), pp. 766–774.

[18] Ike, *op. cit.*, p. 75.

norms are becoming unevenly spread through a dynamic society. Traditional attitudes are more pronounced in upper- than in lower-class families; more in rural than in urban groups; more in the older than in the younger generation. In rural Japan age, property and family status form the three legs on the stool of political power. In urban Japan accomplishment of the individual out of an atomic family, like that found in the West, is beginning to carry more weight.

It is actually the corrosion of traditional mores and the parallel emergence of a baffling middle-class attitude—rather than any short-term experiment in democratization or subsequent superficial conflict in party platforms—which constitute the modern political revolution of Japan. And this is a revolution, although at times it seems to move with the speed of a glacier.

In the opinion of Professor Maruyama Masao, Japan's outstanding authority on nationalism, the center of gravity of political power is located in a wide sector of the middle class. This is one of two strata which embraces small enterprisers and retailers, labor foremen and contractors, craftsmen, landowners, primary school teachers, priests, and the lower rungs of the national and local bureaucracy. The other includes the urban white-collar class, journalists, lawyers, professors and students.[19] It is the considered personal observation of the author of this book that the middle class is increasingly Japan's most important though largely unorganized interest group.

Japan's political parties have, indeed, come up against the increased political apathy of the middle class, a studied indifference which is also the product of expanding technology and bureaucracy. This is one of the reasons why the ruling Liberal-Democratic Party has begun to parrot the aims of the welfare state in its political philosophy of neo-conservatism. One young organizer in a renovationist party said that, in his political activity, he felt as though he were driving a stake into loose sand. The Socialists, who had monotonously spoken of the need for revolution based on the class struggle, in January, 1960, admitted the necessity of shaping more practical policies standing for the interests of the masses. As we shall see, the emergence of the new Democratic Socialist Party in December, 1959, was heralded by the demand that socialism and parliamentary democracy be inseparable and was marked by self-criticism of previous socialist dogmatism.[20]

[19] *Ibid.*, p. 16.
[20] An article on political trends by Muto Mitsuro, in *Jiyu,* April, 1960.

To the right and outside Japan's middle class is a new power elite, which has ruled Japan more or less by default since the peace treaty. It is a product of the destruction of prewar semi-feudal elements, of some influences from the Occupation, and of the emergence of what some Japanese call the new bourgeois democracy.[21] Absent are the symbol of the emperor's authority, the power of the armed forces and the leadership of land owners. Still present is the pervasive force of the bureaucracy. There are also the newly arisen tycoons, often different from prewar *zaibatsu* heads, like President Ishizaku Taizo of *Keidanren* (Federation of Economic Organizations; this and other business groups are further described below, in Chapter 9) and President Sato Kiichiro of Mitsui Bank. In close alliance are politicians like Ikeda Hayato, who had been Minister of International Trade & Industry and who became premier in 1960; and like former cabinet members Premier Kishi Nobusuke, Finance Minister Sato Eisaku and Foreign Minister Fujiyama Aiichiro.

The link between business, particularly financial circles, and the conservative politicians is a strong one. It is estimated that *Keidanren,* for example, poured 170 million yen (about $472,000) into the 1955 House of Councillors campaign. Based on data provided by the Autonomy Agency, total donations received by the Liberal-Democrats from January to December, 1958, reached the staggering total of 2,380 million yen (over $6,600,000 through official channels; the unofficial total may have reached 5,000 million yen.) [22]

Three types and several subtypes have been identified within the new power elite of Japan. First are the newly risen entrepreneurs. These in turn can be subdivided into executives who started as salaried workers and department chiefs who worked their way up to become directors and presidents. They are the economic politicians, who profited from the turmoil of defeat, deconcentration and reconcentration. Then there are the executives sent out to subsidiary firms. There are also executives who were formerly government officials. And there are still some who, with their sons, are the owners of companies. All these constitute the managerial class, a postwar phenomenon.

[21] Japanese writers have borrowed the terminology of C. Wright Mills, who described the power elite of the United States as consisting of businessmen, politicians and the military. See the article by Hayashi Shozo in *Chuo Koron,* January, 1960.

[22] Ando Yoshio, on the role of financial circles and their organizations, in *Economist,* December 15, 1957; also the article on pressure groups and the budget, *Chuo Koron,* May 10, 1958; and Hayashi Shozo, *loc. cit.*

Second, there are the top-level bureaucrats, who maintain close if informal contacts with the world of business and finance.

Third, there are the politicians who represent both the bureaucrats in government and the managerial class in business.[23]

To the left and also outside Japan's rapidly emergent middle class is another power bloc consisting of the great labor federations. Enjoying perhaps too close ties with the various socialist parties, labor has remained even more out of touch with the middle class, although it has drawn sporadic support from intellectuals, professors and students. Labor federations have been listed above (Chap. 3) and labor's relations with government are described below (Chap. 9). At this point it is important to note that Japan's labor organizations, as pressure groups, have been characterized by rigid ideology, intense factionalism, and political platforms largely out of touch with the phenomenon of the consumer economy.

It has been charged that what reigns in Japan's labor movement is not a practical code formed of experience gained from collective bargaining and strikes for better working conditions. Rather, labor leaders are infected by dogma inherited from Marxism-Leninism, which they learned when they were young. The ideology of trade unions is therefore almost altogether political. Such activities have made both the unions and their affiliated parties somewhat undemocratic.[24]

In July, 1950, the Japan General Council of Trade Unions (*Nihon Rodo Kumiai Sohyo Gikai*)—commonly called *Sohyo*— was formally organized with nineteen union groups and a total membership of over 3,000,000. The main constituents of *Sohyo* have been government and public workers' unions (for example, National Railway Workers and Japan Teachers unions). This federation was born of a democratization movement to fight dogmatic tendencies in the old Congress of Industrial Unions (*Sambetsu*), but actually it has inherited many of those very tendencies. Rightist-leftist disputes became so sharp that, in April, 1954, four labor organizations seceded from *Sohyo* and merged with the older Japan General Federation of Labor Unions (*Nihon Rodo Kumiai Sodomei*, known as *Sodomei*), which was long affiliated with the right wing of the Socialists. They formed a new Congress of Industrial Unions (*Zenro Kaigi*), composed

[23] Hayashi Shozo on the power elite, *loc. cit.*

[24] Seki Yoshihiko (Professor, Tokyo Metropolitan University), on the anachronistic ideology of renovationist political and labor movements, *Jiyu,* May, 1960.

of about 800,000 members of private industrial unions (such as the National Federation of Textile Workers and Japan Seamen's unions). In short, after 1957 all major unions were affiliated with either *Sohyo* or its rival, *Zenro*.[25]

When *Zenro* split off from *Sohyo* it made the following criticism of the parent federation: (1) wavering leadership and confusion in the guidance of labor; (2) loss of confidence because of participation principally in leftist political movements; (3) deviation from its own basic policies; and (4) decisions made in private group conferences.[26]

Efforts to reunite the labor federations broke down in August, 1959, when *Sohyo* Chairman Ohta Kaoru announced a joint struggle with the Japan Communist Party against revision of the Japanese-American security treaty. Beyond these tactics *Sohyo* and *Zenro* were rapidly dividing the Socialists into class party and people's party wings. Eventually dissatisfaction invaded the ranks of *Sohyo* itself. Significantly, on January 23, 1960, the day before the appearance of the new Democratic Socialist Party, certain Socialist leaders of *Sohyo* issued a manifesto entitled "Some Suggestions for the Advancement of the Labor Movement." [27] The manifesto called upon *Sohyo* to revise its undue emphasis on political movements and to back political parties only indirectly. In reply, Secretary General Iwai Akira explained that "*Sohyo* has been fighting against the war policies of monopoly capital and its fight has inevitably become a political struggle . . . because the socialist parties of Japan are weak." [28] Despite this widening split in labor, which was soon reflected in a division of the Socialists as well, *Sohyo* took the leadership in the cam-

[25] In addition, there are a federation of industrial organizations called *Shin Sambetsu* with 430,000 members and the old *Sambetsu*, which still had about 12,000 members. "Postwar Labor Movements," Nakamura & Matsumura, *op. cit.*, p. 49. At the time of writing, a new publication from Japan had just come to the author's attention: *Summary of the Labor Press,* compiled and published monthly by the Gotham Foundation Research Center, Sophia University, Tokyo (Issue No. 1, May, 1960). A project begun by Dr. Gaston Sigur, formerly of the Asia Foundation, the *Summary* digests organ papers of *Sohyo*, *Zenro, Sodomei* and others.

[26] Isa Hideo, "Collapsing *Sohyo,* Advancing *Zenro*," *Nippon Shuho,* March 5, 1960.

[27] These were members of the *Rodosha Doshi Kai* (Workers' Brotherhood), who were in turn probably inspired by the National Railway Workers' Union *(Kokutetsu).* The latter had begun to insist that *Sohyo* pay stricter attention to economic demands of labor. *Seiji Keizai,* August, 1959; *Economist,* March 1, 1960.

[28] *Asahi Journal,* February 14, 1960 (interview with Iwai Akira); and *Shakaishugi,* March, 1960 (interview with Ohta Kaoru).

paign against revision of the American security treaty and, in its effort, won support of most labor organizations and socialists.

The Political Parties

BACKGROUND. The seeds of political parties in Japan were sown even before the adoption of the Meiji Constitution. Itagaki Taisuke and Okuma Shigenobu founded the first modern political parties in the late nineteenth century, stirred the oligarchs to fulfill the vague promise to adopt a constitutional form of government and then withdrew in face of severe government oppression.

In 1889, on the eve of elections for the first Diet, the parties were revived. From original Liberal and Progressive party lines, a bewildering network of branches split off at tangents and then coalesced in basic groups. Yet the personality of the parties was preserved through the following years, even across war into the Occupation. The Liberals eventually became the *Seiyukai* (or *Rikken Seiyukai,* literally Society for Political Friends of Constitutional Government), in 1900; one branch of the Progressives finally became the *Minseito* (Party for Popular Government), in 1927. These were Japan's two main bourgeois parties.[29]

In the early Taisho era (1912-1925) and especially after World War I, ideas of democracy spread rapidly in Japan. Japan's most distinguished liberal, Ozaki Yukio, and Inukai Tsuyoshi became leaders of the opposition to bureaucratic government. In 1918 Japan's first genuine party cabinet was formed by the *Seiyukai* under the leadership of Hara Takashi and the historic universal manhood suffrage bill was passed in 1925.

Meanwhile, the growth of democracy and the rapid industrialization of Japan had also produced the appearance of so-called proletarian parties. In 1901, the Social Democratic Party (*Shakai Minshuto*) put in a brief appearance but was dissolved by the government on the day it was founded. In 1928, under the new suffrage act, four such parties succeeded in sending eight members to the Diet; in April, 1937, socialists reached a high-water mark of thirty-six representatives in the Diet. Even in these early days of social democracy adherents of proletarian parties

[29] Japanese political scientists distinguish between two classes of parties, bourgeois and proletarian. Professor Robert E. Ward has arranged selected Japanese literature on parties under such headings in *A Guide to Japanese Reference and Research Materials in the Field of Political Science* (Ann Arbor: Center for Japanese Studies, Bibliography Series No. 1, University of Michigan, 1950), pp. 86–91.

were split into two main factions, the theorists and the direct actionists.

Party governments received crushing blows from 1930 on, when young officers of the Imperial Army adventured into the era of government by assassination. Party leaders then tried only to rationalize the *faits accomplis* of the army, and party government was literally and figuratively dead.[30] The 1930s saw a succession of whole-nation and transcendental cabinets; the 1940s, a cycle of shabby, cut-rate political associations successively called the Imperial Rule Assistance Political Council, the I.R.A. Political Association and, finally, the Japan Political Party. These all had pretensions toward, but never succeeded in establishing, the one-party state of fascism.

Although the immediate postwar period produced a maze of parties (there were over 1,000 registered groups at one point), Japan had a paucity of true political parties. Even the three or four major ones offered a bewildering shift of names, symptomatic of the bland transfer of members' allegiance, and an almost total lack of true political principles.[31] Two conservative parties which contended, merged, split off, and coalesced again were the Liberals (*Jiyuto*: Liberal Party, Democratic-Liberals, Liberals— Yoshida and Hatoyama factions—and finally Liberal-Democrats) and the Democrats (*Minshuto*: Progressives, Democrats, People's Democratic Party, Progressives, Democrats and, finally, Liberal-Democrats). Both were grandsons, at least by marriage, of the old prewar *Seiyukai* and *Minseito*. The great purges beginning in 1946, however, effectively ended the advisability and possibility of direct lineal inheritance.

The Liberals (as the Yoshida coalition) were the first in postwar Japan to obtain an absolute majority in the lower house, in the elections of 1949. Despite its glittering name, the Liberal Party was far to the Right among conservative groups. It enjoyed the support of new business and industrial interests as well as the votes of rural conservative Japan. At one stage the Democrats allied with the Socialists in the Katayama government and later

[30] The most thorough study is Robert A. Scalapino, *Democracy and the Party Movement in Prewar Japan: The Failure of the First Attempt* (Berkeley: University of California, 1953).

[31] For early, searching articles written by experienced (former SCAP) officials, see the symposium edited by Professor Harold S. Quigley, *American Political Science Review*, XLII, No. 5 (October, 1948) and No. 6 (December, 1948), especially Kenneth E. Colton, "Pre-war Political Influences in Post-war Conservative Parties"; and John Saffell, "Japan's Post-war Socialist Party," pp. 940–969.

formed a cabinet under their own president, Ashida Hitoshi. The Democrats were, however, only a little less conservative and differed on minor points from the Liberal Party.

The only major and somewhat more effective opposition was provided by the Social Democratic Party of Japan (*Nihon Sha-kaito*),[32] formally organized in November, 1945. From the beginning, the Socialists represented a conglomeration of the Left; the party included divergent elements such as were represented by the late Kagawa Toyohiko, Christian leader; Abe Isoo, war-horse socialist from the 1900s who died in 1949; and Takano Iwasaburo, former adviser to the Social Mass Party. In June, 1947, Katayama Tetsu, Chairman of the Socialist Central Executive Committee, became premier and formed the first socialist government in Japan's history. Management of party affairs fell to Nishio Suehiro, a Right-wing Socialist. Unfortunately for the Socialists, they came to power when Japan was at a low economic ebb, and the cabinet fell in 1948.

For the remainder of the Occupation period and for two years beyond the peace Liberal Yoshida Shigeru gave the nation leadership, but it can scarcely be said to have rested on genuine party organization. Five times premier of Japan, Yoshida broke the fifty-year-old record of Prince Ito. His iron bureaucratic rule eventually divided the Liberals and paved the way for the rise of Japan's most famous purgee, Hatoyama Ichiro. The split in turn led to the resignation of Yoshida in 1954 and, paradoxically, to the merger of Hatoyama Liberals, Progressives and Democrats into a new Liberal-Democratic Party (*Jiyu-Minshuto*) in 1955.

The Socialists had been even more impractically divided than their conservative rivals. Indeed, the Right- (*U-ha*) split off from the Left-wing (*Sa-ha*) because the former supported both the peace treaty and limited rearmament, while the Left opposed both.[33] In October, 1955, a complex compromise was completed whereby Suzuki Mosaburo (with the backing of the

[32] The literal translation would be "Japan Socialist Party," but the group early adopted as an official English translation "Social Democratic Party of Japan," to suggest its relationship to the international socialist movement. See Cecil H. Uyehara, "The Social Democratic Movement," *The Annals* of the American Academy of Political and Social Science, CCCVIII (November, 1956), p. 54.

[33] Left, Right and eventually unified platforms of the Socialists may be conveniently found in Uyehara, Royama, & Ogata, *Comparative Platforms of Japan's Major Political Parties*, mimeographed (Medford, Mass., 1955). Further reference to a project which has studied Japan's social democratic movement —of which this symposium is a part—will be made below. The project has been directed by Professor Allan B. Cole and Dr. George Totten.

militant *Sohyo*) became chairman and Asanuma Inejiro (with
the support of the more moderate *Zenro*) became secretary-general.

Thus in 1955 there was a great deal of talk about the
fortunate emergence in Japan of a genuine two-party system.
The discussion was, however, ill-founded for a number of reasons.
In the first place, Japanese voters continued to weigh personality
of candidates more heavily than the platforms of the political
parties in casting their ballots in elections.[34] Second, neither of
the blocs had come to believe in the party system. President
Suzuki, at a party congress in 1958 stated openly that the two-
party system neither existed nor was desired by the Socialists.
The parties, he said, were "based on capitalism, and on the
working classes under capitalism." The party's aim was the establishment of a socialist state. On the other side of the political
fence, conservative opinion had frequently expressed, even if
not so blatantly, that the two-party system is satisfactory and
desirable if the governing party can remain in control, and if the
opposition can be kept more or less permanently in the political
wilderness.[35]

Today, Japan may well be what Professor Robert Scalapino
has called a one and one-half party state or what we call a six
quarter-parties state. During the 1950s, the Socialists were filled
with hope for the future. They moved moderately but steadily
upward, both in percentage of votes and seats won in the Diet.
Some even saw the approach of a socialist era. Then they reached
a ceiling in the general election of May, 1958. Their percentage
of votes continued to decline in the House of Councillors election
of June, 1959. Under these blows of defeat, the party split once
again. The Socialists had come up against the barriers of organization, leadership and policies which separated them from two-
thirds of the voters. The longer they were denied the opportunity
of taking office, the more doctrinaire, revolutionary and impractical their policies became and, consequently, the less chance of
gaining broad support by appealing to the middle-class floating
vote, which alone could bring them to power. And yet, as they
efficiently demonstrated in the security treaty revision crisis in

---

[34] A public opinion survey conducted by the Autonomy Agency, for example, demonstrated that 38 per cent of those polled took into consideration
the personality of the candidate first (this was particularly true of supporters
of Liberal-Democratic candidates), while 28 per cent said they cast their
ballots on the basis of party principles. *The Japan Times,* February 3, 1959.

[35] "The Two Party System," *The Japan Times, June* 9, 1959.

1959–1960, in alliance with other groups of the Left, the Socialists could effectively block the will of the majority as expressed in the Diet. Meanwhile, conservative governments continued to roll up majorities but at the same time (as clearly evidenced by opinion polls) continued to be unpopular and suspect. Liberal-Democrats were, in turn, fragmented into at least four power factions. Herein lay another reason why glowing predictions, a few years back, of the stability of the two-party state were at least premature.[36]

THE CONSERVATIVES. A number of reasons have been given for the continued dominance by the conservative parties, despite public suspicion of them. Although the dynamic process of further industrialization and urbanization has eroded traditional values, the emerging middle class is still essentially conservative within the context of the socio-political system. If, under land reform, a large measure of equality and social mobility has been intruded into agrarian Japan, this very movement has served as a positive asset to the conservatives. The old earthquakes of rural unrest have been greatly subdued; and the Socialists have shown little or no imagination in trying to invade the rural conservative strongholds. The conservatives have been able to tap the traditional and pervasive strength of the bureaucracy and, at the same time, have shown some political flair for seeking support of public opinion. In the latter area, the Socialists have often walked with two left feet. Conservatives have also been able to siphon off currents of nationalism among all political elements. In terms of party organization, although the conservatives too have been faction-ridden, they have presented new faces of political leadership and, at the same time, successfully assimilated the older purgees. All has not been strength, of course. As one writer put it,

Less spectacular but no less significant were changes in conservative party organization, function, power and policies; the continued existence of factionalism; the threat of an invigorated and growing Socialist movement; and the development of party color in local governmental jurisdiction.[37]

The Liberal-Democratic Party (*Jiyu-Minshuto*) was formed, as we have noted, in November, 1955. It is characteristic of the party that it had no president until April, 1956, when Hatoyama

[36] Robert A. Scalapino, "Japanese Socialism in Crisis," reprint from *Foreign Affairs,* January, 1960.

[37] Kenneth E. Colton, "The Conservative Political Movement," *The Annals* of the American Academy of Political and Social Science, CCCVIII (November, 1956), p. 40.

Ichiro was named. After his retirement Ishibashi Tanzan was elected president but held office only briefly. Kishi Nobusuke succeeded both as president and prime minister in February, 1957. In July, 1960, after the rigors of the battle to revise the American-Japanese security treaty, Kishi announced that he would retire. The maneuvers to select a successor once again revealed the intense factionalism in party circles.

In its domestic policy the Liberal-Democratic Party set as one goal of its administration the elimination of poverty. In the series of campaigns of 1959 which culminated in the House of Councillors elections of June 2, its basic policies were defined as follows:

> To adhere to parliamentarianism, eliminate undemocratic activities, stabilize farm and fisheries management on the principles of free enterprise; to secure the structural improvement of medium and smaller enterprises, improvement of roads, flood prevention, stabilization of national economy, effective enforcement of the social security system.[38]

As the party in power, it had developed a keen sense of public relations. For example, in the same upper house campaign it published a number of eye-catching pamphlets entitled "How Are Taxes Used?" and "A Bright Japan, an Abundant Life." [39]

The foreign policy platform of the Liberal-Democrats in the late 1950s naturally paralleled the policy of the government as defined by Prime Minister Kishi and Foreign Minister Fujiyama:

> To contribute to world peace and to elevate Japan's international status through cooperation with the free nations; to adhere to the policies of the United Nations, and maintain good neighborly relations with the Asian countries.[40]

[38] *The Japan Times,* May 7, 1959.

[39] Many such pamphlets were collected by the author in Kyoto during the election campaign in 1959: *"Zeikin wa do tsukawareru ka? Akarui kurashi no san-ju-yon-nen-do yosan"* (How are taxes used? The Showa 34 [1959] budget for a bright life), *Jiyu-Minshuto* (Tokyo), May, 1959, containing explanations of plans for tax reduction, people's livelihood, expansion of industry, widening of social welfare, broadening of education, services for women, youth, and children, and slogans, *"Akarui Nippon yutakana seikatsu"* (A bright Japan, an abundant life), *Jiyu-Minshuto* (Tokyo), 1959 was a popular platform, illustrated with clever cartoons: "The Course toward Liberty and Prosperity," the economy, education, social security, agriculture and forestry, medium and small enterprises, labor, use of national land, measures for youth and women, diplomacy, and national security.

[40] *The Japan Times,* May 7, 1959.

The platform for the 1958 general election further spelled out these general aims: (1) prohibition of nuclear tests: strongly push forward general disarmament, prohibit atomic and hydrogen bombs, pursue an independent foreign policy based on the UN, and maintain Japan's position as an Asian nation; (2) security: build up defense forces commensurate with resources and then consider withdrawal of American forces; no nuclear arms for self-defense forces; (3) the two Chinas: endeavor to increase trade with the People's Republic, but no recognition for the present; (4) Southeast Asia: cooperation in economic development, technical and financial assistance; (5) foreign trade: increase of exports to $5 billion by 1962.[41] Although the Liberal-Democrats have regularly supported close economic and political ties with the United States, they have also bowed to the force of nationalism by favoring the return of Okinawa to Japanese control.

The potential power of Japan's emergent middle class received the deep bow of the Liberal-Democrats in 1960, when the party's so-called Philosophers Group announced its "Political Philosophy of Neo-Conservatism." This group was spearheaded by the party's brain-trusters, including Kiyose Ichiro (Speaker of the House of Representatives), forty-three-year-old Hayakawa Takashi (formerly a member of the Progressives), and other Diet members. The policy statement, in typical political party style, tried to strike a happy medium based on neo-conservatism and neo-nationalism while repudiating racism and class supremacy. It thus rejected dogmas of Marxism but argued for the necessity of revised capitalism, rectification of the imbalance of wealth and full employment. The Liberal-Democrats, then, "stress that the entire people should be turned into the middle class and owners of capital." [42]

To publicize its platform and to help elect its candidates to office, the Liberal-Democratic Party established its "Principles of Organization" when it was first formed in 1955. In its "Policies for Organization Activities for 1960," stress was laid on 20,000,000 small enterprisers, farmers and fishermen. In theory, the organizational structure of the party is headed by the president; in practice, even in normal times there is a form of collective factional

[41] Based on a questionnaire submitted by *Asahi Shimbun*, April 26, 1958 (for the directly contrasting Socialist stand, see below), reproduced in *Japan Report*, IV, No. 9 (May 1, 1958), pp. 4–5.
[42] See the analysis of the platform by Uzaki Kohei, critic, in *Jitsugyo no Nippon*, February 15, 1960.

leadership among six officials, who act as an inner executive. These include the secretary general and chairmen of the executive board, Political Affairs Research committee, Diet Strategy committee, National Organization committee and Party Discipline committee.

Similarly, the forty-man Executive Board has officially been the agency for policy decisions; under President Kishi, however, the board was relegated to secondary importance because of the need to balance factions among the six primary offices. Other principal officers have included a vice-president, six deputy secretaries, and four bureau chiefs (general affairs, accounts, propaganda, and publications). The National Organization committee has included, in addition to the chairman, six bureau chiefs (organization, industry, labor, culture, youth and women). Finally, on the sixteen-man Political Affairs Research committee have served members responsible for cabinet, local administration and defense problems, as well as affairs connected with each of the cabinet ministries. Members of both houses have been represented on party general councils.[43]

In April, 1959, the Party Discipline committee demonstrated that it had real teeth. It reprimanded two prominent members of the Liberal-Democratic Party and decided to expel Dietman Tsuji Masanobu—the famous wartime strategist of the Imperial Army, author of a best seller about his escape from war crimes trials, and amazingly successful post-treaty candidate among ex-servicemen. He was ruled out for leading an anti-Kishi drive within the party.[44]

The Liberal-Democratic Party established a local organizers' system in 1958, further evidence that it was far more vigorous in driving stakes at the rice roots than was its rival, the Socialist Party. To illustrate by describing one prefectural federation with which the author is familiar, Kyoto-*fu* was divided into sixteen districts, each with a branch office chief representing the party. The organization of the federation is presented in simplified form in Figure 1.

---

[43] Panel discussion by members of the National Organization committee, *Chuo Koron*, April, 1960; Nakamura & Matsumura, *op. cit.*, "Organizations and Platforms of Major Political Parties (as of February 1, 1958)," pp. 52–53; also Kenneth Colton, "Japan's Leaders, 1958," *Current History*, XXXIV, No. 200 (April, 1958).

[44] Ikeda Hajime, "Reprimand of Dietmen," *The Japan Times*, April 29, 1959.

FIGURE 1 *Kyoto-fu Federal Association of the Liberal-Democratic Party*

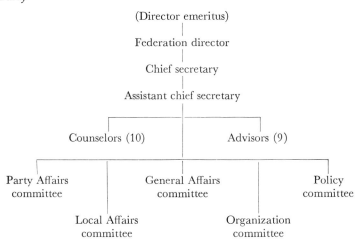

SOURCE: *Jiyu-Minshuto Kyoto-fu shibu rengokai yakuin meibo* (Register of names of officers of the Liberal-Democratic Party, Kyoto-*fu* branch federation), 23 pp. (Kyoto: September, 1957), presented to the author by Executive Secretary Kanagawa Buichi, on June 2, 1959 (the day of the House of Councillors election). Mr. Kanagawa shyly apologized, "All the famous people are out!"

There is no doubt that the ruling Liberal-Democrats have by far outsubscribed and outspent their Socialist rivals. For example, accounts released by the Autonomy Agency for a six month period (July-December, 1957) showed that party subscriptions totaled 619,000,000 yen ($1,700,000) and expenditures 477,000,000 yen ($1,300,000). Principal donors included the so-called Economic Rehabilitation council, the Japan Coal association, Tokyo Gas company, the Spiritous Liquors manufacturers council and the Ship Owners association.[45]

Turning from organization and finances to intra-party politics, one is immediately confronted by a labyrinth of factions and counter-factions. Perhaps these can be best illustrated by a brief mention of Liberal-Democratic Party personalities keyed to the speculation which surrounded selection of a successor to Premier Kishi in 1960. Kishi himself had already attained the highest post of political power and was on the decline. Nevertheless, his rise to the top had been rapid (he joined a party for the first time in

[45] Table of Political Party Funds, *The Japan Times*, December 4, 1958.

1953) and remarkable (in his early sixties he was relatively young as Japanese politicians go). Graduated from the former Tokyo Imperial University, Kishi had spent twenty-four years as a reform bureaucrat, mostly in the commerce and industry ministry, in Manchuria and, later, in the Tojo Cabinet. Because of the greatly enhanced political power position of the parties in post-treaty Japan, he may well have represented one of the last of the bureaucrats, prewar pattern, to assume leadership.

Prominently mentioned as a successor to Kishi was Ikeda Hayato, a financial specialist, new type bureaucrat, and ex-bureaucrat politician. He headed the main current of the Party but was handicapped for the expert's lack of sympathy with public sentiment. Ikeda once said, "It is better to make huge investments abroad than to make warships and airplanes." [46]

Quite different from either Kishi or Ikeda, Vice-President Ohno Bamboku was a real throwback to an old-fashioned politician. Whether throwing beans at the devil in a traditional *Setsubun* ceremony from the dizzy heights of the new Tokyo Tower, or serving as Speaker of the House, or maneuvering in the cabinets of Yoshida, Hatoyama or Kishi, Ohno was the prototype of a politician. By normal standards, his words and deeds often proved inconsistent, but that was his trademark. As the party's first tactician, he considered himself the legitimate heir. He depended for his strength, however, on men behind the scenes like Ikeda and Kono.

Kono Ichiro, man of action and former strong arm of both the Hatoyama and Kishi cabinets, led the so-called *Shunju-kai* (spring-and-autumn group). He quit the main current after the cabinet reshuffle of May, 1959. Although a world tour (including an interview with Khrushchev) took him out of the domestic political scene, it did give him a new and somewhat unorthodox perspective. When he returned, he remarked, "Making a trip outside the country, I came to wonder why I ever discussed such minor things." He advocated a thorough discussion of the revised Japanese-American security treaty and a United States-backed, Japan-led Asian economic sphere.

Perhaps the most powerful leader of the anti-main stream

[46] On March 30, 1960, when West German Chancellor Adenauer visited ex-Premier Yoshida (whom the press prominently mentioned as a possible successor to Kishi), Minister of International Trade & Industry Ikeda, Finance Minister Sato Eisaku, and Executive Board Chairman Ishii Mitsujiro were present at a luncheon. Yoshida introduced them, saying, "These three are candidates for the future prime ministership." *Yomiuri,* March 31, 1960.

camp was Matsumura Kenzo, former Minister of Agriculture & Forestry (who worked out details of land reform) and Education Minister (who invited to Japan the Chinese Communist leader Kuo Mo-jo). Miki Takeo, chairman of the Political Affairs Research committee, was not quite as friendly toward Communist China. It was said that, whenever an important decision had to be made in party circles, he made a trip abroad! At the other end of the policy group was former Premier Ishibashi Tanzan, an economist whose mild anti-Americanism dated from Occupation days. Ishibashi became more heretical and isolated, because of his jaundiced view of the revised security treaty and proposed policy of reconciliation with Communist China and the Soviet Union.[47]

On July 14, 1960, Ikeda Hayato, Minister of International Trade and Industry in the outgoing Kishi Cabinet, was elected president of the Liberal Democratic Party. Mr. Ikeda's new cabinet was formally inaugurated on July 19. He headed a caretaker government until the elections of November.

Mr. Ikeda was born in 1899, second son of a well-to-do brewer. After graduation in 1925 from the law department of Kyoto Imperial University he entered upon a twenty-three-year career in the finance ministry. In 1949 he retired from government service and embarked on his political career. He soon became closely associated with former Premier Yoshida.[48]

Now a few words should be added to describe certain minor conservative groups. The *Ryokufukai* (Green Breeze Society), although it enjoyed an intriguing name, has never really been a political party. Established in the House of Councillors by a group of independent, nonprofessional politicians, after the first postwar election in May, 1947, the *Ryokufukai* was more like a negotiating caucus of conservatives. With dwindling representation of independents in the upper house elections of 1959 (see Chap. 6), the future of the Green Breeze was in grave doubt. In February, 1960, with only eleven representatives in the 250-seat House of Councillors, the society changed its name to *Doshikai* (Society of Comrades).

Coming up fast to replace the *Ryokufukai* in public atten-

[47] The above profiles of Liberal-Democratic leaders were drawn from the following sources: Shinohara Hajime, "Profiles of Seven LDP Leaders," *Asahi Journal,* March 27, 1960; Kuzo Yuzo's sketch of Kono, *Economist,* May 22, 1960; Hosokawa Ryugen on LDP leaders, *Shukan Sankei,* January 10, 1960; an anonymous panel, *Doko,* March, 1960; Uzaki Kohei, critic, *Jitsugyo no Nippon,* February 15, 1960; and Kenneth Colton, "Japan's Leaders, 1958," *op. cit.,* pp. 229–232.

[48] *Japan Report,* VI, No. 14 (July 20, 1960).

tion was the probably conservative, possibly reactionary *Soka Gakkai* (Value Creation Academic Society). Its creation of political values was certainly not academic. In the July, 1956, upper house election, the society of Nichiren worshipers ran six candidates (four from national and two from local constituencies); three of them were elected (total ballots cast, about 1,000,000). Three years later in the June, 1959, election, the society again put up six candidates (five national and one local). This time all six were successful (total ballots, about 3,000,000). Known for *shakubuku,* its high-pressure conversion method (literally "break and subdue," words once used by Nichiren himself), the *Soka Gakkai* had little money but a world of enthusiasm. On the one hand, the sect boasted a strong military coloration: fifteen families constituted a squad, six squads a company, ten companies a district, thirty districts a regional chapter, which was directly responsible to headquarters in Tokyo. On the other hand, the sect liked to think of itself as an academic society: professors, associate professors and lecturers were appointed among followers who felt inferior in educational background. Emergence of this party of purgation, which has denounced both conservatives and communists, has called forth the warning that it a form of fascism. Whether this be exaggeration or not, the *Soka Gakkai* in a troubled Japan bears watching.[49]

THE RENOVATIONISTS. Sufficient comment has already been made of the prewar disabilities, postwar opportunities and yet decline in voting power of Japan's proletarian parties. Before turning to the renovationist parties, and particularly to the agony of the Socialists, some general remarks can usefully be made about their supporters.

With regard to interest groups, earlier described, the predominant characteristic of the Socialists has been the fact that they became increasingly a one-pressure-group party. The party has remained small (at the time of the 1958 elections, only about 60,000 members), even though it has polled 13,000,000 votes. This means that labor union members have provided disproportionate support. At prefectural levels the interlocking directorate of party and union officials has been striking. In national elections in the 1950s almost three-fourths of all candidates sponsored by *Sohyo* were successful; over two-thirds of those backed by *Zenro* were elected; and almost 85 per cent of those jointly sponsored won.

[49] Murata Kiyoaki, "Soka Gakkai: Communist Envy," *The Japan Times,* June 25, 1959; Ueda Haruo, "Unique Buddhist Organization Now a Political Factor," *Mainichi,* July 24, 1959.

Incidentally, as Japan's labor movement split so the Socialists divided. Despite these facts, no former major leader of postwar labor has been able to gain the top echelon of policy organs.[50]

Behind the labor-supported party have also stood Japan's intellectuals. And it is precisely in the *interi* (almost anyone who has had a college education), where one finds the strength of theoretical Japanese Marxism. Japanese intellectuals have shown a remarkable and frustrating talent for confusing fact and value judgments. They have perhaps had a disproportionate influence on public opinion. They accounted, to some degree, for the highly impractical policies of the renovationists, who often appeared remote from the dynamics of Japan's fast-changing society.[51]

Another source of internal friction has been the age brackets into which renovationists have fallen. Top leaders have been almost entirely veterans of the suppressed prewar movement: they have been trained in mass struggle, theoretical controversy, agitation and factional infighting. It has been estimated that 70 per cent of the Right and 40 per cent of the Left Socialist Representatives are over fifty. Only the Left Socialists have even approached the militant radicalism of the student movement, for example, the *Zengakuren;* and the Right has been almost permanently alienated from the younger generation.[52]

Whence the support of the renovationist parties? Despite the fact that they have never fully capitalized on their sources of strength, renovationist parties have drawn support from professional and technical personnel, white-collar workers (particularly lower-level bureaucrats), a minority of small merchants and industrialists, the younger generation and women. They were all attracted by the party's opposition to corruption charged against conservatives, to rearmament, to military bases, and to revision of the constitution. In his studies of social stratification and mobility Professor Allan Cole has pointed out that the subcontract system and its inherent frictions help explain why some small businessmen support reformist parties, particularly the Right wing of the Socialists. The urban proletariat, referred to by Cole as "indus-

[50] For expert analysis of these factors, see Scalapino, *op. cit.;* Uyehara, "The Social Democratic Movement," *op. cit.,* p. 59; Colton, "Japan's Leaders," *op. cit.,* p. 232.

[51] Murata Kiyoaki, "Japan's Intellectuals," *The Japan Times,* June 23, 1960; for an opposite view, see "Japanese Intellectuals Discuss Japanese-American Relations," *Far Eastern Survey,* October, 1960.

[52] George O. Totten, "Problems of Japanese Socialist Leadership," *Pacific Affairs,* XXVIII, No. 2 (June, 1955), pp. 160–161.

trial peasants," have shown marked ability to bow to authority as well as a penchant for intense political radicalism. These characteristics are also true of some white-collar workers, specifically members of the Japan Teachers Union.[53]

The Social Democratic Party of Japan (*Nihon Shakaito*) was formed in October, 1955, as we have noted, by reuniting the Left and Right wings. The new party platform, adopted after months of negotiation, sought to reconcile obvious areas of disagreement but turned out to be a congeries of contradictory compromises. It was, at best, a dazzling wallpaper design which merely pasted over the structural cracks in the Socialist wall. Struggles over the platform continued right down to the eventual re-splitting of the party. After the miserable showing of candidates in the June, 1959, election for the upper house, the Left faction redefined the character of the party as a class-mass party. Such a platform was correct because, although the aim of the party was socialist revolution, under existent conditions in Japan this revolution could be achieved only by peaceful means.[54] Such tortured reasoning did not convince sectors of the Right.

Socialist platforms have been more wordy, more highly theoretical and more intensely concentrated on foreign policy. By way of contrast with Liberal-Democratic policy, it will be interesting to note the basic policies set down by the Socialists in the House of Councillors election of 1959:

> To block all reactionary movements of the Kishi Cabinet, including the amendment of the constitution, revision of the Japanese-American security pact and enactment of the antiespionage law, which threaten the maintenance of peace and democratic government. To increase the income of the working public and reform the economic system to prevent large enterprises and millionaires from getting the lion's share. Special emphasis to be placed on boosting backward industries (agriculture, fisheries and forestry) as well as smaller enterprises, and perfecting the social insurance system.[55]

[53] Allan B. Cole, "Social Stratification and Mobility: Some Political Implications," *The Annals, op. cit.*, pp. 121–129; for a fuller account, see his *Japanese Society and Politics: The Impact of Social Stratification and Mobility on Politics* (Boston: Boston University, 1956); finally, for a case study based on society in Kyoto, *Political Tendencies of Japanese in Small Enterprises, with Special Reference to the Social Democratic Party* (New York: Institute of Pacific Relations, 1959).

[54] *The Japan Times,* June 25, 1959.

[55] *The Japan Times,* May 7, 1959 (for LDP basic policies, see above, p. 78).

Propaganda issued by the Socialists also displayed promises and slogans. Unlike the slick publications of the Liberal-Democrats, pamphlets had an undertone of radical, sometimes even Marxist mood. Even local elections were called struggles; defense expenditures by the Government were said to come out of the people's livelihood.[56]

Again in contrast with those of the Liberal-Democrats, the foreign policies of the Socialists can be briefly summarized from the platform for the 1958 general election as follows: (1) prohibition of nuclear tests: immediate and unconditional prohibition of tests by the United States, Great Britain and the Soviet Union, setting this question apart from disarmament (the unilateral suspension of tests by the Soviet was welcomed); (2) security: strive for collective security among Japan, the Soviet Union, mainland China, and the United States; simultaneous annulment of the Japanese-American security and Sino-Soviet friendship treaties; establishment in Asia of a nuclear-free area; (3) the two Chinas: conclude peace treaty with the People's Republic, and support representation in the UN; peaceful, independent solution of status of Nationalist Government of China (a domestic Chinese question); (4) Southeast Asia: friendly relations with Afro-Asian countries on basis of the "Five Principles of Peace"; (5) foreign trade: correct lopsided patterns by abolition of controls on trade with mainland China. Finally, the Socialists demanded an immediate return of Okinawa and the Bonins; and rational settlement of territorial issues with Russia by means of peaceful relations.[57]

[56] Pamphlets collected by the author in Kyoto, 1959: Nihon Shakaito, *Shakaito wa yakusoku suru* (The Social Democratic Party promises) (Tokyo: Policies Deliberation Council, April 1, 1959); *San-in giin senkyo seisaku, surogan, seisakushu* (A collection of policies and slogans for the House of Councillors election), (Tokyo: Policies Deliberation Council, 1959). The latter, for example, contained a general explanation of policies, foreign affairs, economic policy, finance and the tax system, labor, agriculture, medium and small enterprises, secular education, social security, policies for youth and women, and proposals for reform of the administrative structure of the state.

[57] Questionaire by *Asahi Shimbun*, April 26, 1958, reproduced in *Japan Report, loc. cit.,* pp. 4–5. For the upper house elections, a Socialist publication set out the foreign policy platform of the party in greater detail; Nihon Shakaito, *"Seisaku,"* (Policies), *Shakai Tsushin* (organ of the Socialists), No. 292 (September 25, 1958): (1) declarations on safety & security, relations with the Soviet Union, Asian Socialist parties, nuclear tests; (2) platforms on Chinese relations, the Near East; (3) representation of China in the UN; (4) talks on nuclear tests, Quemoy & Matsu, Okinawa (presented to the author by Fujimaki Shimpei of the Policies Deliberation committee).

Factionalism inherent in the unified Socialist Party was as much revealed by organization problems as by compromise platforms. Official national leadership was located in three major bodies (as of 1958): (1) seven top officials, including the chairman (Left Socialist Suzuki Mosaburo), secretary-general (Right Socialist Asanuma Inejiro), and chairmen of the Finance, Discipline, Policies Deliberation, Diet Affairs and Elections committees; (2) a thirty-six-man Central Executive committee, chief policy instrument next to the annual convention; and (3) twelve advisers or elder statesmen. In addition, the central headquarters of the party included a Disciplinary committe, auditors, and seven chiefs of departments of general affairs, organization, education and public information, youth and women, international affairs, planning and Diet.[58]

In June, 1959, a party structural reform council completed a reorganization embodying the reduction of the Central Executive committee to ten members. The move only heightened the factional strife, however, and after the split (at the seventeenth national convention in March, 1960) there were protests from local chapters to improve the organization of the party. On the other hand, delegates turned down by overwhelming majority a proposal to increase the Central Executive committee by five. It was then evident there was a gap between Socialist leadership and the lower echelons.[59]

As a matter of fact, the Socialists were—on paper—as well organized locally as was the rival Liberal-Democratic Party. The federation of party chapters in Kyoto-*fu,* for example, had jurisdiction over twenty-four branches in cities and villages of the prefecture. It held a plenary session of all members once a year and elected representatives to the Federal Executive committee, which is represented in simplified outline in Figure 2.

Nevertheless, after the local and upper house elections of 1959 local organizers were increasingly engaging in self-criticism concerning factionalism in the Party, the crisis in union alliances, and failure to elicit support among youth and in the villages.[60]

Even more so than the rival Liberal-Democratic Party, the Socialists have been plagued by factionalism. Although Socialist factions are immensely complicated, brief mention should be

[58] *Nihon Shakaito hombu, Yakuin meibo* (Register of officers), extra issue of *Shakai Tsushin,* Tokyo, April 25, 1958.

[59] *The Japan Times,* July 6, 1959; *Sekai,* May, 1960.

[60] *Sekai,* September, 1959 (a panel discussion by JSP organizers).

FIGURE 2 *Kyoto-fu Federal Executive committee of Social Democratic Party*

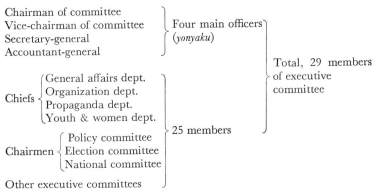

SOURCE: Based on interview with Kamigura Tetsuo, manager of secretariat, Kyoto-*fu* federal executive committee, SDP. Other publications of the committee: *Dai ju-ni kai teiki daikai* (Twelfth regular plenary session, report) (Kyoto: Okazaki Public Hall, March 2, 1958); *Fu-shi-sei koryo* (Platforms for *Fu* and city governments) (Kyoto: Nihon Shakaito Kyoto-fu Rengokai, 1959).

made of their general characteristics. As has been previously described, there has been a major split between Right and Left, severe enough to create two Socialist parties. These in turn have inherited different policies and tactics from at least three broad cliques: (1) the Social Democrats (*Shaminkei*), relatively more conservative veteran politicians; (2) the sharply divergent Labor-Farmer faction (*Ronoha*), a Marxist group and (3) the Japan labor clique (*Nichirokei*), which dominated the Right.

During 1959–60 the party was driven to another split because of the increasing dominance of the extreme Left, criticism of policies by Nishio Suehiro, and the struggle to find a successor to Chairman Suzuki.

During 1959, the Socialists gradually came under the influence of the so-called Council to Strengthen the Socialist Party, led by Professor Sakisaka Itsuro, formerly of Kyushu University. He in turn had received the support of Chairman Ohta of *Sohyo*. In brief, Professor Sakisaka blamed the failure on its previous people's party rather than class party emphasis. With a warmed-over analysis borrowed from Marxism, Sakisaka pointed to an inevitable conflict between working and capitalist classes. The purification of the Socialists could come only with a return to a class party basis. To this analysis, Right-wing Nishio Suehiro promptly issued a rebuttal and, eventually, led a bolt from the party.[61]

Even a split in the Socialists did not eliminate factionalism. Indeed, the struggle went even further over who would succeed Suzuki as chairman, in 1960. His own faction was anxious to salvage at least the Suzuki-Asanuma axis, and so the Left favored Asanuma Inejiro as the new chairman. The Kawakami, remaining Right-wing faction to which Asanuma belonged, was opposed. Nevertheless, on March 25, 1960, Asanuma was named by a slim margin and took over a party whose Diet strength was falling in both houses. According to one account the new chairman immediately sought to widen the breadth of the party by attending sumo and professional wrestling tournaments. The audience, he reported, seemed friendly! [62]

Considerably less friendly were ultra-Right-wing groups who believed that Asanuma was trying to establish a communist-type government in Japan. On October 12, 1960, in Hibiya Hall in downtown Tokyo, before a horrified audience and with Premier Ikeda a few yards away, Chairman Asanuma was stabbed to death by an eighteen-year-old fanatic student. Ironically, the occasion was a candidates' meeting attended by representatives of major parties.

In October, 1959, the long-simmering rebellion against the domination of the Socialists by left-wing and labor factions, its preoccupation with politics as essentially a class struggle, and its contempt for parliamentary procedure led the sixty-eight-year-old former labor leader and former Deputy Premier (in the Ashida Cabinet) Nishio Suehiro to bolt from the party with about forty of his faction in the Diet. On January 24, 1960, the dissidents established the *Minshu-Shakaito,* officially translated as Democratic Socialist Party.[63]

Almost immediately the new party became embroiled in squabbles with the Socialists (who denounced them as a bourgeois party) and the campaign against revision of the Japanese-American security treaty. On the latter issue, the Democratic Socialists condemned both Liberal Democrats and Socialists for failure to support parliamentary procedures. The primary cause of the mass demonstrations of 1960, they claimed, was the outrageous

[61] Seki Yoshihiko, "Outdated Sakisaka Theory on Socialism," condensed from *Keizai Orai,* February, 1959, by *The Japan Times,* February 2, 1959; Nishio's reply was contained in *Nippon Shuho,* August 5, 1959.

[62] Interview with Asanuma Inejiro, *Shukan Yomiuri,* April 10, 1960.

[63] *The Japan Times,* January 25, 1960.

manner in which the Kishi Cabinet tried to win parliamentary
ratification of the new treaty. The behavior of the Socialists gave
the government an excuse for undemocratic actions.[64] Nevertheless, the Democratic Socialists proposed postponement of the revision until the people could be heard; at the same time they
joined the government in the futile attempt to separate the scheduled visit of President Eisenhower from issues of domestic politics.

Once the crisis of June, 1960, was over, Premier Kishi had re-
signed, and the general election of November had been scheduled,
the Democratic Socialists tried to model their new organization
after the British Labour Party. Most significant was its pro-
nouncement, "The new party's basic aim lies in making the whole
nation a middle class." [65]

Treatment of renovationist parties would not seem complete,
of course, without mention of the Japan Communist Party
(Nihon Kyosanto). A summary can be brief, fortunately, for the
party qua party has recently been no more effective than its counterpart in the United States.[66]

The Japan Communist Party was strangely reborn in October, 1945, when General MacArthur ordered the Japanese Government to release all political prisoners, with the result that
Tokuda Kyuichi, Shiga Yoshio, and other communists came out
of prison. The party expanded even more rapidly after the return
in January, 1946, of Nosaka Sanzo from Yenan in China. Nosaka,
thoroughly trained in the tactics of Mao Tse-tung, brought with
him the peaceful revolution line and the slogan embracing the
"beloved Communist Party." The peak of its influence came in

[64] Sone Eki, Secretary-General of the Democratic Socialist Party, in
Sekai, October, 1960.

[65] Royama Masamichi in Minshu Shakaishugi Kenkyu, July, 1960. The
tentative platform of the new party had been drafted by the Minsharen
(Democratic Socialist League) and was strongly influenced by the prewar
tactics of Abe Isoo and postwar principles of Professor Royama. It had been
drafted by Professor Seki Yoshihiko, Tokyo Metropolitan University, whose
criticism of the Sakisaka thesis has been noted. It contained five major
sections: (1) basic principles; (2) a record of forerunners; (3) problems; (4)
goals of reform; and (5) path for the party. Asahi Journal, January 24, 1960.
See also article by Murashima Kiyuki on leaders of the DSP, Sekai Orai,
April, 1960.

[66] An early survey, somewhat colored by the author's position in Govern-
ment Section, SCAP, was J. P. Napier, A Survey of the Japan Communist
Party (Tokyo: The Nippon Times, 1952); a more recent analysis was con-
tained in a series of two articles ("By a Correspondent"), "The Japanese
Communist Record in 1957," Far Eastern Economic Review, XXVI, Nos. 2–3
(January 8–15, 1959).

January, 1949, when the Communists rolled up almost 3,000,000 votes (9.7 per cent of the total cast) and won thirty-five seats in the House of Representatives.

Japanese Communists' troubles began in 1950—and have continued ever since—when the party was hit by the government's organization control law, which drove most leaders underground; and, at the same time, by the Cominform's criticism that it had watered down revolutionary principles.

Party leaders have since reemerged, only to find that the initiative for communist propaganda and political warfare emanates from outside the country. Furthermore, the cause has been more vigorously pushed within Japan by nominal noncommunists. These have included Left Socialists, *Sohyo* and—when the organization has not proved too radical even for the Communists—the *Zengakuren*. Above all, mainland Chinese and Russians have depended on an amorphous but nevertheless powerful Leftist cultural front.[67]

The headquarters of the Japan Communist Party in Tokyo is organized like any other political party and gives little evidence of the trials and tribulations beneath the surface. There is a party convention, a central committee, a fourteen-member central executive committee (which includes Nosaka and Shiga), a secretariat, a discipline committee, and conferences and committees established in each local branch. Recent estimates of membership run as low as 40,000, far less than that of the militant *Soka Gakkai,* for example.

Beginning in 1955, certain communist intellectuals and students (shaken by anti-Stalin criticism), organized the Revolutionary Communist League. By 1958, the group had succeeded in establishing cells within the student group, *Zengakuren.* The league defined itself as a truly vanguard organization, and pledged itself to uncompromising struggle with the Japan Communist Party. The latter promptly denounced its rival as Trotskyite. The RCL is thus antigovernment, anti-Soviet, anti-American and anti-Communist! In the spring of 1960, when Mr. James Hagerty was harassed by demonstrators at Haneda airport, the American President's press secretary might have found it difficult

[67] Further details may be found in People's Cultural Research Association, *The Leftist Cultural Front; Its Organization and Activities* (Tokyo: March, 1956), which the author received courtesy of Dr. Robert B. Hall, Tokyo representative of the Asia Foundation; and the author's article, "Japan's Relations with the Communist World," *Current History,* XXXIV, No. 22 (April, 1958).

to believe that he was confronted by the "moderate" wing of
Zengarkuren.[68]

Japanese Elections

Certainly one of the more encouraging features of recent
Japanese political behavior has been the increase in participation
by citizens in the electoral process. Japan's first law of elections,
for members of the House of Representatives, was promulgated in
1889 (the year the Meiji Constitution was adopted). It provided
that only males who were twenty-five years of age and over and
who paid 15 yen or more in direct national tax could vote. Voting
citizens elected one member per district by open ballot. A law of
1900 brought in the secret ballot. And the law of 1925 brought in
universal male suffrage for the first time. Laws of 1945, passed
under the Occupation, gave all over the age of twenty the right
to vote, females as well as males (the constitution, adopted two
years later, guaranteed universal adult suffrage and secret ballot).
Finally, in 1950 the Public Offices Election Law was promulgated,
absorbing previous laws for the separate houses. The steady increase in the Japanese electorate, as a result of these successive
laws, is clearly illustrated in Table 1.

According to statistics (of the prime minister's office and the
Autonomy agency) released in late 1957, of the 51,800,000 Japanese voters almost 25,000,000 were males and over 27,000,000
females. A decline in rate of increase of registered voters mirrored
the lowering birth rate around 1937. One other set of statistics is
significant: rural registrations were at 20,850,000 (a decrease of
about 227,000 per year); urban registrations were at 31,046,923
(and increasing at a rate of over one million per year).[69]

Statistics such as these might rather coldly indicate a steady
increase in Socialist, as against Liberal-Democratic voters. These
projections would have to be offset, however, by the internal
difficulties of the Socialists described above.

Under the present legislation, all Japanese over twenty years
of age (except as deprived for criminal acts) are entitled to vote
for the House of Representatives. A citizen must reside for three
months in a village, a town, or a city, in order to register on
the electors' list; without registration, he cannot vote. Candidates must notify an election meeting chairman (appointed by

[68] Interview with Iwabayashi Toranosuke, organization department, Japan
Communist Party in *Zenei* (organ of the party), February, 1960.

[69] *Japan Report,* IV, No. 4 (February 15, 1958).

TABLE 1 *Comparison of electorate with population (from statistics of the Autonomy agency)*

Election year	Right to vote (1,000s)	Population (1,000s)	Electorate as percentage of population
1890	450.9	39,902	1.13
1924	3,274.6	58,350	5.61
1928	12,405.1	62,070	19.98
1946	36,878.4	75,800	48.65
1947	40,907.5	78,101	52.38
1949	42,105.3	81,780	51.49
1952	46,772.6	85,900	54.45
1953	47,090.2	86,000	54.25
1955	49,235.4	88,700	55.51
1956	50,177.9	89,500	56.06
1958	51,807.5	91,100	56.86
1960	56,554.5	93,540	60.46

SOURCE: *Fusen sanju shunen; fujin sansei ju shunen kinen kai, hen* (Committee for the commemoration of thirtieth year of universal suffrage; tenth year of women suffrage, ed.), *Sansei-ken kukucho shiko* (Outline history of the enlargement of suffrage), (Tokyo: Komei Senkyo Remmei, 1957), with an introduction by Maeda Tamon: see p. 321 for table; and *Japan Report*, IV, No. 4 (February 15, 1958); special issue (December 15, 1960).

the commission concerned), a stipulated number of days before the election. He must deposit for himself, or have deposited, the sum of 100,000 yen (about $280). Campaigns are severely restricted and maximum campaign expenses are prescribed by law.[70]

Japan has had an election management commission system since 1946. (For operations of the prefectural commissions, see below, Chap. 10.)

Writing in an American election year (1960), the author of this book has tried to recall and contrast Japanese campaigns in two general elections (1952, 1953), in local elections (1959), and in an upper house election (1959), which he observed. By and large, it is his recollection that the Japanese campaigns were mercifully shorter, if noisier, than the American variety. Newspapers in both countries did a fine job of identifying issues and maintaining the tradition of conveying political news. The Japa-

[70] In October, 1959, Japanese headlines were occupied by one of the biggest postwar election scandals. Newspapers speculated that as much as 100 million yen (over $275,000) might have been given as bribes to buy votes for the thirty-year-old wonder boy, Ayukawa Kinjiro. Two of his campaigners, who had secretly fled to Okinawa, were returned and arrested.

nese press was more active, more neutral and, if anything, more sophisticated about party claims. Japanese candidates made more use of the local meeting, particularly the panel of candidates so familiar to League of Women Voters' sessions in America. Up to 1960, the radio was still the favorite medium of Japanese candidates; television was yet to reach the dramatic proportions it had in the United States. Ordinarily, although the Japanese candidate might appear to the American guest in slightly unfamiliar surroundings—perched precariously with several party workers on the back of a three-wheel *bata-bata*—he was easily identifiable as his American counterpart. Both were of the same species, rapidly repeating their own names over loudspeakers, equipped with big smiles, and decked out with large lapel boutonnieres.

Several nonpartisan organizations make special efforts to provide voters with information. Especially worthy of mention is the Clean Election League in Tokyo, under the direction of former Education Minister Maeda Tamon. The Autonomy agency also makes available detailed statistics on party affiliation, voting behavior and similar data.[71]

Further details of methods of electing Dietmen, as well as the nature of the constituencies of the two houses, are described below (Chap. 6). Here it will be sufficient to look briefly at the results of two recent general elections as examples of voting behavior.

In this election seven women, including the widow of Asanuma Inejiro, were elected (eleven were chosen in 1958). The following compares the 1960 voting rate with previous elections:[72]

Category	1960 election (%)	Highest previous rate (%)
Men	76.00	80.74 (1949)
Women	71.22	74.42 (1958)
Both sexes	73.50	76.99 (1958)

[71] Komei Senkyo Remmei (Clean Election League), *1959 Komei senkyo no shiori; Sangiin giin tsujo senkyo; chiho senkyo, han* (Guide to clean elections in 1959; regular election for the House of Councillors; local elections, edition) (Tokyo: Zaidan Hojin, 1959); *Komei senkyo no jitai; seron chosa kekka no gaiyo* (The status of clean elections; outline of results of research in public opinion) (Tokyo: Komei Senkyo Remmei, 1958); the latter was based, to some extent, on *Sosenkyo no jitai; seron chosa kekka no gaiyo* (Trends in general elections; outline of results of research in public opinion) (Tokyo: Autonomy Agency, Elections Bureau, December, 1958).

[72] *Japan Report,* Special (December 15, 1960), p. 2.

TABLE 2   *General election of 1960, votes and percentages gained by parties*

Party	Number of votes	Percentage	(Percentage in 1958)
Liberal-Democrats	22,740,258	57.6	(57.8)
Socialists	10,887,134	27.5 ⎫	(32.9)
Democratic Socialists	3,464,144	8.8 ⎭	
Communists	1,156,722	2.9	(2.6)
Minor parties	141,940	0.4	(0.7)
Independents	1,118,906	2.8	(6.0)
TOTAL	39,509,104	100.0	(100.0)

SOURCE: *Japan Report*, Special (December 15, 1960), p. 2. For seats held in the Diet before and during 1960, see Chap. 6.

Political commentators dubbed 1959 the year of elections. Voting took place for twenty-nine prefectural governors, five large city mayors (Yokohama, Nagoya, Osaka, Kyoto, Kobe), officials in twenty-three special wards (Tokyo-*to*), 512 ordinary city mayors, 3,154 town and village heads and 3,671 local assemblymen; in June, voters filled one-half the seats of the House of Councillors. In both the local and upper house campaigns, three major issues regularly appeared in party platforms: (1) revision of the Japanese-American security pact; (2) Japan-Communist China relations; (3) and social security. Table 3 presents data on the upper house election.

TABLE 3   *House of Councillors election, 1959*

Party	National constituency			Local constituency			Seats in H. of C.	
	Votes	Per cent	Seats	Votes	Per cent	Seats	Total won	Strength
Lib.-Demo.	12,119,711	41.2	22	15,667,022	51.9	49	71	132
Socialist	7,794,900	26.5	17	10,265,393	34.2	21	38	85
Green Breeze	2,381,997	8.1	4	731,383	2.4	2	6	11
Communist	551,823	1.9	1	999,255	3.3	0	1	3
Minor	753,246	2.5	1	155,189	0.5	0	1	1
Independ.	5,817,938	19.8	7	2,311,112	7.7	3	10	18
TOTAL	29,419,615	100.0	52 *	30,129,354	100.0	75	127	250

* Two extra seats, to fill vacancies caused by deaths.

SOURCE: *Japan Report*, V, No. 12 (June 15, 1959). For seats held in the Diet before and during 1960, see Chap. 6.

Japan's leading newspapers saw a challenge to both parties in the sharp rise of independent candidates. *Asahi Shimbun* singled out the defeat of Socialists particularly in urban districts.

"The clearest indication is their crushing defeat in metropolitan Tokyo. . . . There is something in the Socialist Party at present, whether it be its nature as a party or its policies, that prevents it from winning the increased confidence of the public." Questions on the future of the national constituency system were also raised, and comments made on the change in character of the House of Councillors.[73]

On October 24, 1960, Premier Ikeda dissolved the Diet and later set November 20 as the date for Japan's eighth general election for the lower house. The government deliberately declared its intention to clarify the political situation by "liquidating without delay the social tensions brought about over the question of revising the United States-Japanese security treaty." Socialists, hopeful of translating the public revulsion against political violence into opposition to the Liberal-Democrats, ran on a platform of neutralism in foreign affairs. In the election, Liberal-Democrats got 57.6 per cent of the total vote and 296 seats in the lower house; Socialists, 27.5 per cent and 145 seats; the new Democratic Socialists, 8.8 per cent and seventeen seats.[74]

5 - The New Japanese Executive

Toward the end of February, 1960, at the Togu residence of Crown Prince Akihito in Shibuya, Tokyo, a ceremonial bathing rite was held to pray for the health and literary ability of a male child. Shortly thereafter in a *Meimei-no-gi,* or naming ceremony, the little boy was identified as Hironomiya (Prince Hiro) and named Naruhito. This name consisted of two Chinese ideographs, personally selected by Emperor Hirohito from a list recommended by noted scholars of the Chinese classics. For many Japanese,

[73] For further comment on the upper house, see below, Chap. 6; for data on the 1959 election, based on *Asahi, Mainichi* and *Yomiuri,* see "Results of June 2, 1959 Elections for the House of Councillors (compared with 1953 and 1956 Results)," mimeographed (Tokyo: American Embassy, June 4, 1959); and "Notes and Comment: Behind the 1959 Japanese Elections," by Douglas H. Mendel, Jr., in *Pacific Affairs,* XXXII, No. 3 (September, 1959).

[74] *The New York Times,* November 22, 1960.

the long line of Japanese emperors was thus assured for another generation and the stability of Japan thus freshly guaranteed.

As has been pointed out (Chap. 1), it was simply impossible to put in the formal words of an organic law the symbolic importance of this event as evidence of the unity of the Japanese people. On the other hand, it was easy to see that the Japanese press, taking its cue from the attitudes of Crown Prince Akihito and Princess Michiko, demonstrated an entirely new emphasis with respect to the new heir. For example, it was candidly pointed out that when the princess was taken to the hospital, her mother, Mrs. Shoda, hastened to her bedside and remained there until the time of birth. This was unheard of in the past.

In the months before the birth of Naruhito, the crown prince and his wife gave every indication that they hoped to maintain direct contact with their children by rearing them rather than entrusting them to appointed guardians and tutors, as in the past. The *Mainichi* hoped the new prince could grow, as does any Japanese child, in an atmosphere of freedom. A *Yomiuri* editorial underlined the departure from traditional mysticism.[1]

Shortly thereafter, Crown Prince Akihito and the princess visited America, at the invitation of the President, to commemorate the centennial of diplomatic relations between the two countries.[2]

The Emperor and the Executive

As a matter of fact, young Naruhito entered the world's oldest imperial family but one which has been considerably reduced in number under law. In 1960, it consisted of Emperor Hirohito (age fifty-nine), Empress Nagako, Crown Prince Akihito (age twenty-seven) and Princess Michiko. Five other children included Akihito's younger brother, Prince Yoshi (age twenty-five), and four married daughters who had technically left the family. There were, in addition, nine others belonging to families of the children or grandchildren of an emperor, called *Shinno*.[3]

In principle, the imperial family is now subject to all the laws which the ordinary Japanese citizen must obey; in practice,

---

[1] "Birth of Prince Hailed by Japanese Nation," *Japan Report,* VI, No. 5 (March 1, 1960), pp. 2–3.

[2] The Japanese Government hoped the tour would erase some of the bitterness resulting from cancellation of President Eisenhower's trip to Japan the previous June. *Japan Report,* special issue (September 19, 1960).

[3] Law No. 3, Imperial House Law, January 16, 1947 (Chap. 2).

numerous exemptions are legally made. Formerly, the Imperial House Law stood alongside the Meiji Constitution itself and was part of Japan's organic law. Now its affairs are governed by a statute which was passed by the Diet. And this law is executed by an Imperial House council of ten, only two of whom are members of the imperial family. Of the remaining eight, seven serve *ex officio* during their own terms of office; the prime minister, the presidents and vice presidents of the houses of the Diet, the chief justice of the Supreme Court, and the head of the Imperial Household agency. The Supreme Court elects one other justice to serve on the council and his term, as well as those of the two family representatives, is four years. The prime minister presides over meetings of the council, in which six members constitute a quorum and decisions are taken by majority vote. Expenses of running household affairs are managed under the Imperial House Economy Law, which is also passed by the Diet, and appropriated in the regular national budget. Affairs of the imperial family are administered from the Imperial Household agency (*Kunai cho*), an external organ of the prime minister's office. The agency's structure may be represented as follows:

FIGURE 3 *Imperial Household agency (Kunai cho) (932)*

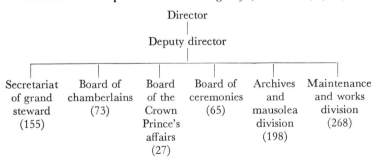

SOURCE: This chart and those throughout text are based on the following sources: *Gyosei-Kanri cho, Gyosei Kanri Kyoku* (Administrative Management agency, Management Bureau, ed.), *Gyosei kiko zu (Showa 33 nempan)* [Charts of administrative structure (1958)] (Tokyo: Ministry of Finance, 1958), p. 14; and *Revised Japanese and English Language Listing of the Government Organization of Japan* (with names of bureau, division and section chiefs), mimeographed (Tokyo: Publications of the Administrative Management agency and others, September 1, 1959). The numbers on the chart indicate the approximate personnel level, 1958.

The precise role of the emperor within the executive power, under the new constitution, is still a matter of legal dispute.

One can only sense (see Chap. 1, above) that it lies somewhere between the traditional and mystical *kokutai*, the theory of national polity, and popular sovereignty. For example, the present emperor's part in the decision to accept surrender in 1945 and his subsequent role in persuading the Japanese to adopt the Occupation-inspired constitution itself, would seem to make key provisions of that constitution sound redundant. The emperor is the symbol of the state and of the unity of the people (Art. 1). Furthermore, as Professor Harold Quigley has pointed out, through his quiet example Emperor Hirohito set postwar Japan on the path of constitutional monarchy.[4]

Paradoxically the Constitution, which provides (Art. 4) that the emperor shall not have powers, elsewhere (Arts. 3, 6, 7) assigns to him duties of appointment (of the prime minister and chief justice), attestation (of appointments of ministers of state and ambassadors), promulgation (of amendments to the constitution, laws, treaties and cabinet orders), and ratification (of diplomatic instruments). He also convokes the Diet, dissolves the House of Representatives, and proclaims the need for a general election. He attests general and special amnesties and awards honors. He receives ambassadors and engages in numerous ceremonial functions. Of course, under the new constitution the emperor undertakes all these responsibilities "with the advice and approval of the cabinet," which most often represents a majority party in the Diet; and yet all of these are governmental acts undertaken "on behalf of the people." Therein lies the paradox, already sufficiently discussed, of the status of the emperor in the executive.

The Cabinet Tradition

The appearance of a modern cabinet system in Japan marked the beginning of a tradition of central administrative organization. Indeed, Japan's first cabinet—after the Prussian model— was formed in 1885 and only later justified in the Meiji Constitution and by usage. From one point of view, at the start the cabinet was doomed in any attempt to exercise independent executive power. The competence of the cabinet was limited to assisting the emperor in the exercise of executive power; it was organized by imperial ordinance and all ministers were appointed by the emperor; the cabinet was responsible solely to the emperor.

---

[4] See Chap. 15, "The Powers of the Executive: Constitutional Monarchy," in Harold S. Quigley & John E. Turner, *The New Japan: Government and Politics* (Minneapolis: University of Minnesota, 1956).

Moreover, there were other executive agencies like the powerful privy council. All of this meant that the premier and the cabinet, under the Meiji Constitution, became a link between seen and unseen organs of government.

Nevertheless, the old cabinet soon became the major battle-ground for contending aristocrats, militarists, financier-indus-trialists, party leaders and bureaucrats. Even a brief summary reveals that all the great events of modern Japanese political history swirled around the cabinet. From 1890 to 1898, powerful clansmen converted into politicians and soon to become elder statesmen (*Genro*)—men like Ito, Matsukata and Yamagata—dominated the executive and maneuvered from a position of strength in the cabinet. For the next twenty years, semi-party cabinets built around *Genro* and their lieges gave opportunity for leadership to men like Okuma, Ito, Saionji, Katsura and Yamamoto. For a single decade, 1921–1931, party cabinets were tried, mostly on the advice of the last elder statesman, Prince Saionji. Thereafter, the power of the parties in the cabinet was stifled and the period 1931–1945 saw the steady rise in prestige of the military bureaucracy. Through all of this prewar experience, the cabinet was always responsible to the amorphous group who defined the imperial will; it was usually checked by the military services, which had privileged access to the throne; and it was occasionally responsive to political parties.[5]

During this same period, an administrative precedent was set whereby the cabinet was actually thought of in two senses. First, the cabinet council (*Kakugi*) consisted of the Emperor's ministers of state, including the prime minister, who acted for the emperor in a consultative fashion in a policy-making body. Second, the cabinet was composed of executive housekeeping agencies, including special offices directly responsible to the prime minister but set apart from the ministries. Both aspects of the cabinet have carried over to the postwar period.

The Prime Minister and His Office

Under the new Constitution (Chap. 5) and in postwar politics, the prime minister (*Sori Daijin*) has attained a superior

[5] The Japanese government has published a handsome set of volumes, *Naikaku seido shichi-ju nen shi* (A 70-year history of the cabinet system) (Tokyo: Ministry of Finance, 1955), 690 pp. A companion volume contains a series of charts, diagramatically representing the evolution of the various ministries within the cabinet and agencies under the prime minister.

executive status both in law and in fact. Appointed by the emperor, after election by the Diet, he is the head of the cabinet. Within the cabinet itself, he is in an enviable political position, for he appoints and removes all other ministers. The premier presides over cabinet meetings, declares a consensus of cabinet opinion, and represents his colleagues in submission of the budget, ordinary bills and proposals to the Diet. Finally, he exercises control and supervision over all executive branches.[6] With few exceptions, postwar prime ministers have been skilled bureaucrats, who have also managed to bridge the rushing streams of Japanese politics.

There are several reasons for the powerful position of the prime minister in the new Japanese executive. Legally, ministers of state are responsible to him (rather than to the Crown, as in the case of Great Britain). Also the typical rapid growth of the administrative state in Japan has centered in the prime minister's office (*Sori Fu*),[7] which has come to handle a myriad important tasks not assigned to specific ministries. These include matters dealt with in the name of the imperial household, statistical research, administrative management, public safety, defense, economic planning, local autonomy, science and technological development. To aid the prime minister in handling these multifold affairs, there is a whole complex of offices and agencies.

The office proper is headed by the prime minister himself, who holds the post of office chief. He is aided by a director-general, a deputy, a secretariat containing fourteen counselors and various sections. The secretariat maintains two offices in Chiyoda-*ku*, near the Diet building. In addition, there are two bureaus handling pensions and statistics, and three separate divisions concerned with decorations, tabulations and various investigations.

Auxiliary organs attached to the office have in recent years grown in number by leaps and bounds. Altogether these included (1959) some thirty-five institutes (for example, statistician training), committees (for example, central disaster relief planning), councils (for example, employment), and commissions (for exam-

[6] Constitution, Chap. 5, Arts. 66, 68, 72; Law No. 5, the Cabinet Law, January 16, 1945, Arts 2, 4, 5, 6, 8.

[7] The prime minister's office is dealt with in a series of small manuals, each titled *Sori Fu*, 1 (Cabinet, office proper); 2 (Imperial Household agency, Police agency, National Fire Defense headquarters); 3 (Defense agency, Procurement agency); 4 (Administrative Management agency, Hokkaido Development agency, Autonomy agency); 5 (Economic Planning agency, Science and Technics agency), (Tokyo: Ministry of Finance, 1958.)

ple, atomic energy). The important Science Council of Japan is also an organ of the prime minister's office.

External organs include the Fair Trade commission, to which belongs the job of administering Japan's postwar anti-monopoly laws. The commission has a chairman and four commissioners. Equally controversial has been the jurisdiction of the National Public Safety commission. Its chairman and five members have been involved in the ticklish process of recentralization of police power, within limits of the civil liberties guaranteed by the new constitution. The commission supervises the police directly and coordinates indirectly the work of the Tokyo safety commission and police, as well as all the prefectural commissions (Chap. 10). Similarly, national fire headquarters coordinates the work of local fire departments.

Staff or housekeeping chores of the prime minister's office (indeed, of the entire executive) are in the hands of the relatively new Administrative Management agency. Like the American Bureau of the Budget, this agency has a great deal to do with the civil service and, as such, is discussed later (Chap. 7).

The Autonomy agency was originally established as a sort of watchdog for the new principle of local autonomy, provided directly in the constitution. (In 1960, the agency was raised to ministry status). Autonomy functions and the national capital region development commission are discussed below (Chap. 10).

Because of constitutional limitations, previously discussed, Japan cannot afford to have its growing military forces legitimized by a full-fledged ministry. This accounts for the appearance of the Defense agency (and its collateral Procurement agency) under the prime minister's office. It too is dealt with below (Chap. 11). A competitor for budgetary attention is the important Economic Planning agency, also discussed below (Chap. 9).

Finally, the Science and Technics agency, with its three councillors, is engaged in planning in the fields of atomic energy, natural resources, aeronautics, electronics, radiology and the like.

With a position astride this great, inner bureaucracy—to say nothing of the cabinet and ministries proper—the Japanese prime ministership has become a focus for intense political pressure. After the resignation of a prime minister or after a general election, whether the government is supported or not, the speaker of the lower house takes the initiative in finding a new leader, by seeking party agreement. Normally, but not necessarily, he will be the head of the party with the largest number of seats in the House of Representatives. The Diet elects the prime min-

ister by a simple majority, each house voting separately. If they
fail to agree, the election is thrown into joint committee and,
if disagreement continues, the vote of the House of Representatives is decisive. If the cabinet resigns *en bloc,* for a brief period
the prime minister is the sole member of the new government.
(Outgoing ministers attend the administration until replaced).

Once the prime minister is identified, the formation of a
cabinet proves to be a slow, difficult and often painful process
because party factions now come into play. Usually a sort of
headquarters for choosing a cabinet is set up, and the struggle
swirls around the secretary-general of the party. In theory, fewer
than half the prime minister's cabinet may be chosen from outside
the Diet but actually, party pressure through the Diet is too
fierce to be ignored. According to the constitution (Art. 66), the
prime minister and all his colleagues must be civilians.

The Cabinet System

It should be clear, from the above description, that under
the constitution of 1947 (Art. 65) executive power has been
clearly vested in the prime minister and his cabinet (*Naikaku*).
The cabinet is (Art. 66) collectively responsible to the Diet, which
in turn (Art. 73) establishes general standards of administrative
organization. In other words, powers which were (under the
Meiji Constitution) assigned to an amorphous executive, appointed in the name of, and responsible solely to the emperor,
have now been shifted to the cabinet.

Furthermore, the cabinet—unlike the pre-war executive—
constitutes an organic unity; put the other way around, under
the National Government Organization Law of 1948 components
must maintain liaison under cabinet direction.[8] Cabinet meetings, ordinarily held on Tuesday and Friday in the prime minister's official residence, tend to reflect this characteristic. The
prime minister presides (in his absence, the vice-premier), there
is no quorum, and discussions are secret. Because of the cabinet's
collective responsibility, decisions must appear to be unanimous.

---

[8] Basic revision of the law in 1948 had as its purpose the provision
". . . of a clear delineation of the scope of duties and powers, in line fashion,
under control of the cabinet." *Naikaku Kambo* (Cabinet secretariat), *Kokka
gyosei soshiki ho* (National government organization law) ([Tokyo:] Law No.
120, July 10, 1948); of special interest are the revisions which carry the law
to the immediate post-surrender period: (1) to (34), mimeographed, December
10, 1948 to July 31, 1952. See further discussion of the law below (Chap. 7).

Those who are absent from a meeting may be asked to initial an agreement later.

With regard to housekeeping functions of the government, then, the cabinet is the highest administrative organ. Under it are grouped one office (*Fu*), that of the prime minister, and the twelve ministries (*Sho*).

Only the Board of Audit, singled out in the constitution (Art. 90), is independent of the cabinet. Its three auditors are appointed by the prime minister, with the consent of the Diet. In addition there are a number of external organs attached to the cabinet. The National Personnel authority, often destined to become a regular commission under the prime minister's office, remains a minor fourth power (with the cabinet, Diet and courts). It handles matters relating to public officials and, as such, is discussed further below (Chap. 7).

Two external organs closely resemble American interdepartmental committees. The Ministerial council consists of the prime minister (chairman) and the ministers of foreign affairs, finance, agriculture and forestry, international trade and industry, transportation and the director-general of the Economic Planning agency (with the governor, Bank of Japan as consultant).[9] The National Defense council (more like the American National Security council) also has the prime minister as chairman and as members, the deputy prime minister, ministers of foreign affairs, finance, and the directors-general of the Defense agency and of the Economic Planning agency.

Attached at cabinet level there is, finally, the controversial Constitution Research council (see above, Chap. 2) with its president, two vice-presidents, forty members, and a secretariat.

By 1960 the complete cabinet list has risen to twenty-two posts, twelve identified by the names of departments and the remainder held either concurrently or by men who were, in effect, ministers without portfolio in charge of the semi-independent agencies.[10] Assisting each minister who headed a depart-

[9] In 1959–60, during the critical discussions preceding revision of the Japanese-American security treaty, the cabinet established a foreign affairs council attended, from the Government, by the premier, the foreign minister, finance minister, director-general of the defense agency, director-general of the economic planning agency, and, from the ruling Liberal-Democratic Party, by its president, secretary-general and three other party executives. *Japan Times*, February 25 and 27, 1959.

[10] The first Ikeda Cabinet, installed July 19, 1960, for example listed: the prime minister and twelve ministers with portfolio; the minister of education

ment was one parliamentary vice-minister, except for the ministers of finance, agriculture and forestry and international trade and industry, who each had two. There were, in addition, six parliamentary vice ministers in various independent agencies.

Recently, when a newly formed cabinet has been announced, the names of four close associates of the prime minister have always been included. The deputy prime minister has come to be the spokesman for his chief, a liaison man in the cabinet, and a powerful voice in policy making. With a position somewhat analogous to that of the vice president of the United States, the deputy has come to occupy a position of even greater prestige and influence. The chief cabinet secretary has traditionally been the liaison between the cabinet and powerful interests outside the government, particularly the majority party. As director of the cabinet secretariat, he has also filled the role of chief of staff to the cabinet. The director of the Cabinet Legislation bureau has traditionally been the legal adviser to the cabinet, charged with preparing draft bills, and the chief liaison officer with the Diet. Most recently the fourth name has been that of the director-general of the prime minister's office, previously discussed.

Cabinet Powers and Responsibility

In the prewar executive, as it has already been described, even a majority-party cabinet found it difficult to frame and carry out administrative policy because of the maze of legal and extra-legal forces in the government. This weakness has been corrected under the new constitution and in the practical politics of the postwar era.

It is quite true that no definition of executive power (Art. 65) is given in the Constitution or in the Cabinet Law (Art. 2). Clearly such power is not vested in the crown to be exercised by the cabinet, as in England. Nor has the power of the cabinet grown in an entirely extra-constitutional fashion, as in the United States. Indeed, in Japanese constitutional theory, the cabinet holds an inferior status as compared with the Diet, the highest organ of state power (Art. 41). Nevertheless, the constitution

---

also served as director-general, science and technics agency and chairman, atomic energy commission; the minister of autonomy affairs, as chairman, national public safety commission; other state ministers directed the Administrative Management, Hokkaido Development, Defense and Economic Planning agencies. *Government Organization*, pp. 15–16; see also "Members of Ikeda Cabinet," *Japan Report*, VI, No. 15 (August 1, 1960).

directs the cabinet to administer the law faithfully (Art. 73). And in practice, the cabinet participates in the legislative process and stands at the crossroads of national policy formation.

There is, under the new constitution, no imperial ordinance power, and so policy making is shared only with the Diet. In the drafting of legislation and particularly of the budget, the cabinet takes the lead. Supported by a political party with an absolute majority in the Diet, it is all-powerful in deciding administrative policy.[11] Coupled with its legislative leadership is the fact that statutes are supplemented and executed by cabinet orders so complex as to defy understanding by the ordinary legislator. The cabinet exercises other powers of legislation: it advises the emperor to convoke the Diet, to dissolve the lower house, to proclaim elections, to promulgate constitutional amendments, treaties and laws. Statutes require the signature of the prime minister and the counter-signature of the appropriate minister. The cabinet does not, however, hold a power of veto.

Certainly not the least of cabinet powers is the right to manage foreign affairs and to conclude treaties (Art. 73). The latter are to receive the approval of the Diet, in advance if possible. As a matter of fact, Premier Yoshida Shigeru practically ignored the Diet during negotiation of the San Francisco peace treaty. Although the revised security treaty with the United States was extensively discussed in the Diet, the cabinet did not formally submit it to the legislators until after signature in Washington, in 1960.

Within the realm of public administration, as the major executive organ the cabinet stands supreme. For one thing, it exercises the power of appointment of the regular, classified civil service and shares the same power with regard to the special services (ambassadors, commissioners of the National Personnel authority, and members of the Board of Audit). For another, it holds the power of removal of regular officers, in accordance with the National Public Service Law, and of special officials (unless protected by law in cases of judges, members of the National Personnel authority and Board of Audit). Finally, in the cabinet are centered the advice and approval of executive

[11] For a discussion of the emergence of cabinet strength, see Tsuji Kiyoaki, "The Cabinet, Administrative Organization, and the Bureaucracy," *The Annals* of the American Academy of Political and Social Science, CCCVIII (November, 1956), pp. 10–17. This issue was a symposium devoted to "Japan Since Recovery of Independence," edited by Professor and Mrs. Kenneth E. Colton and Dr. George O. Totten.

acts done in the name of the emperor, as described above. All ministers are protected against legal action, during their tenure, except by permission of the prime minister.

Under the constitution (Art. 66) the cabinet is, in the exercise of executive power, collectively responsible to the Diet. In the normal pattern of the parliamentary-cabinet form of government, if the House of Representatives passes a nonconfidence resolution or rejects a vote of confidence, the cabinet must resign *en bloc* or choose to dissolve the lower house within ten days. Similarly, when there is a vacancy in the post of prime minister or when the Diet is first convoked after a general election for the House of Representatives, the cabinet resigns.

One problem of executive-legislative relationship remains unsettled, save in practice. In 1948, Premier Yoshida attempted to set a precedent by dissolving the House of Representatives without a vote of nonconfidence. He justified this action under one section of the constitution (Art. 7), which provides for imperial dissolution with the advice of the cabinet, but in the face of another (Art. 69), which clearly stipulates the need for a nonconfidence vote. The first time, Mr. Yoshida eventually got his nonconfidence vote; he exercised the power again in 1952 and once again in 1953, without protest.

Trends in Postwar Cabinets

In postwar Japan, as in many another modern state faced with complex problems, there has been an almost inexorable rise of bureaucrats to positions of political power. Indeed, so great has been the incidence of former bureaucrats among prime ministers and cabinets on the postsurrender scene, that Japanese critics themselves have cast doubt on the viability of the free political market and have even predicted the revival of fascism in Japan. Bureaucracy is not, however, a characteristic unique to Japanese officialdom. Political parties have become highly centralized and integrated. Big business, as it has grown bigger, has felt the need for bureaucratic organization. And even the leftist labor federation, *Sohyo,* outspoken in its criticism of ruling circles, has itself become highly bureaucratized.

After the surrender cabinet of Admiral Suzuki Kantaro, Prince Higashikuni formed a caretaker cabinet of consolidation. Both were considered exceptional. Of seven other postwar prime ministers, four had originally distinguished themselves in bureaucratic careers. From the diplomatic service came Shidehara Kijuro,

Yoshida Shigeru, and Dr. Ashida Hitoshi. Of these three, Yoshida left an indelible stamp on the cabinet system.

Five Yoshida cabinets, 1946–47 and 1948–54, saw two major trends in executive growth. First, the Occupation naturally demanded a tight-knit Japanese leadership. To this Premier Yoshida responded by making full use of his constitutional powers and by strengthening the office, through which the patronage from SCAP flowed. With most of the familiar politicians purged, Yoshida soon became a strong, individualistic party leader, who easily dominated the new faces in the Diet. Looking back, one can only wonder if an Occupation can ever create the climate conducive to strong legislative initiative.

Second, Occupation reforms led to a vast New Deal-like undergrowth of boards, agencies, and independent commissions. In Tokyo, any more than in Washington, these have never really been streamlined.

A brief flirtation with opposition party government occurred in 1947–1948, when Katayama Tetsu, a lawyer, headed Japan's first postwar Socialist government. Beginning about September, 1951, Yoshida began to see his own party control and, therefore, leadership eroded away. As depression deepened after the Korean conflict boom, opposition to his economic policies grew; as revisionism mounted after the end of the Occupation, criticism of his foreign policy became strident. Purged politicians returned to the political arena and, finally, scandals and corruption brought down the last Yoshida Cabinet, in December, 1954.

Hatoyama Ichiro, lawyer, prewar *Seiyukai* Party leader, and the only politician personally purged by SCAP, led three cabinets between 1954 and 1956. Resting on an uneasy merger of shifting parties, the Hatoyama governments were perhaps more democratic, as compared with those of Yoshida. Beyond doubt, they were also weaker than previous cabinets. Ishibashi Tanzan, a journalist, held the premiership only briefly from December, 1956 to February, 1957.

From 1957 until July, 1960, Prime Minister Kishi Nobusuke skillfully manipulated his way among party factions and three successive cabinets. He was the fourth of the postwar bureaucrat premiers. Although not a powerful figure—despite election successes it might even be said, paradoxically, that he headed Japan's most unpopular postwar cabinets—Kishi continued the tradition of an executive dominated largely by bureaucrats and businessmen. Such a simple characterization is, however, apt to be misleading. In Prime Minister Kishi's third cabinet (1959–1960), all members had previously been elected to one of the houses of the Diet. Many had scored political successes several times and one (Deputy Prime Minister Masutani Shuji) had been elected to the lower house ten times.

With the election of Premier Ikeda Hayato, in 1960, there was little doubt that the old-fashioned bureaucrat had begun to disappear at least at the higher levels. It was perhaps too much to expect—in Japan as in the United States—the appearance of a completely new personality type, combining the sensitivity of a politician, the initiative of an entrepreneur, and the dedication of a civil servant wedded to the public welfare.[12]

6 - The National Diet

In May of 1953 in Tokyo, workmen in the impressive Diet building—the Japanese version of the British Houses of Parliament—were busily readying the premises for the sixteenth special session, which opened June 16, 1953. (A general election had just been held, in April). The Occupation had subsided into memories then a year old. Guides explained, with a sort of revived pride, features of the huge lobby, with its line of statues of the founding fathers of Meiji Japan, the young *samurai* turned politicians, who had a hundred years before led Japan out of isolation. The more privileged tourist could actually enter the emperor's waiting room, where he rests before formally opening a Diet, and gape at its magnificent Momoyama-style gold-leaf ceiling. A small, elegant, solid gold clock occupied a conspicuous place before a mirror above the mantelpiece. The whole atmosphere was one of dignity and quiet, particularly in the adjacent chambers of the House of Councillors (*Sangiin*), where attendants were putting up the little vertical name boards for the members of the upper house.[1]

[12] Kuroda Kazuo, "The Role of Bureaucrats," *The Japan Times,* January 17, 1959.

[1] The author was conducted on this tour, in May, 1953, by Mr. Kobayashi Munesaburo, International Exchange division of the National Diet Library,

In March, 1959, again in Tokyo, the same impressive Diet building was almost obscured by the dust from frantic construction all around. The *Sori Fu,* where Premier Kishi had a somewhat tenuous hold on the reins of government, appeared old-fashioned and almost drab by comparison with the splendid Diet building, built in 1936, and the newer functional structures rapidly taking shape in 1959, like the National Diet Library, the *Gaimusho* or foreign ministry, and the extra-legally huge Defense agency. This time the author's host was Fujimaki Shimpei, Deputy Director, Bureau of Policy Research, Social Democratic Party.[2] Although Mr. Fujimaki was not a member of the House of Representatives (*Shugiin*), he was able to offer his guest coffee in the lounge. Conversation was difficult since it had to be pitched over the sound of a television set tuned to a baseball game. The vocal, slightly diffident Socialist talked almost entirely about foreign policy. Cultural and possible diplomatic relations with the People's Republic of China (which Mr. Fujimaki had just visited) were touched on, as was the political issue of the day, the forthcoming revision of the United States-Japan security treaty.

These two brief personal impressions are to some extent symbolic of the dignity and tradition, the modern vigor and political hurley-burley of Japan's Diet. Neither, of course, gives much hint as to the place of the legislature in the system of government or as to the future of the Diet within Japanese democracy.

The Diet Tradition

The Japanese Diet (*Kokkai*) is the oldest and most experienced legislature of the non-Western world. Almost 100 years ago, Japanese visitors to America had been shocked by what they heard from the gallery of the United States Congress and remarked that it reminded them of one of their own fish markets.

---

through whose courtesy he met and interviewed Mr. Kondo Hideaki, Secretary-General of the House of Councillors. The most frequently discussed organizational problem then, as now, was the fate of the national constituency which returns 100 councillors-at-large of the 250-member body.

[2] Mr. Fujimaki, who supplied the author with many of the Socialist Party materials cited above (Chap. 4), had visited the United States and had been at Yale University for a summer. The author first met him in Boston, at meetings of the Association for Asian Studies. Young, eager, almost scholarly, he represented a type of party (and, therefore indirectly, Diet) bureaucrat not uncommon in the Socialist Party.

By June, 1954, loud insults and grim fights on the floor of the
Japanese Diet were bringing down the wrath of newspapers,
which denounced the performances as the most disgraceful in
the history of the legislature. It is perhaps facetious to ask if
such developments mark the democratization of Japan or its
progress into modern parliamentary government.

On the one hand, Japan thus enjoys a seventy-year tradition
of parliamentary participation in government. On the other hand,
the old Diet was quite literally a talking society *(Gikai)*. It
always grasped at the shadow but never really held the substance
of prerequisites for an effective legislature. These might be
briefly listed as: (1) the backing of a universal suffrage; (2) responsibility to the electorate; (3) freedom from executive domination;
and (4) plenary legislative authority with a decisive voice particularly in the budget. The competence of the old Diet was
limited, specifically by the ordinance power, which lay with the
executive in the name of the emperor. If the Diet did screw up
its courage sufficiently to disapprove a budget, the cabinet could
simply pass the previous year's schedule of expenditures. Declaration of war, command of the military services, making of treaties,
and matters concerned with the imperial house—all were outside
Diet competence. Prince Ito, architect of the Meiji Constitution,
put it simply: "The use of the Diet is to enable the Head of
State to perform his function and to keep the State in a well-
disciplined, strong, and healthy condition." A modern observer
has pointed to the overwhelming power of the Meiji executive.
Professor Chitoshi Yanaga wrote:

> Consequently, the Diet was a lawmaking body in name and form
> but in practice was little more than a body which rubber-stamped
> policies and enacted them into laws.[3]

Even with the upsurge of political activity after passage of
the universal manhood suffrage act, in 1925, parliamentary government was severely circumscribed. By 1940, with the demise
of parties, parliamentary government under the old constitution
came to an end.

Under the new constitution (Chap. 4, Art. 41) the Diet is
the highest organ of state power and the sole law-making body
of the state. In constitutional theory (see previous chapter), even

[3] The prince's comment was drawn from Ito Hirobumi, *Teikoku Kempo
koshitsu tempan gikai,* cited (Chap. 1), pp. 9–10; see also Chitoshi Yanaga,
Japanese People and Politics (New York: Wiley, 1956), particularly the excellent chapters on the Diet, 8, 9 (the quotation is from p. 171).

the executive power, which belongs to the cabinet, is responsible to the legislature.

Recruitment and Selection of Dietmen

In the general election for the House of Representatives in 1955, the total number of eligible voters was 49,235,375.[4] Natural increases in population, expansion of the suffrage to women and lowering of the voting age to twenty, all were factors in this spectacular increase from the 14,000,000 voters who had participated in elections in 1937. Another factor contributing to the large turnout is the fact that registration is handled by the government. It is therefore uniform and virtually complete.

In direct contrast with American experience, Japanese rural areas have a much higher voting rate (only one absentee of five or six registered) than do urban districts (one nonvoter of three registered). Such national averages have also been borne out where detailed studies have been applied to specific areas: for example, an urban Osaka sample produced a large proportion of nonvoters (and radical party adherents), whereas a rural Izumo Shimane Prefecture sample produced a small number of absentees (and a large conservative majority).[5]

Under present election procedures (see above, Chap. 4), 467 members are returned to the lower House of Representatives from 118 electoral districts (*senkyo ku*). Each district chooses from three to five representatives according to population (except for Tokyo-*to,* the capital, seven). Thus urban Osaka, for example, has two districts returning four seats each. There are 250 members of the upper House of Councillors, with 150 chosen on a geographical basis (prefectures have from two to eight seats) and 100 from the nation at large. Osaka Prefecture, for example, is a single district, returning six councillors to the upper house.

There are up to three times as many candidates for the lower house as there are seats. To be elected, a candidate must

[4] Statistics from the election department, Autonomy agency; see Nakamura Kikuo & Matsumura Yutaka, *Political Handbook of Japan, 1958* (Tokyo: Tokyo News Service, 1958), pp. 24–25.

[5] Jun-ichi Kyogoku & Nobutaka Ike, "Urban-rural Differences in Voting Behavior in Postwar Japan," Stanford University Political Science Series, No. 66 (1960) reprinted from *Proceedings* of the Department of Social Sciences, College of General Education, University of Tokyo (Tokyo, 1959), p. 9. See also Douglas H. Mendel, Jr., *Political Behavior in Post-Treaty Japan: A Survey of Constituencies and Leaders in Two Selected Areas,* unpublished Ph.D. thesis at University of Michigan, 1954, p. 43.

place in the top three to five, depending on size of district. Each voter writes in the name of only one candidate. Thus the successful candidate needs the support of only a minority of voters (his percentage of vote can vary depending on the number to be elected, the number of candidates, and the distribution of votes).

Representatives must be twenty-five years of age and must have had legal residence in one city, town, or village for three months. Legal registry, rather than physical residence, is the criterion. Members of the lower house are elected for four years but, because of frequent dissolutions, seldom fill out this term. On the other hand, there is a strong tendency to reelect experienced members. Councillors must be thirty years old and enjoy an uninterrupted term of six years.

Constitutionally, no prospective member of the Diet may be discriminated against because of race, creed, sex, social status, family, education, property or income. Moreover, members are not liable outside the Diet for their participation in debates or votes; during a session, they are exempt from legal jurisdiction, except for criminal offenses. No one may be a member of both houses at the same time or occupy a staff position in any other national, local, or public corporation (except, of course, the prime minister, state ministers, director and deputy of the cabinet secretariat, and parliamentary vice-ministers, who are members of the Diet).

Ordinary members of the Diet receive, in addition to a monthly salary of 78,000 yen (about $216), *per diem* expenses, allowances, rail passes and postal fees. Chairmen of committees enjoy the use of government automobiles. On the other side of the ledger, Dietmen are now accessible to their constituents and expenses run high. It has been estimated that campaign expenditures per election have amounted to almost twenty times annual salaries.[6]

Sociological Basis

Aside from the constitutional and legal technicalities described, whom does the Japanese legislature actually represent? Do electoral institutions influence the manner in which votes are used, that is, the distribution of party strength? What of

[6] A speaker received 110,000 yen (about $305) per month, equivalent to the salary of a prime minister or chief justice; a vice-speaker, 80,000 yen (about $244), equivalent to the salary of a state minister. See Yanaga, *op. cit.,* p. 188.

equality of representation, a perennial problem in the history of all parliamentary systems?

First, it can be safely said—despite popular misconceptions —that no significant differences have been found among districts in terms of the number of representatives allotted. There is, however, an urban-rural disparity in percentages of successful candidates: beginning in 1947 about one-fifth of total number of candidates were elected from metropolitan districts, while one of three candidates were returned from rural areas.[7]

Turning to equality of representation, the urban-rural gap described earlier is directly translated into practical politics to the disadvantage of the city. Beginning with the January, 1949, election, rather significant differences began to appear among various kinds of districts. By May, 1958, the discrepancy had become so great that, on the average, for every ten representatives being returned from a rural constituency, thirteen should have been sent from urban, and nineteen from metropolitan districts. There were several reasons for this lag. Population growth had not been uniform: there was a tremendous increase of urban voters without a corresponding increase in the number of representatives apportioned. Adjustment to census statistics was not rapid enough: changes had to come through legislation, since there was no constitutional provision for reapportionment. Various political interests blocked changes.[8] One result has been continued under-representation of urban areas (where socialist parties' strength is to be found) coupled with over-representation of rural districts (where traditionally conservative parties are strong).

When we consider electoral institutions, representation and party strength, all factors do not favor the conservative parties. The Japanese system obviously has certain characteristics which seem to combine features of American primaries (with cross-filing) and those of British general elections. To the extent that candidates can win votes on their own, they can through the plural-member districts become independent from the control of local party machines and even central party leadership. On the other hand, they must often compete against other candidates of their

[7] Kyogoku & Ike, *op. cit.*, p. 24. These authors studied six general elections from 1947 to 1958. They divided all electoral districts into four broad categories, metropolitan, urban, semi-rural and rural, and into three institutional classes, depending on whether districts returned three, four, or five members; they then chose at random two electoral districts from each different group, or a total of twenty-four sample districts.

[8] Kyogoku & Ike, *ibid.*, p. 18.

own party. Liberal-Democrats, as the plurality party, have had to put up candidates for almost all contested seats. Under the multi-member district system, they have thus been at a slight disadvantage compared with the Socialists, who could concentrate on one candidate per district. The multi-member and national constituencies for the upper house, as in a system of proportional representation, have been permissive of radical parties, who concentrate on fewer candidates.

As to the political parties themselves, to enjoy some stability and coherence, they should bear some meaningful relationship to social classes and groups (as described above, Chap. 4). What interests, whom do the members of the Diet represent?

Conservative strength has been traditionally drawn from former *Seiyukai*-Liberal strongholds and, to a lesser extent, from former *Minseito*-Progressive urban centers. It has profited from a growing trend toward political coloration in prefectural governorships and assemblies. Evidence of conservative dominance of local politics was seen in the fact that, by the mid-1950s, the Liberal-Democratic Party held a comfortable majority in every prefectural assembly.[9] Before the war Socialists had some voting strength and even political leadership from rural areas. Since land reform, however, radical (and often, at the same time, reactionary) farmers' movements seem to have evaporated. "Until recently, Socialist leaders tended to ignore the agricultural community and to adopt the path of least resistance by relying on the collective vote of organized labor." [10] In the postwar era, Socialists began to challenge conservatives in the largest five-man urban-industrial districts. By the end of the 1950s, they were poised to invade the traditional agrarian constituencies.

In the post-treaty era, both conservative and radical parties have tended to run candidates fairly evenly through the country. Conservatives in rural constituencies, however, get relatively more votes and thus more rural representatives are returned. Of 117 districts studied by Professors Kyogoku and Ike, about 80 per cent were found to be rural or semirural. On this basis, conservatives by themselves have been able to form governments on a continuing basis. Since the Socialists have endorsed many more candidates in the urban and metropolitan districts, their Diet members have come from the cities.[11]

[9] Kenneth E. Colton, "The Conservative Political Movement," 7 *Annals* of the American Academy of Political and Social Science, CCCV (November, 1956).

[10] Cecil H. Uyehara, "The Social Democratic Movement," *ibid.*

[11] Kyogoku & Ike, *loc. cit.*, p. 32.

To be somewhat more specific, the degree of support for conservative parties, with few exceptions, has been inversely related to the degree of urbanization. A little over six of every ten voters in rural areas (as against four or five of ten in metropolitan districts) have supported the conservative bloc. Conservatives draw from various occupational groups, with strongest support from business, management and the bureaucracy. Socialists, on the other hand, have been getting the support of four of every

TABLE 4   *Composition of the House of Representatives, September 1, 1958*

Description	Lib.-Demo. Party	Socialist Party
Total no. in House	298	166
Average age	55.7	51.2
University graduates	222	100
from Tokyo University	91	20
from Kyoto University	24	8
from other institutions*	107	72
Professions†		
Business, management	105	20
Bureaucracy (incl. parties)	83	13
Law	35	21
Newspaper, publishing	29	8
Agriculture, farming	16	23
Academic, teaching	15	20
Diplomacy	5	1
Military	3	0
Medicine, dentistry	2	9
Women	3	7
Labor, labor organizations	0	41
Others‡	4	3
Present, former prime ministers§	4	1

One independent (formerly a Socialist) age: 41; profession: labor; one Communist, age: 57; profession: former editor, *Akahata* (Red Flag).

* Graduates from other institutions including (Lib.-Demo.) 9 who studied in the U.S., 1 in France, 2 in Germany; (Soc.) 1 in U.S., 2 in China, 1 in Austria.

† Categories are often difficult to establish, or overlap; these are the author's subjective judgments based on predominant activity.

‡ Including (Lib.-Demo.) sports, 2; priest, 1; miscellany, 1; (Soc.) social welfare, 1; civil liberties organization, 1; pastor, 1.

§ (Lib.-Demo.) Kishi Nobusuke; Ishibashi Tanzan; Yoshida Shigeru; toyama Ichiro (since deceased); Ashida Hitoshi (since deceased). (Soc.) ayama Tetsu.

SOURCE: From official Diet and party publications, compiled in *Brief les of the Members of the House of Representatives*, mimeographed (Tokyo: rican Embassy, September 1, 1958).

ten voters in metropolitan districts (in contrast to two or three of ten in rural areas). As might be expected, left-wing parties are preferred by members of the working class.

Finally, how are these characteristics of electoral institutions and of the distribution of party strength reflected in the Diet itself? A composite profile of membership of the lower house (the House of Councillors is discussed in some detail below) reveals a number of interesting results. For example, despite the traditional reverence for elders throughout the Far East, the average age of membership is not markedly higher than that of the American lower house. The percentage of members who have enjoyed higher education is startlingly high. Moreover, a glance at the data in Table 4 will quickly reveal the apparent pathways to political prestige in Japan. Outstanding are the number of businessmen and bureaucrats. Compared with the situation in the Congress of the United States, lawyers are relatively scarce. Former academicians are relatively more numerous. Farmers and, to a lesser extent, laborers are under-represented.

Diet Organization

The national Diet, sole law-making organ of the state, consists of the House of Representatives (*Shugiin*) and the House of Councillors (*Sangiin*). A simplified outline of its organization is presented in Figure 4.

Each house is responsible for judging disputes relating to the qualifications of members. A majority of two-thirds of members present may by resolution deny a candidate his seat. Each house also elects its own officers, establishes its rules of procedure, consents to the arrest of members during sessions and punishes member for disorderly conduct. (Problems of discipline are discussed more fully below). A majority of two-thirds present in a house must vote to expel a member.

Sessions of the Diet are of three types. The ordinary (*tsujo*) session is convoked in late December, when the houses organize. A recess, covering the traditional New Year's festivities, ordinarily lasts until late January, whereupon the Diet is convened again for the constitutional minimum of 150 days (the record 13th session lasted for 235 days). An extraordinary (*rinji*) session is convoked by the emperor, on advice of the cabinet, or when one-fourth of all members of either house petitions the cabinet. When the House of Representatives is dissolved, a general election must soon follow and, after that, a special (*tokubetsu*) session is man-

FIGURE 4 *Organization of the Diet*
Diet (*Kokkai*)

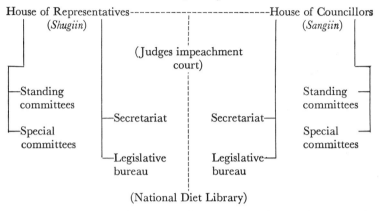

(National Diet Library)

SOURCE: Law No. 79 (the Diet Law), April 28, 1947 (in force May 3, 1947); Oika Makoto, *Shin Kokkai kaisetsu* (An explanation of the new Diet) (Tokyo, 1947) (Oike was chief clerk of the Diet); *Government Organization*, pp. 2–13; *Kiko zu*, pp. 104–107 (both previously cited, Chap. 5).

datory within thirty days of the election, or seventy days of the dissolution. The major purpose of a special session is the election of a new prime minister and formation of a new government.[12]

Although the Japanese have adopted the parliamentary system, the physical arrangement of the House of Representatives is in a semi-circle, like the Congress of the United States. Members of the cabinet and their assistants are seated to one side, on a raised level. The House of Representatives meets at 1 p.m. (after committees, in the morning). The House of Councillors reverses this process, holding its plenary at 10 a.m. (committees in the afternoon). One-third or more of the total membership constitutes a quorum but attendance is very poor, probably because of the complexity of the committee system. The agenda of all meetings must be published and circulated in advance but, of course, significant deliberations have already occurred in committee. Deliberations on the floor are public; an executive session must be voted by two-thirds of all members present. Voting is accomplished by standing, showing of hands, or the more cumbersome

[12] During an emergency, if the House of Representatives has been dissolved, the cabinet may summon the House of Councillors in an emergency (*kinkyu*) session. Any action is, however, subject to subsequent House of Representatives approval. Up to 1958, such emergencies arose twice.

method of individually depositing a ballot on the rostrum. Unless otherwise provided by the constitution, decisions of both houses are by simple majority and ties are broken by the speaker or president. As critical maneuvers have come to be concentrated more and more in party caucuses and in committees, many provisions for plenary debate, incorporated in early rules of the postwar Diet have been abandoned.[13]

Actually the first step in Diet organization is the selection of officers. The speaker is normally drawn from the majority party (in the 16th special session, 1953–55, Speaker Tsutsumi Yasujiro set a precedent by resigning from his party post in order to maintain neutrality). Often the vice-speaker comes from the next largest party. The speaker determines the schedule of business, is responsible for maintaining order, holds the disciplinary power and refers bills to committees.

The speaker of the House of Representatives has become more and more enmeshed in problems of discipline. As a result of dangerous riots in the Diet compound on November 27, 1959, for example, Speaker Kato Ryogoro was eventually forced to resign, prior to reopening of the 24th ordinary Diet session. Premier Kishi, Liberal-Democratic Vice-President Ohno Bamboku and Secretary-General Kawashima Shojiro made the ultimate decision on resignation; and chairmen of Diet policy committees of the Liberal-Democratic, Socialist, and Social-Democratic parties negotiated the reorganization of the Diet offices. When the session reopened on February 1, 1960, Kato announced his resignation despite the fact he refused to take responsibility for the anti-security treaty revision riots and subsequent threat to discipline Secretary-General Asanuma Inejiro (Socialist) for his complicity in the demonstration. The speakership passed, by agreement within the majority party, to Kiyose Ichiro and the vice-speakership went to Socialist Kawakami Jotaro. Only then could the house proceed with its business.[14]

One of the most important sections of the postwar Diet Law (Chap. V, Art. 42) has been that which established standing committees. There is one shared by both houses, the legislative committee, made up of ten members from the lower and eight from the upper house, with a chairman rotating between the houses. It provides the forum for discussion of mutual problems. In addi-

[13] For an early account of postwar operations, see Justin H. Williams, "The Japanese Diet under the New Constitution," *American Political Science Review*, XLII (October, 1948), pp. 927–939.

[14] See *The Japan Times*, January 30, February 1, 1960.

tion, the law originally provided no less than twenty-one standing committees, identical in each house.

Fortunately, by 1960 the number of standing committees had been reduced to sixteen, identical in name for each house: cabinet, local administration, judicial affairs, foreign affairs, finance, education, social and labor affairs, agriculture-forestry and fisheries, commerce and industry, transportation, postal services, construction, budget, audit, discipline, and house management (or steering) committees.[15] The finance committee is probably the most powerful for it assigns, in the first instance, party strengths among the other committees. In the budget committee the bitterest political battles are fought between the government and the opposition.

According to the Diet Law, each member must serve on at least one and on not more than three standing committees. In fact, allocation of assignments and selection of chairmen are strictly in accordance with party strengths (since May, 1953). Training and experience (rather than seniority, as in the United States) determine the members of committees. Although members formally elect and the speaker formally appoints committee chairmen, they are actually determined in the government party high command.

As in the American Congress, committees maintain an absolute control over the flow of all bills. Although meetings are technically public, strategy is all worked out in an executive directorate (*rijikai,* consisting of the chairman and key members), which meets behind closed doors. Hearings are, however, open and under subpoena and it is here that the private is adjusted to the public interest.

Sometimes, of course, more spectacular are the special committees. In February, 1960, the Diet regarded the debate over the revised Japan-United States security treaty revision as being so vital as to necessitate a forty-five-man special committee.

Aside from serious concern over the House of Councillors, to which we shall turn next, the greatest volume of criticism is directed at postwar Diet committees. In the first place, the committee system is charged with being suited to a presidential, not a parliamentary structure of government. The larger the number, the greater the opportunity for delay, particularly on the part of a minority; also, the more inordinate amount of time spent by cabinet members in answering questions. Second, the Diet has become infamous for promotion of narrow committee interests,

[15] *Government Organization, op. cit.,* pp. 3-7.

rather than coherent, overall legislative programs. There is too much opportunity for special interests to dominate the attitudes of committees. Third, it is often charged that the fragmented Diet committees have become outposts of the respective departments of administration. In any case, committee members are not yet a match for their bureaucratic counterparts. Fourth, many legislative decisions are made outside the committees, in party caucuses. On the other hand, individual members' bills involving appropriations must now receive prior approval of fifty members and have become, in effect, party bills. The committee system, it is argued, ends up by insisting that more, not less, money be spent.[16]

The House of Councillors

Usually a nation has a bicameral legislature either because it is a federal state or because it wants to perpetuate, in modern style, an older tradition of aristocracy. One of the few changes the Occupation allowed the Japanese to make in the original draft constitution did, nevertheless, provide an upper house. In theory it was not to be a replica of the old House of Peers, not a powerful body like the American Senate, nor yet a powerless organ like the French Council of the Republic. In short, the Japanese House of Representatives was to be like the American lower house, but even more responsive to public will since it could be dissolved. The House of Councillors, since it could not be dissolved, was designed to lend continuity and stability to the political scene. The compromise with SCAP, which wanted a unicameral system, resulted in provision for the 100-member national constituency. Now it is for this, however, that the system is most often criticized.

By 1956, even the staid House of Councillors had been torn by riots on the floor of the Diet, on that occasion involving protests against the remodeling of local boards of education. That was not, as one editorial put it, the basic issue.

The problem in brief is that the House of Councillors has all but become a duplicate of the Lower House, thus depriving itself of much of its raison d'etre.[17]

[16] For an excellent summary of criticism, see Hattie Kawahara Colton, "The National Diet after Independence," *The Annals* of the American Academy of Political and Social Science, CCCVIII (November, 1956), pp. 24–26; and also Yanaga, *op. cit.*, pp. 182–185.

[17] Murata Kiyoaki, "Whither the Upper House?" *The Japan Times*, May 13, 1959.

The trend toward politicizing the House of Councillors has been unmistakable. In April, 1947, the largest bloc in the House (111) were independents holding 44 per cent of the total seats. Twelve years later, in May of 1959, 82 per cent of the Councillors were closely affiliated with political parties and only 5.2 per cent were independents. With the further dwindling of such independent groups as the *Doshikai* (formerly the *Ryokufukai*), which fell off to 11 seats after the upper house elections of June 2, 1959, the function of the House of Councillors has become more difficult than ever. Nevertheless, Japanese newspapers still exhort the Councillors to act independently of lower house blocs and to arrest the extreme actions of the House of Representatives.[18]

The prime weakness is that, in any given election, some 100 candidates vie for fifty at-large seats in the national constituency (half are elected every three years). Campaigning throughout the nation in one month would involve enormous expense, even if it were possible. The electorate can scarcely be expected to know such candidates unless they enjoy powerful backing. This backing candidates have increasingly received from the parties. Some conservatives want to abolish the national constituency and redistribute the seats among the local, prefectural constituencies where they are strong. Others propose an experiment with functional representation, in an appointive upper chamber, of professional, occupational and cultural groups.

Functions and the Legislative Process

The chief function of the new Diet is to serve as a national forum, in which popular opinion is expressed, and in which the people are educated as to both government and opposition objectives. In theory all state matters are now regulated under laws approved by the Diet, or under orders on delegated authority.

The Diet can even act as a constituent assembly, since amendments to the constitution are to be initiated by means of a concurring vote of two-thirds of each house. Thereafter, the proposed amendment is submitted to the people for referendum in a special election or one specified by the Diet.

Supervisory power over public administration (see below, Chap. 7) stems from the right to name the prime minister himself; to vote confidence or nonconfidence in him and his colleagues; and to investigate both national and prefectural governmental operations. Each house conducts such investigations, can

[18] *Mainichi Shimbun,* June 5, 1959; *Nihon Keizai Shimbun,* June 5, 1959.

insist upon the presence of government officials, can impound records and can take testimony. Similarly, the Diet's power to check the judiciary lies in its ability to impeach judges.

Although the initiative in the conduct of foreign relations is delegated to the cabinet, nevertheless the latter is required by law to report on policy to the Diet. Treaties must receive the approval of both houses.

The ultimate weapon of the Diet is of course its control over all appropriations and expenditures, over taxation and revenue, and over auditing of final accounts.

Although legally the legislature thus enjoys constitutional supremacy over the executive, planning of the legislative program is in fact a function of the cabinet. Drafting of a bill usually begins in an administrative department. (Individual members' bills are scarce). The tortuous path leads from the section to the bureau to the documents section of the departmental secretariat to the parliamentary vice-minister to the minister. All bills then go through the cabinet secretariat to the Cabinet Bureau of Legislation, which carefully scrutinizes the draft statute. At this cabinet level there is an increasing use of public commissions to study, modify and even implement the stated objectives.

Next, the bill is placed on the cabinet agenda but, before the ministers discuss it, it is submitted to rigorous study by all vice-ministers. The following day, the deputy chief secretary explains the purport of the bill to the cabinet. Once approved, the bill goes to the speaker of the lower, or president of the upper house in the name of the prime minister. It is then assigned to committee according to agreed-upon party strategy. In committees the government is closely questioned and opposition testimony taken.

The Diet ordinarily follows its committees' recommendations on bills. If disagreement persists in a joint committee, or when the House of Councillors fails to act within sixty days after receipt of a bill approved by the lower house, the draft becomes law when passed a second time in the House of Representatives by a majority of two-thirds or more of members present. Once the law is passed, the speaker reports this fact to the emperor. The premier's signature follows that of the emperor, and the statute is published in *Kampo* (the "Official Gazette").[19]

[19] It should be noted here that the Diet may not pass a special law affecting a local public entity without the parallel, majority consent of the voters within the local jurisdiction. The basic source for information on laws, ordinances, regulations, and orders is *Kampo*, Tokyo, July 2, 1883 + (daily).

The above is a capsule summary of the ordinary legislative process. To understand thoroughly the functions of the Diet, however, somewhat closer scrutiny should be paid to several features of Diet operations. Let us now turn to the critical budget power, treaties and, finally, certain problems of discipline.

THE BUDGET. The drafters of Japan's organic law regarded the power of the purse to be so important as to devote to it an entire section (Chap. 7) of the new constitution. Constitutionally (Chap. 4, Art. 60), the power of the House of Representatives is predominant. Technically (Chap. 7, Art. 86) the cabinet prepares and submits to the Diet for its consideration and decision, a budget for each fiscal year.

The estimates of various departments are gathered together by the Budget Bureau of the Finance Ministry by August 31 prior to a given fiscal year (April 1-March 31). September and October are devoted to reconciling and trimming these requests. The Japanese budget procedure is, however, unique in that most attempts are made to increase rather than decrease expenditures. Pressure emanates from not only the bureaucracy but also from politicians. A draft budget is usually ready by January, and there follow deliberations within party circles and in two or three cabinet meetings. In late January, the draft budget goes to the House of Representatives and, within five days, to the House of Councillors. This is the occasion for administrative speeches by the government: the premier, on general policy; the foreign minister, on foreign affairs; the finance minister, on fiscal policy; and the director-general, Economic Planning agency, on economic planning.

For example in February, 1960, before the 24th ordinary session of the Diet, Prime Minister Kishi reviewed his recent trip to the United States and Canada, the revision of the security treaty, and problems of the forthcoming summit conference. He spoke of the need for Asian economic development. He pledged that the government would devote its attention to raising Japan's living standard, in terms of consumption per capita, to 30 per cent above prewar levels. He introduced a draft budget which included loan and investment plans which he said rested on sound fiscal policy. Japan's immediate priorities were said to be land

---

Stenographic records of proceedings in both houses are contained in *Kampo gogai* (supplement to *Kampo*), Tokyo, December, 1890 + (daily during sessions). Beginning with records of the 90th Diet, which convened in May, 1946, an English-language minutes of proceedings was added to the English edition of *Kampo*.

conservation, relief of disaster damage (he launched a ten-year plan for flood control), and wide support of agriculture, small and medium industries, and a program of social security. Foreign Minister Fujiyama Aiichiro then followed with a more detailed summary of foreign policy.[20]

After the government's administrative speeches, members of the government appear before the standing committees on the budget and parties begin their interpellation. Public hearings on the budget are mandatory. Committees then report back to the plenary sessions, which may or may not follow their recommendations. In case of failure to reconcile the differing views of the houses, or in case the upper house fails to take decisive action within thirty days (as compared with sixty in the case of ordinary bills), the decision of the House of Representatives becomes that of the Diet. After the fiscal year has closed, departments submit their accounts by July 31 to the Finance Ministry; from there they wend their way to the cabinet, to the Diet, and, by November 30, to the Board of Audit.

Let us now take a closer look at an actual budget, to get some idea of the size and scope of the fiscal operation of the Japanese government. On November 14, 1959, the government's 61,408 million yen ($170.5 million) supplementary budget passed a plenary session of the House of Representatives and was soon thereafter approved by the House of Councillors. This sum was designed chiefly to aid flood-devastated areas hard hit by Typhoon Ise Bay that Fall. On November 25, the executive board of the Liberal-Democratic Party approved a skeleton draft 1960 budget, which had been previously endorsed by seven top party leaders. On December 23, Finance Minister Sato Eisaku presented to the cabinet this draft budget of 1,569,000 million yen ($4,353,000,000). This too reflected the construction minister's request for 269,496 million yen ($748,000,000) for river, antiflood, and afforestation measures, in the wake of the typhoon.[21]

On January 13, 1960, the cabinet in extraordinary meeting approved the draft budget for fiscal 1960. The last item to be straightened out between Liberal-Democratic Party and cabinet leaders involved the question of local government subsidies. The general account shown in Table 5 was slightly below the original

[20] "Administrative Speech by Prime Minister Kishi at the 34th Regular Session of the National Diet, Feb. 1, 1960," *Japan Report*, VI, No. 3 (February 1, 1960), pp. 2–6.

[21] *The Japan Times*, Nov. 15, Nov. 25, Dec. 24, 1959.

finance ministry estimates but marked an increase of 150,426 million yen ($418,000,000) over fiscal 1959.

TABLE 5   *Fiscal 1960 budget (in comparison with fiscal 1959)*

Revenue	1960	1959
Tax and stamp revenues	1,336,631	1,121,241
Payments from Monopoly Corp.	136,412	120,125
Receipts from govt. enterprises	17,186	16,076
Other revenues	62,624	81,329
Surplus, preceding fiscal year	16,821	80,477
TOTAL	1,569,674	1,419,248
Expenditure		
Social security	181,609	147,869
Education	180,170	159,712
Development, science & technology	25,180	22,520
National bonds	27,407	55,373
Pensions	130,015	122,915
Grants to local govts.	286,532	248,649
Defense	154,565	153,665
Reparations, other debts	24,023	32,340
Public works	276,673	220,996
Housing and sanitation	15,739	13,742
Agricultural insurance	11,493	10,852
Trade promotion, economic cooperation	4,518	3,813
Development, small & medium enterprises	2,582	1,521
Transfer, staple-food special account	11,200	1,000
Reserves	8,000	8,000
Miscellaneous	229,968	216,281
TOTAL	1,569,674	1,419,248

Figures in millions of yen. 360 yen = $1.00.
SOURCE: *The Japan Times*, January 14, 1960.

In justification of this draft budget, government spokesmen pointed to the facts that the percentage of budget to gross national product was only 12.7 per cent, and that defense occupied only 1.4 per cent of national income and only 9.4 per cent of national expenditure, not unreasonably large figures. Minister of Finance Sato explained that revenue and expenditure were balanced and that the foundations had been laid for a steadily rising standard of living, through (1) rehabilitation of typhoon damage; (2) support of communications and transportation; (3) encouragement of science, technology and foreign trade; (4) widening of social security coverage; and (5) subsidies to depressed (coal, shipping) industries, agriculture and small business.[22]

Critics of this budget centered their fire on the general lack of appeal to the public, and failure to fulfill the government's promise to raise the national income. Interference in budget compilation by parties and pressure groups was distasteful, in that the public responsibility for the budget lay with the cabinet. Even Imamatsu Jiro, Liberal-Democratic Dietman, openly regretted the lack of compromise between party circles and the Finance Ministry, a spirit which delayed preparation of the budget. Steadily rising defense expenditures, plus "favoring big business," came in for denunciation by the Socialist opposition. The new Democratic-Socialist bloc decried the failure of the draft to incorporate foreign trade liberalization measures.[23]

Nevertheless, the fiscal 1960 budget passed the lower house by a vote of 249–140 on March 4, 1960. On March 31, twenty-eight days after it had been forwarded to the upper, and two months after it had been presented to the lower house, the budget passed the House of Councillors on party lines, with a vote of 140–79.[24]

THE DIET AND TREATIES. Mention has already been made of the fact that the Diet maintains indirect control over foreign policy. This is accomplished through the powers of investigation and interpellation, and because treaties must receive Diet approval. Here again, as in the case of the budget, the House of Representatives enjoys seniority. A number of unanswered questions concerning the rights of the Diet in considering treaties remain, however, and these were raised in the hectic debates during 1959–60 over the revised security pact with the United States.[25]

Prime Minister Kishi himself opened the controversy by an offhand statement, made at a Hakone hot spring resort, to the effect that any amendment (for example, reduction of the term of the treaty) would constitute failure of ratification by the Diet. In subsequent public hearings, only one of three distinguished experts supported the government's view. Japan's most famous political scientist, former President of Ochanomizu University Royama Masamichi, argued that the Diet has the right to debate

[22] Interview with Finance Minister Sato, *Economist,* February 2, 1960.
[23] *Ibid.;* Mr. Imamatsu's remarks were carried in *Sekai Orai,* March, 1960; and *The Japan Times,* January 14, 1960.
[24] *The Japan Times,* March 4, April 1, 1960.
[25] See also Chap. 11 below.

treaties extensively. This function, he said, is basically the same regardless of whether it is a law, budget bill or treaty. A Diet amendment would not of course be immediately effective; the resolution would, however, be binding on the government and it would be up to the cabinet to decide how best to renegotiate to follow the will of the Diet. One of the difficulties in this dispute, which waxed warm, was that there was not complete agreement even within the ruling Liberal-Democratic Party. In the Party-Government Foreign Affairs council, a majority felt that the Diet has no power to amend a treaty, as it can laws or budget bills. Powerful members affiliated with Kono Ichiro argued that the Diet ought to be able to add a reservation to a treaty; however, a number of witnesses argued that, in such a controversial issue, the Diet ought to be dissolved in order to seek the people's opinion in a referendum.[26]

DIET DISCIPLINE. One other feature of post-treaty Diet operations has little to do with the legal functions of the legislature, but it certainly has left its stamp on the functioning of the houses. Mention has been made of the fact that the conservative program for Japan, often referred to as "the reserve course," has been bitterly contested by the Left opposition. Finally, in February, 1959, floor leaders of the Liberal-Democratic and Socialist parties agreed to set up a special committee to discuss measures to maintain order in the Diet Building. The Liberal-Democrats appointed four members from the lower and two from the upper house. The opposition Socialists were opposed to inclusion of Councillors because it would endanger the independence of the House of Councillors. In any case, the committee accomplished little.[27]

Even Socialists expressed regrets over the massive demonstration of November 27, 1959, which got out of hand and spilled over into the Diet compound. Liberal-Democratic leaders proposed a bill which would ban demonstrations in the vicinity of the Diet building. Although it was later passed by 203 representatives of the ruling party, all Socialists boycotted the deliberations to the end of the 23rd extraordinary session. In the 34th ordinary session in March, 1960, the bill passed the upper house by a

[26] See, for example, the view of Professor Hoshino Yasusaburo, Tokyo Gakugei University, *Chuo Koron,* March, 1960; also *The Japan Times,* Feb. 22, 24, 1960. Mr. Kono's statements: "The Diet naturally has the power to revise a treaty. If the Dietmen refuse to recognize that, they will be reducing their own powers." *Economist,* March 8, 1960.

[27] *The Japan Times,* February 28, 1959.

vote of 126–81. Under the Diet Law, it had to be referred back to the lower house where Liberal-Democrats were hesitant to force the issue for fear of ruining their chances on the Japan-United States security pact revision.[28] Unseemly conduct around and even in the Diet nevertheless brought sharp criticism from the press and left an air of deep disquiet over the fate of parliamentary government in Japan.

Profile of the Post-independence Diet

Even before the occupation of Japan ended, the potential strength of the new Diet was apparent: for the first time it could call the executive to account and openly audit the activities of the bureaucracy. The Diet could become a powerful arm of democratic government, depending upon the vitality of the political parties. On the other hand, in disturbing fashion some of the weaknesses of the prewar Diet had already made their reappearance: invasion of the committees by cynical party wire-pullers (*kuromaku*); direct intervention by brash lobbyists; and outright rowdiness on the floor of the Diet.

Recovery of the exercise of its sovereignty came to Japan with the 13th session of the Diet (1952) under the new constitution. This long awaited event was also marked by the return of many purged conservative politicians and vigorous challenges by Socialists on the national scene (as against conservative strength at the local level). At first the Diet, with its new-found power, strange procedures, and committee system, proved baffling for the old-timers.

Nevertheless, the 15th session (1952–53) was significant for the steady decline of postwar newcomers, symbolized by Premier Yoshida Shigeru, and the revival of prewar politicians' power, symbolized by Hatoyama Ichiro. The 16th session (1953) saw the Diet plunge into problems of the budget, reborn defense capabilities and antimonopoly law revision. Fateful were the first discussions of United States Mutual Security Aid, beginning in July, 1953. They foreshadowed the approaching agonizing reappraisal of the constitutional, moral and political issues of defense. Conservatives began to use the technique of majority railroading; the opposition, the technique of boycott of sessions.

The 19th session (1954) marked a climax of bitter disputes:

[28] *The Japan Times,* November 29, December 9, December 25, December 27, 1959, March 22, 1960.

in June, the first riots on the floor of the Diet occurred over revision of police powers; in July, the Self-Defense agency and Forces laws passed over strenuous opposition. The pendulum was swinging back and Hatoyama came to power late in 1954, on the eve of the January, 1955 elections.

From the 22nd session in 1955 to the 24th session in 1956, Japan watched the emergence of a so-called two-party system, the confrontation of Liberal-Democratic and Socialist blocs. To assure lasting majorities, conservatives tried their best to introduce new, gerrymandered election districts. The minority, by delaying tactics, succeeded time and again in defeating the absolute majority. All the post-independence Diets struggled with the issue of constitutional revision.

Both constitutional review and rearmament (which would require a two-thirds majority in both houses) received heavy blows in the upper house elections of July 8, 1956. The Japanese voter was apparently shrewd in rejecting the pie-in-the-sky alternatives offered by the Socialist minority, and yet withholding the two-thirds majority needed by the Liberal-Democrats to revise the constitution and set the clock back.

Despite failure to receive a two-thirds vote of confidence, the Liberal-Democratic Government decided, in 1957, to put into effect the Constitution Research council without Socialist permission or participation. From the 30th extraordinary session (1958) to the 24th ordinary session (1960) the Diet was dominated by inflammatory issues like the police bill revision and Japan-United States security treaty revision.[29]

A composite picture of the party composition of post-treaty Diets is offered in Table 6. A mere glance will reveal that the new Diet has been infected with a prewar disease, the shifts and maneuvers around powerful political personalities; it has not been distinguished by the emergence of parties based on political principles. As Japan approached the end of its first decade of independence, there was a crying need for a reappraisal of parliamentary procedure, for both the Liberal-Democratic and Socialist parties were operating under Meiji era concepts. Conservatives became more despotic because of their numerical superiority; the Socialists, swayed by outdated concepts of Marxism, took an all or nothing stand. Especially in Diet committees, these attitudes

[29] For a supplementary detailed review of domestic developments in Japan, see the author's annual contribution (1957–) to the Encyclopaedia Britannica, *Britannica Book of the Year.*

TABLE 6 Party composition of post-treaty Diets, 1952–1960

House of Representatives

Parties	Oct. 1, 1952[a]	May 18, 1953[b]	Dec. 10, 1954[c]	Feb. 27, 1955[d]	Nov. 22, 1955[e]	June 17, 1958[f]	Oct. 26, 1959[g]	Jan. 30, 1960[h]	Nov. 20, 1960[i]
Liberals (Yoshida)	—	202	—	—	—	—	—	—	—
Liberals	240	—	185	—	—	—	—	—	—
Liberals (Hatoyama)	—	35	—	112	—	—	—	—	—
Progressives	85	77	—	—	—	—	—	—	—
Liberal-Democrats	—	—	—	—	300	298	288	288	296
Democrats	—	—	121	185	—	—	—	—	—
Socialists (Left-wing)	54	72	72	89	—	—	—	—	—
Socialists	—	—	—	—	154	167	144	127	145
Socialists (Right-wing)	57	66	61	67	—	—	—	—	—
Democratic Socialists	—	—	—	—	—	—	21	38	17
Communists	0	1	1	2	2	1	1	1	3
Minor parties, vacancies	30	13	27	12	11	1	13	13	5

House of Councillors

Parties	After 1953 election	After 1956 election	After 1959 election
Liberals (Yoshida)	93		
Liberals (Hatoyama)	3		
Liberal-Democrats		122	132
Progressives	17		
Socialists (Left-wing)	43		
Socialists		80	85
Socialists (Right-wing)	26		
Ryokufukai	48	31	11
Communists	0	2	3
Minor parties, vacancies	5	15	19

a After general election of 1952.   b After general election of 1953.   c After general election of 1954.   • After election of Hatoyama.   d After general election of 1955.   e After mergers of Lib.-Dem. and Socialist parties.   f After general election of 1958.   g Opening of 33d extraordinary session.   h Opening of 34th ordinary session.   i After general election of 1960.

SOURCE: Compiled from various sources: Lineberger, Djang & Burks, op. cit., Appendix 19, p. 617; Britannica Book of the Year, 1957, '58, '59, '60 issues; Japan Report, cited, V, No. 22 (November 20, 1959); The Japan Times, January 30, 1960.

resulted in a lack of true legislative compromise and in an either-or choice.[30]

Meanwhile, as far as the Diet's fate is concerned, voices are being heard which propose the reinstitution of executive power, with the emperor at the top of the pyramid; permission for the cabinet to dissolve the Diet and suspend sessions; and even subsequent Diet approval of emergency (cabinet) budget decrees. All of these plans could become dangerous, if public opinion in a crisis reverts to disillusionment with slower Diet proceedings. Once again the fate of Japanese democracy may lie in the hands of the Diet.

7 - Public Administration and the Public Service

The legalism which has persistently dominated the thinking of the *kambatsu* (literally, official clique) has deep historical, roots in the Sino-Japanese tradition of an elite chosen from scholar-statesmen. In addition, the bureaucracy in modern Japan was able, between 1868 and 1945, to build almost unassailable defenses against inroads by any other group desirous of assaulting its citadels of power. It is a tribute to the strength and morale of this elite corps to say that of all the prewar cliques—the aristocracy, the military, the *zaibatsu,* and the bureaucracy—the bureaucracy was the last to change under the impact of Occupation and post-Occupation reforms, if indeed it has changed at all.

It should always be remembered that the Japanese are not novices at public administration. They boast of a centuries-old administrative tradition, within which it was perfectly normal to expect detailed regulation of social, political, economic and even intellectual life. In prewar Japan the *kambatsu* thought of themselves as direct servants of the emperor and as guardians of the national polity. Thus this clique constituted both a formal

[30] See the criticism by Professor Nakamura Kikuo of Keio University, in *Nippon oyobi Nipponjin,* March, 1960.

organ of government, staffing the ministries and public service, and also a powerful semi-independent force set apart from the Japanese public at large.

Theoretically, the prewar bureaucracy was responsible through the cabinet to the emperor. The relatively weak position of the cabinet (see Chap. 5) meant, however, that there was little interference in the day-to-day affairs conducted by bureaucrats. The vast bureaucracy presumably could have clashed head-on with the increasingly powerful militarist clique, save for the fact that military and civilian affairs were kept separate in the executive. At the level of practical politics, there was ample opportunity for conflict with the powerful finance clique, the *zaibatsu,* but more often the bureaucracy bought off, or was bought off by subsidies, government contracts, public land and special favors. The bureaucrats not only looked down on the Diet but were masters of techniques for keeping the mere people's representatives in their place. In fact, bureaucrats moved easily in and out of the political parties and purchased protection for their perquisites by capturing political bosses and floor leaders alike.

In the modern terms in which comparative politics is studied—methods of attaining prestige and nature of a political elite—prewar Japan offered a classic case study of the predominance of the bureaucracy. Orthodox training of the bureaucrats began early and was concentrated overwhelmingly in one institution, Tokyo Imperial University, itself an arm of the dug-in bureaucracy. *Tokyo Teidai* prepared three out of four of those who eventually entered public service. Ambitious young men, many from rural areas, congregated in the law department of the university, where they acquired a highly technical legal education. In order to pass civil service examinations, they spent most of their time memorizing the *Roppo,*[1] practically to the exclusion of courses on politics or economics. Trained as legal technicians, they entered government service with the rigid ideology of the bureaucracy.

One result of this training was a legalistic attitude, which related all administrative decisions to laws, codes and regulations. Another conspicuous characteristic, which Professor Tsuji Kiyoaki feels still haunts the Japanese government, was a deep-

---

[1] The *Roppo,* or six codes, consisted of the constitution, civil code, commercial code, criminal code, code of civil procedure and code of criminal procedure. The outstanding study of the *Kambatsu* is Tsuji Kiyoaki, *Nihon kanryosei no kenkyu* (Research on the Japanese bureaucracy) (Tokyo: Kobundo, 1952).

rooted sense of departmentalism. This was a product of the fact
that each ministry was responsible solely to the emperor. The
weakness of the Diet and, relatively, even of the cabinet meant
that the *kambatsu* was in fact accountable to no one. Within the
bureaucracy itself, legalistic training meant there was nothing
resembling a manual of administrative procedure, no distinction
between line and staff functions, and no responsible administration of the budget.

Administrative Reorganization

In the immediate post-surrender period, which offered
numerous problems of administration, the Japanese and the Occupation authorities alike faced as well difficulties inherent in
the nature of the bureaucracy: its great complexity, diffusion of
jurisdiction and characteristic indirection of method. These
constituted, so to speak, the forces of inertia pitted against the
attempt by Japan to mobilize for modern war, to demobilize in
defeat, and to face the basic reforms proposed by the Occupationaires.[2]

Indeed, the Occupation tried valiantly to help the Japanese
set their bureaucracy on the path of democracy and to modernize
it for the sake of efficiency. One of the prime difficulties lay in
the fact that the Occupation, from the beginning and out of
necessity, used a system of indirect rule through the Japanese
bureaucracy itself, which was in turn perhaps the least changed
of all sectors of Japanese society.

The attempts at reorganization began with the Cabinet Law
of 1945 (amended in 1947; see above, Chap. 5); the National
Government Organization Law of 1948; and the National Public
Service Law of 1947 (amended in 1948, 1949; see below). All of
these steps, as well as an attempt in 1950 to reform administrative
structure, were taken by the Japanese government itself[3] and
proved entirely too halting to suit the impatient Occupationaires.
Whereupon, administrative planners were persuaded to try a
new, American technique.

[2] Milton J. Esman, "Japanese Administration—A Comparative View,"
Public Administration Review, VII, No. 2 (Spring, 1947), pp. 100–112.

[3] [*Naikaku Kambo* (Cabinet Secretariat)] *Kokka gyosei soshiki ho* (National government organization law) (Tokyo: Law No. 120, July 10, 1948)
(hereinafter referred to as Organization Law). A primary source for tracing
successive reorganizations is the publication of the *Gyosei-Kanri cho, Kanri-bu*
(Administrative Management agency, Management division), *Gyosei kiko
nempo* (Annual report on administrative structure), Tokyo, I, 1950 + (annual).

In 1951, the Japanese government turned to the Hoover Commission technique, using a brain trust of prominent citizens called the Government Ordinance Advisory committee. The committee drafted the "Report on Reform of the Administrative System," which was released by the cabinet secretariat in October, 1951. This report constituted perhaps the high watermark of the tide of attempted postwar reform of the bureaucracy. It was drafted just before the Occupation came to an end and in light of the fact that Japan was soon to regain the exercise of its own sovereignty. In some cases, suggestions incorporated in the document were promptly effected; in others, they were never even tried. For these reasons, perhaps a closer look at it will prove worthwhile.[4]

The 1951 report courageously tackled aspects of the problem of administrative reform: (1) under the new constitution, public employees were to become servants of the people; (2) it was necessary to strip off all kinds of emergency functions developed under the Occupation; (3) account had to be taken of approaching treaty status; (4) certain American-inspired reforms had to go.

> The administrative commission system may be necessary for democratization of administrative structure but our social and economic conditions, being different from those in the United States, do not demand the system as an urgent necessity.[5]

The commission then criticized the devolution of responsibility for public personnel and thus sounded the theme of numerous proposals for administrative reform which followed. It singled out the independence of the new National Personnel authority, recommended its abolition, and urged replacement by a personnel committee under the prime minister's office. The Administrative Management agency should continue as the chief instrument of administrative control under jurisdiction of the cabinet.

Under Occupation encouragement, administrative planners who had developed a vested interest in maintaining gains of democratization and modernization of the bureaucracy came to be centered in the agency. Its duties were legally defined to

---

[4] The following paragraphs are based primarily on my previous article, "A Note on the Emerging Administrative Structure of the Post-Treaty Japanese National Government," *Occasional Papers,* Center for Japanese Studies, No. 3, Ann Arbor, University of Michigan (1952).

[5] *Gyosei seido no kaikaku ni kansuru toshin* (Report on reform of the administrative system), Tokyo, August 14, 1951.

include: (1) study of administrative structure; (2) supervision of the planning and operations of administrative organs; (3) recommendations for the creation, reorganization or abolition of organs; and (4) inspection of the work of administrative agencies.[6] The structure of the agency is depicted in Figure 5.

FIGURE 5 *Administrative Management agency (Gyosei-Kanri cho)*

(Prime minister's office)
|
Director-general (state minister)
of the Administrative Management agency
|
Parliamentary vice-minister
|
Administrative vice-minister
|

| Director-general's secretariat | Management bureau | Statistical Standards bureau | Inspection bureau |

SOURCE: *Government Organization*, p. 37; *Kiko zu*, p. 16, both originally cited above, see Chap. 5.

Difficulties faced by the agency, despite a clear definition of its mission, have arisen out of the fact that administrative control has continued to spread among not just two but three agencies. One is the agency itself, another is the National Personnel authority (described in greater detail below); and the third is the Budget Bureau of the Ministry of Finance. Although there have been repeated proposals to transfer this bureau to the jurisdiction of the prime minister's office, where it could work closely with the Administrative Management agency, this particular reform has never been effected. One result, felt ever since 1951, has been the continuation of traditional interministry rivalry. Departmentalism, working through the separate agencies responsible for administrative management, has in turn led to the repeated pigeon-holing of significant features of proposals for reform.

Nevertheless, in 1952 when the Occupation retired behind the screen of security pact arrangements, the Japanese government did accomplish considerable reform in a first rush of

[6] *Gyosei-Kanri cho setchi ho* (Law establishing the Administrative Management agency) mimeographed, Tokyo, rev. to 31 July, 1952.

rationalization of administrative structure. The new treaty status of Japan, for example, called immediately for the revival of the Foreign Ministry. Consistency in the internal structure of the various ministries was accomplished by revision of the National Government Organization Law. The number of agencies was reduced and the labor force in public service (excluding government corporations) was cut 1.3 per cent or by 383,000 personnel. Sample results are presented in Table 7.

TABLE 7 *Comparative chart of agencies, before and after reform, 1952*

	Number before reform	Number after reform
Offices, ministries	14	12
External organs	46	27
Bureaus	92	82
Divisions	129	83
Personnel	1,520,604	1,423,840

SOURCE: Organization Law (No. 120, July 20, 1948), mimeographed, rev. (1) to (34), Dec. 10, 1948–July 31, 1952; Gyosei-kanri cho, Kanri-bu (Administrative Management agency, Management division), *Gyosei kiko kikaku hyo* (Comparative charts, reform of administrative structure) mimeographed, Tokyo, Aug. 1, 1952.

In 1955 the Hatoyama Cabinet, which had campaigned on the issue of rationalization of administrative structure, again took up the problem of reorganization and ordered an administrative council to draw up a plan. The council's report, released in February, 1956, advocated the creation of a top-management agency, a cabinet committee on budget, an independent board of trade, re-establishment of the Home Ministry (by amalgamating functions of the Autonomy agency and Construction Ministry) and, once again, complete abolition of the National Personnel authority. These proposals were bitterly opposed both by factions within the Liberal-Democratic Party and intrenched bureaucrats, so that compromises resulted in a considerably watered-down plan released in March, 1956. This plan called for establishment of a home ministry and, once again, creation of a cabinet committee on budget, and abolition of the National Personnel authority. A brief summary of the present status of departments and agencies will reveal that none of these changes has been carried out.

Departments and Agencies

Actual post-treaty changes in the administrative structure of the national government can now be added up to a brief description of present ministries, commissions and agencies. First and most obvious, as has been mentioned, was the reappearance of the Ministry of Foreign Affairs (*Gaimu Sho,* described below, in Chap. 11). Second, the Japanese government soon adopted one recommendation of the 1951 report by returning to a Ministry of Justice (*Homu Sho*), from the unfamiliar, American-type office of Attorney General. Work of the assistant attorney general for legislative opinion was shifted to the Cabinet Legislation bureau.

In a third instance, the government refused to follow the recommendations of the 1951 report. The Ordinance commission had bravely proposed a full-fledged security ministry, which would control the police, the growing paramilitary self-defense forces (then called National Police Reserve), immigration and maritime security. Instead, on July 1, 1954, the Defense agency (*Boei cho,* described below, Chap. 11) was established under a minister of state. Also in 1954, the separate National Public Safety commission (*Kokka Hoan iinkai*) got a minister of state and jurisdiction over the recentralized police system. Moreover, the new Autonomy agency (*Jichi cho*) began to hedge in local autonomy by means of strong pressures. Allocation of subsidies, influence on recruitment of prefectural personnel, and indirect control over personnel changes, all these represented first evidences of a reverse course toward re-centralization. In 1960 the agency was converted into a Ministry of Autonomy Affairs. Finally, in March, 1956, the National Personnel authority suffered a reduction in staff. Nevertheless, it remained a separate administrative organ of the cabinet, its president (*Sosai*) ranking with but after the prime minister himself. The authority, as we shall see, retains control over public service personnel. As of the end of 1958, these personnel were grouped in the departments, commissions, and agencies of the Japanese national government as is shown in Table 8.

Powers and Functions

The prime minister and ministers of state act as administrative chiefs of the prime minister's office and of the various ministries and agencies respectively. Each departmental minister is directed by the prime minister, without interference, and each in

TABLE 8 *Departments, commissions and agencies of the Japanese national government (with number of incumbent, regular public service employees) as of October 1, 1958*

Semi-Independent agencies			Agencies of prime minister's office	
Board of Audit (*Kaikei-Kensa In*)	1,174		Police (*Keisatsu Cho*)	7,594
National Personnel Authority (*Jinji In*)	725		National Fire Defense HQ	
Constitutional Research Council			(*Kokka Shobo Hombu*)	107
(*Kempo Chosa Kai*)	8		Imperial Household Agency	
Defense Council (*Kokubo Kaigi*)	12		(*Kunai Cho*)	932
			Defense (*Boei Cho*)	19,396
Cabinet Secretariat (*Naikaku Kambo*)	36		Procurement (*Chotatsu Cho*)	3,272
			Administrative management	
Ministries			(*Gyosei-Kanri Cho*)	1,591
Justice (*Homu Sho*)	40,840		Hokkaido Development	
Foreign Affairs (*Gaimu Sho*)	1,843		(*Hokkaido Kaihatsu Cho*)	3,222
Finance (*Okura Sho*)	13,556		Autonomy (*Jichi Cho*)	244*
Education (*Mombu Sho*)	63,947		Economic Planning	
Welfare (*Kosei Sho*)	49,916		(*Keizai Kikaku Cho*)	367
Agriculture & Forestry			Science & Technics	
(*No-Rin Sho*)	25,733		(*Kagaku-Gijutsu Cho*)	417
International Trade & Industry				
(*Tsusho-Sangyo Sho*)	6,376		Agencies of ministries	
Transportation (*Unyu Sho*)	12,154		Public Security Investigation	
Postal services (*Yusei Sho*)	3,077		[Justice] (*Koan-Iin Cho*)	1,617
Labor (*Rodo Sho*)	22,732		Mint [Finance] (*Zohei Kyoku*)	9
Construction (*Kensetsu Sho*)	16,275		Government Printing Office	
			[Finance] (*Insatsu Kyoku*)	13
Independent commissions			Tax Administration [Finance]	
Fair Trade (*Kosei-Torihiki Iinkai*)	237		(*Kokuzei Cho*)	49,483
Land Coordination			Food [Agriculture & Forestry]	
(*Tochi-Chosei Iinkai*)	18		(*Shokuryo Cho*)	27,018
National Capital Regional Develop-			Forestry [Agriculture & Forestry]	
ment (*Shutoken Seibi Iinkai*)	40		(*Rinya Cho*)	1,032
			Fishery [Agriculture & Forestry]	
Ministry commissions			(*Suisan Cho*)	1,460
Public Security Examination			Industrial Science & Technology	
[Justice] (*Koan Shinsai Iinkai*)	9		[International Trade & Industry]	
Cultural Property Protection			(*Kogyo-Gijuku In*)	4,143
[Education] (*Bunkazai Hogo Iinkai*)	426		Patent [International Trade &	
Mariners' Labor Relations			Industry] (*Tokkyo Cho*)	941
[Transportation] (*Senin-Rodo Iinkai*)	52		Medium & Small Enterprises	
Prize Courts Decisions Review			[International Trade & Industry]	
[Transportation] (*Hokaku-Shiken			(*Chusho-Kigyo Cho*)	133
Saishinsa Iinkai*)	10		Meteorological [Transportation]	
Central Labor Relations [Labor]			(*Kisho Cho*)	5,232
(*Chuo Rodo Iinkai*)	85		Marine Accident Inquiry	
Public Corporations Arbitration &			[Transportation] (*Kainan-Shimpan	
Mediation [Labor] (*Kokyo			Cho*)	188
Kigyotai to Rodo Iinkai*)	119		Maritime Safety [Transportation]	
			(*Kaiji Hoan Cho*)	10,599

* Became ministry, 1960.

SOURCE: National Personnel authority, *Annual Report*, 1958, Tokyo, mimeographed, (1959); *Government Organization, passim.*

turn distributes and supervises the administrative duties of his ministry. Similarly a commission is headed by a chairman (*incho*), an agency, by a director-general (*chokan*). The powers and duties of the various agencies and subdivisions are regularized by law, ordinances and administrative orders. Reconciliation of conflicting jurisdiction among ministries, commissions, and agencies is effected through a cabinet conference (*kakugi*) in accordance with the Cabinet Law. Conflicts between a field agency of the national government and the governor of a prefecture are adjusted, in the first instance, through the Autonomy Ministry and by reference to the Local Autonomy Law.[7]

Each ministry is subdivided into a secretariat, bureaus (numbering four to nine depending on the ministry) and sections (in some cases called offices or rooms). Where necessary, examination and training institutes, temporary councils, conferences, and committees, research institutes and medical institutions are provided by law. Secretariat, bureau and section chiefs must be specifically authorized by statute; all remaining administrative employees are periodically authorized under personnel ceiling laws.[8]

The administrative structure of the Ministry of Finance is presented in simplified form in Figure 6.

The administrative pattern of most departments is similar to those represented graphically. The minister is assisted by an administrative vice-minister, who is a career civil servant and the intra-ministry administrator; he is also aided by one or more parliamentary vice-ministers, who are party men serving in a liaison capacity between the department and the Diet. Interdepartmental administrative coordination is provided by a meeting of all vice-ministers. Assembling twice a week, Monday and Thursday (that is, ordinarily one day ahead of the cabinet), the vice-ministers are aided by directors of the cabinet Secretariat and Legislation bureau. They constitute the highest administrative liaison conference in the government.

Day-to-day staff duties in each ministry are handled by the minister's secretariat. Among the many matters it handles, the following are illustrative of the range of secretariat duties: confidential affairs for the minister; appointment, training, promotion and dismissal of ministry personnel and supervision of their health and welfare activities; study of legislative statutes and orders; budget and final accounting.[9]

[7] Organization Law, Arts. 3, 4, 5, 6, 10–16; Law No. 5, the Cabinet Law, January 16, 1945, amended to 1947; Law No. 67, Local Autonomy Law, May 3, 1947, amended to 1952, especially Arts. 145, 150.

[8] Organization Law, Arts. 17–20; *Gyosei kikan shokuin teiin ho* (Law for fixed number of personnel in administrative organs), Law No. 126, May 31, 1949, revisions (1) to (30), December 24, 1949 to July 31, 1952.

[9] Chapter 7, "The Prime Minister and His Cabinet," of Professor Chitoshi Yanaga's *Japanese People and Politics* (New York: Wiley, 1956), offers a sufficiently factual account of such activities, with shrewd insights on the inner workings of the bureaucracy.

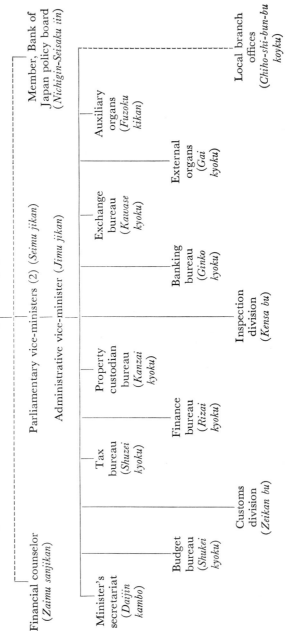

FIGURE 6 *Ministry of Finance (Okura Sho)*

Minister (*Okura Daijin*)

Parliamentary vice-ministers (2) (*Seimu jikan*)

Administrative vice-minister (*Jimu jikan*)

Financial counselor (*Zaimu sanjikan*)

Member, Bank of Japan policy board (*Nichigin-Seisaku iin*)

Minister's secretariat (*Daijin kambo*)

Budget bureau (*Shukei kyoku*)

Customs division (*Zeikan bu*)

Tax bureau (*Shuzei kyoku*)

Finance bureau (*Rizai kyoku*)

Property custodian bureau (*Kanzai kyoku*)

Inspection division (*Kensa bu*)

Banking bureau (*Ginko kyoku*)

Exchange bureau (*Kawase kyoku*)

External organs (*Gai kyoku*)

Auxiliary organs (*Fuzoku kikan*)

Local branch offices (*Chiho-shi-bun-bu koyku*)

SOURCE: *Government Organization*, p. 85; *Kiko zu*, p. 46.

142

The Public Service

ORGANIZATION. The Japanese civil service dates from the enforcement of Public Service regulations of 1887. Perhaps enough
has already been said about the position of the cabinet (Chap. 5)
and the nature of the bureaucracy to indicate the characteristics
of the prewar public service. Members owed absolute allegiance
to the emperor and his government. Recruitment of personnel,
divided into A-class and B-class, was by examination, but their
status was regularized by imperial ordinance rather than by law.
There was always open discrimination in favor of permanent
employees.

It is also clear that the new constitution demanded radical
changes whereby public officials would become servants of the
community. As in the case of administrative structure, the public
service too was to be reformed according to modern techniques
and standards of efficiency. The National Public Service Law
of October 1, 1947, attempted to implement these requirements
for a democratic and efficient administration.

Under the new, postwar system governmental employees are
divided into two broad categories. Special personnel include
political appointees (the prime minister, ministers, chief cabinet
secretary, and parliamentary vice-ministers); independent officials
(judges); persons elected or appointed with consent of the Diet
(National Public Safety commissioners); and officers with special
qualifications (ambassadors, staff of the Imperial Household
agency). A separate law governs the status of such public servants.
Regular personnel include incumbents in all positions other than
those called special and to these the National Public Service Law
applies. Special provisions are passed to cover specialized personnel in the fields of education, foreign service and the field
service of agencies.

There are, in other words, different manners in which one
can speak of the total number of personnel employed by the
Japanese government. For example, in June, 1954, special personnel numbered 190,282; regular, 645,683; total, 835,965. In
addition, public corporations (in the government monopoly,
railway, and communications fields) employed 653,760. More
meaningful and more recent statistics, for March, 1958, showed
420,604 ordinary and 318,354 industrial employees (in govern-
ment-managed enterprises), for an aggregate of 738,959. For fiscal
1957, the accession rate of public employees was 5.9 per cent

and the separation rate was 5.6 per cent, of the total government work force.[10]

The agency primarily responsible for maintaining unified personnel standards throughout the government as well as for placing obstacles in the way of harmful political patronage is the controversial National Personnel authority, already mentioned several times in connection with the campaigns for administrative reform. Separated from the cabinet, it holds semi-legislative and semi-judicial powers. The authority consists of a president and two commissioners and meets weekly. It is assisted by a National Personnel council, a liaison organ for the various ministries and agencies. In 1951, it was linked to the Civil Service Assembly of the United States and Canada (later renamed the Public Personnel Association). In 1958, the authority sent representatives to the Regional Conference on Public Administration, held in Manila. Through the United Nations Technical Assistance Program, it has sent out delegations to study personnel procedures in Europe and in America. As of August, 1959, it employed 725 public servants.

Perhaps nothing will better illustrate the work of the authority than a brief summary of its activities in a single year. The year 1958 was the tenth anniversary of its birth as the central personnel agency responsible for the enforcement of the National Public Service Law; and a milestone along the road to its mission, the establishment of a democratic and efficient public service. During that year the authority submitted its (tenth) annual recommendations on pay for public servants. It put into effect a new commutation allowance for personnel, and recommended establishment of a so-called cold-district allowance (to pay for fuel in extremely cold areas). Meanwhile, it supervised the administration of various public service entrance examinations and screened candidates for appointments in various agencies. (The percentage of appointments by ministries and agencies of candidates who had been successful in examinations increased during the year). Also during the year, the authority conducted a survey of the employment situation in 17,022 government establishments throughout the country. For the third year,

---

[10] *Japan: Its Land, People and Culture,* compiled by Japanese National Commission for UNESCO (Tokyo: Ministry of Finance, 1958), Chap. 5, "Government and Political Organization," pp. 157–159; NPA, *Annual Report,* 1958, *op. cit.,* pp. 1–2. For a comparison of the number of local government personnel, see below, Chapter 10, Figure 11.

it presented in-service training for high-level management personnel (2,400 officers had gone through the courses by 1958). It made strenuous efforts to preserve safety and health of public employees (in 1958, some 28,000 employees or 10.6 per cent of those examined in routine tests were found to have tuberculosis of the respiratory organs). Finally, it reviewed in equity various actions adverse to public employees, a total of 518 grievances and 4,148 representations.

On the other hand, in 1958 the National Personnel authority had still not achieved one of its goals: classification of personnel resting on job descriptions. In May, 1950, it had developed a position-classification plan and in May, 1952, had determined titles and publicized them. A storm of criticism soon led the authority to realize the system was inappropriate in spots and it was suspended. During 1958, the authority was still studying the classification problem.[11]

RECRUITMENT. The National Public Service Law prescribes that all appointments to the regular service be made on the basis of entrance examination, evaluation of performance or demonstration of ability. Authority rules implement this basic principle.[12] First of all, appointments to posts of section chief and above are all subject to approval by the authority. Second, appointments to posts below those levels have increasingly come to be influenced by its entrance examinations. The first such examinations were held in January, 1949. To the end of fiscal 1957, the authority had handled over 2,000,000 applicants, had actually examined 1,500,000 candidates, and had certified 152,040 as having passed. Appointees as a direct result of examinations totaled 66,927.

If the total number of examined appointees is not too impressive, at least the standards of the authority appeared to remain high. During 1958 it also checked the examination techniques of ministries which chose to recruit independently as well as various field agencies.

WORKING CONDITIONS. The National Personnel authority is responsible for constant investigation of public service pay scales, compared with cost of living indices and with prevailing wages paid in private industry. There is little doubt that the average

[11] NPA, *Annual Report, op. cit.,* pp. 1–3, 28.
[12] NPA Rule 8–12, Appointment and Dismissal of Personnel, May, 1952; amended by Rules 8–13, 8–14, August, 1955, for appointment of temporary employees; see *ibid.,* p. 4.

pay of government employees is running below that of the privately employed; the differential is most marked in the case of university graduates.

From an average monthly scale of 6,307 yen (about $14; December, 1948) ten annual recommendations of the authority succeeded in bringing the average monthly pay up to 19,390 yen (about $54; March, 1958). In addition, employees received semi-annual bonuses, special work and diligence allowances which added up to an average of 255 per cent of monthly pay. Correspondingly, in fiscal 1957, the average monthly base pay in private industry was 20,859 yen (about $58) for white-collar, and 12,947 yen (about $36) for blue-collar workers. The authority's own estimates of standard living costs in Tokyo, in March, 1958, for a single adult male was 7,560 yen (about $21); a senior high school graduate newly appointed to government post was receiving 7,200 yen ($20).[13]

The National Personnel authority had, by 1958, perfected a performance rating system. The system rested on findings of a public service efficiency study group, which had met between 1952 and 1955,[14] but ratings met the stiff opposition of employee organizations, particularly of teachers' associations. The authority was more successful in its training program, aimed primarily at middle-level managerial and supervisory personnel. For the first time, a wide use of case studies was employed.

It must always be kept in mind, of course, that even the Japanese bureaucracy is staffed by human beings. The whole story of their working conditions cannot be told simply in symmetrical organization charts or through recital of regulations. Mention has already been made of the new equity system whereby Japanese public servants can obtain a review of actions taken by the government against them. A sampling of some of these actions will quickly demonstrate that government employees in Japan are equipped with all the human foibles, fears and fancies encountered in any service. Here are a few cases lifted from actual hearings:

[13] *Ibid.*, pp. 19–22; the official source for government pay scales is *Okura Sho, Shukei Kyoku, Kyuyo seido chosa-kai hen* (Finance Ministry, Budget Bureau, committee to investigate salary-allowance system, ed.) *Shinhen, Komuin kyuyo benran* (Public Service salary & allowance manual, rev. ed.) (Tokyo: Ministry of Finance, 1958). See especially the tipped-in chart showing legal structure of allowances, and salaries at a glance, facing p. 12.

[14] One interesting result of the group's work was the widespread introduction of horizontal—in place of the traditional vertical—writing of Japanese ideographs in government documents.

Case 1. Disciplinary dismissal, Mie prefectural labor standards office (April 26, 1958): The original action of disciplinary dismissal is approved as the authority is satisfied that the appellant, by taking an under-age girl to a red-district restaurant run by his wife in the full knowledge that she would be compelled to engage in prostitution, committed an act discreditable to his official position as chief of a labor standards inspection office, in which capacity he ought to have given utmost attention to the protection of minors.

Case 2. Disciplinary suspension from duty; Osaka tax administration bureau (June 16, 1958) : When serving as the three key executive officers of the Osaka tax administration bureau employees labor union, the appellants, in an effort to secure compliance with a wage demand of their union by a show of force, issued a joint directive calling on the employees to carry out delaying tactics in violation of the duties of their positions. The authority rejects their appeals. . . .

Case 3. Disciplinary dismissal, Uno post office (June 28, 1958): The original action of disciplinary dismissal is approved, as the authority is satisfied that the appellant (chief of a stamp sales counter), embezzled the proceeds of stamp sales, repetitiously and continuously, over a long period of time by utilizing his official position.

Case 4. Renewal of temporary retirement, Kyoto imperial guard post (June 28, 1958) : At the time of the action, the appellant had not been completely cured of his tuberculosis but had recovered to such an extent that he was capable of carrying on ordinary desk work while receiving medical treatment. It was difficult to assign him to clerical duties, however. The regular police duties of an imperial guard policeman require a strong physical constitution and preclude any reduction of work hours. After reviewing the case, the authority has recognized that the appellant will still require at least six months' rest before he is able to return to work, and approved the renewal of the period of his temporary retirement for another six months.[15]

RESPONSIBILITY. Accountability of the bureaucracy is of course to the respective ministers, to the cabinet and prime minister and, ultimately, to the Diet, which as highest organ of state power enjoys virtually unlimited power of investigation, at least in legal theory. It holds the power of the purse. The investigative power extends not only to the executive, but to the judiciary as well, so long as the courts' independence is not threatened.

The Diet, in exercising its new powers of investigation, has worked through a special committee on administrative supervision. This committee is something like the well-known Senate Government Operations Committee in the United States. There have been charges that the other standing committees have tended to become spokesmen for the various administrative de-

[15] *Ibid.,* pp. 39 *ff.*

partments. There seems little doubt, however, that the relatively stronger position of the Diet has curbed what was in prewar days the almost unlimited power of the bureaucracy.

Furthermore there is a growing trend, also tied to the new legal position of the Diet, wherein the bureaucracy has come to bypass even the cabinet in order to link its own technical know-how with the growing political prestige of the parties. This is, as has been pointed out (Chap. 4), in turn a product of the tendency of parties—and particularly the factions within the major parties—to overshadow both the bureaucracy and the cabinet. Whether this development will eventually lead to a shift of effective power to the Diet itself, what earlier reforms and constitutional law prescribed, is not yet entirely clear. It certainly does mean, however, that the bureaucracy's former solid phalanx is slowly being pierced and influenced by more mundane and democratic political forces. Should this trend continue too far, of course, it would mean a threat to the independence of public servants.

To inhibit political excesses in the public service, the law rather strictly limits the outside activities of government employees. Leaves of absence designed to cover heavy engagement in outside organizations (even of employees), are forbidden. There are restrictions on political activities. Strict watch is kept over participation in private business outside government service, and over engagement of former public service employees after separation, in activities which might represent conflict of interest.

In the late 1950s the greatest number of disciplinary actions against government employees was, however, connected with illegal organization and union activities. (In 1958, such actions increased almost 70 per cent because of demonstrations against the government's police revision bill). Government employees (except police) enjoy limited rights of organization, as long as groups are promptly registered with the National Personnel authority. They have no real right of collective bargaining, however, and the right to strike is disapproved. In 1958, about 60 per cent of the regular public service (excluding those employed in government corporations) were organized.

8 - Law and Order

Old Japan, in contrast with Old China, very early drafted legal blueprints for the superstructure of the state. In this fundamental sense, Japan has always been—at least until the recent emergence of the People's Republic of China—far more legalistic in its governing process, as compared with the Middle Kingdom of China. Over the very edge of Japanese history (as we have seen in Chap. 1) marched grand constitutions and law codes, evidence that the Japanese tried to accept literally what the Chinese meant figuratively.

In Japanese feudal experience too, there was a strong sense of legal rights and obligations, which may well have laid down the foundations for the remarkably rapid modernization of the Japanese nation-state. In that process, the Japanese used law as a powerful instrument of social control.

During the twentieth century, Japan has slowly developed a unique combination of Japanese mores, traditional Confucian ethics, and modern legal norms derived—to the extent they owe a debt to Western inspiration—from continental rather than common law. Post-surrender Japan, as we are about to discover, has been equipped with a highly articulated system of courts and attendant rule-making powers, with familiar and yet hauntingly different sets of criminal and civil procedures. To this extent, the American lawyer who visits Japan at first feels as much at home in the comfortable confines of the law as he would in most Western states.

One word of warning must be added. Prodded by the Occupation, Japanese adopted elaborate measures to reform their entire legal system. In the countryside, however, such reforms have beaten vainly against the widespread aversion to the judicial process in any shape or form.

Field studies have made quite clear that only in a matter of vital importance does a villager of rural Japan voluntarily seek the assistance of the new courts in the settlement of a dispute. Even this step is taken only when all other means have been exhausted. The rural community highly values its harmony and solidarity and dislikes seeing them breached in any flagrant fashion. This does not mean there are not disputes, even bitter quarrels, in the *buraku* of agrarian, rural Japan. It does mean that the symmetrical structure of the court system and the rhythm of the judicial process must be matched off against familiar and traditional methods of consensus, conciliation and decisions by elders.[1]

Law in Japanese Society

The literature on law, either Japanese or Western languages, clearly illustrates the above-mentioned cultural lag. An American legal expert, long resident in Japan, has pointed to the largely historical nature of materials on Japanese law, the paucity of data on actual, contemporary practice and, above all, the sad neglect of "law as an operative social institution." [2]

Japan's first written ethical code was the so-called Constitution of Seventeen Articles, produced in A.D. 604. Actually, the first written laws were the regulations (in Chinese style) of the Taika Reform, 646, and of the Taiho Code, 702. These formal and artificial codes slowly dissolved to a nucleus of indigenous and largely unwritten law, after the tenth century.

At about the same time as Anglo-Norman law began to emerge in an island kingdom on the rimland at the other side of Eurasia, in 1232 an administrative council of the Kamakura *Bakufu* adopted a set of laws known as the Joei Code.[3]

Whereas the previous Taiko-Taiho codes had represented the Chinese Empire, adapted to Japan's felt needs, the Joei Code marked the florescence of Japanese feudalism, expressed through

[1] See Richard K. Beardsley, John W. Hall and Robert E. Ward, *Village Japan* (Chicago: University of Chicago, 1959), pp. 390–395.

[2] Dr. Richard W. Rabinowitz, Research Associate in Law, Harvard Law School, has been the key American figure in the (Ford Foundation-backed) Program for Intellectual Cooperation between American and Japanese law faculties. The author is grateful for the opportunity to participate in an informal discussion, in Tokyo, March 15, 1959, with Dr. Rabinowitz; the author's neighbor in Kyoto, Mr. Timothy Williams, member of the Program; and with the author's Fulbright colleague, Professor John M. Maki, University of Washington, an authority on Japanese constitutional law. See Richard W. Rabinowitz, "Materials on Japanese Law in Western Languages," *The American Journal of Comparative Law*, IV, No. 1 (Winter, 1955), pp. 97–104.

[3] The statute law of Old Japan has been compiled in one volume of less than 1,000 pages: Hagino Yoshiyuki, ed., *Nihon kodai hoten* (Legal records of Old Japan), Tokyo, 1892.

a military-landed nobility. In general the military headquarters of the Muromachi (1339–1573) and of the great Tokugawa (1600–1868) faithfully followed the provisions of the Joei Code. Throughout these periods, the chief field of legal interest was the regulation of land tenure and rights.

In feudal theory, each domain under the shogunate tended to legislate independently for its own people. Uniformity arose out of the similarity of language, custom and social background. At the top, the Tokugawa was able to compile house laws in general codes. Thus there were Tokugawa Ieyasu's Law of the Military Houses, 1615; the Edict of a Hundred Articles; special laws for the imperial court and for the shogunate; and specific regulations such as the Orders Posted in Edo. Most noteworthy in Japanese feudal criminal law were the principles of consanguineous and joint responsibility.[4] Resort to the courts was however a socially suspect act and was therefore rare. The overwhelming majority of disputes were settled within villages by the arbitration of headmen or elders.

After 1867, the privilege of making law returned to the central (Meiji) government. Japan's modern, basic codes were constructed parallel to the Meiji Constitution itself and borrowed heavily from continental European, specifically German principles.

To say, however, that Japan's first modern laws were products of an innate trait of imitation would be an oversimplification. First, in universal legal history the absorption of foreign principles is too familiar an occurrence. Second, Japanese law very carefully skirted any alien influences which challenged deep-seated customs and practices, particularly the all-powerful family system. Modern criminal law and procedure date back to 1882; modern jurisprudence to 1889 and the adoption of the Meiji Constitution, which went into effect in 1890. As we have seen (Chap. 2), extensive legal freedoms were granted in theory, but human rights were nominal in practice. A new criminal law, modelled on Germany's appeared in 1907 and a criminal procedure code followed in 1922. At about the same time, the other civil and commercial codes went into effect.[5]

[4] The most complete survey in English was prepared by John Henry Wigmore, "Materials for the study of Private Law in Old Japan," *Transactions* of the Asiatic Society of Japan, XX, Supplement (1892), especially Part 1, introduction.

[5] See *Japan: Its Land, People and Culture,* compiled by Japanese National Commission for UNESCO (Tokyo: Ministry of Finance, 1958), esp. Chap. 5, pp. 140–141.

The new constitution of 1947 brought to Japan not only a so-called induced revolution but also a fundamentally altered legal system, the full effects of which have yet to be felt, especially in the area of inviolable human rights. It must be emphatically stated, however, that subsequent legal reforms under the constitution have not changed the basic character of Japanese law by making it a member of our own common law family. Occupationaires tried to avoid the mistake, perhaps made in the constitution itself, of imposing American-born innovations out of tune with the Japanese system which is based on essentially different continental law.[6]

Nevertheless, revision of the code of criminal procedure, beginning in 1948, provided sweeping and time-consuming reforms. It implemented and strengthened the familiar and numerous constitutional safeguards, such as the right to counsel, the right to examine witnesses, and the requirement of judicial warrants for arrest, search and seizure. Changes in the penal code, eliminating the key provision for *lèse majesté,* dramatized the new principle of equality before the law. Alterations in the definition of defamation and libel widened the right of freedom of expression. Finally, by way of illustration, renunciation of war in Article 9 of the constitution required a modification of the whole Japanese concept of treason.

In the critical field of domestic relations, amendments to the civil code in 1947–1948 abolished the old household system in legal theory, and substituted the principles of the dignity of the individual and equality of the sexes. Of course, the Japanese have no more been able to sweep away the traditional house by law than we Americans have been able to bring about integration of racial minorities simply by court order. Amendments to the code of civil procedure simplified the appeal system and laid down the revolutionary principle that illegal acts of administrative agencies can be challenged by bringing actions in court. Revisions of the commercial code aimed primarily at democratizing corporations by strengthening the influence of stockholders and of the minority. Here again, the letter of the law may well be far in advance of the actual changes.

It might be well, at this point, to summarize the different types of law which now exist in Japan, if only to illustrate the

[6] An authoritative summary by one who aided the Japanese in reform is contained in Alfred C. Oppler, "Courts and Law in Transition," *Contemporary Japan* (Special Peace Edition), XXI, Nos. 1–3 (1952), pp. 19–55.

thoroughly modern legal structure which Japanese enjoy or with which they are freighted, depending upon the point of view. The keystone in the legal arch is now, of course,

1. *The constitution of Japan* itself. Rather difficult to amend, the organic act has the strongest formal validity compared with other laws and regulations.

2. *Laws* are now promulgated by the Diet, the sole law-making organ of the state. They are inferior to the constitution but superior to other regulations.

3. *Parliamentary rules* govern only the Diet and pertain to meetings, proceedings and internal discipline of the houses.

4. *Supreme Court rules* determine procedure, practice and discipline of the courts.

5. *Cabinet orders* execute provisions of the constitution and of law.

6. *Ministerial ordinances* execute cabinet orders and provisions of law.

7. *Other rules* emanate from the Audit Board, the National Personnel authority and similar external agencies. There are also regulations and rules issued by local public bodies.

The above classification is by legal type. Perhaps more meaningful is an illustrative list of actual laws on the books in post-treaty Japan. Among the most famous public laws are those of the imperial house, imperial house economy, nationality, habeas corpus, the Diet, court organization, cabinet, local autonomy, and regulation of political funds and expenditures. Among the well known laws governing civil affairs are those dealing with the civil code, commercial code and family registration. Then there are those concerning criminal affairs: the criminal code, criminal procedure code and the juvenile law. Finally, there are a host of statutes concerning social and economic affairs: labor standards, labor unions, labor relations adjustment, and child welfare. Altogether there were, in 1958, approximately 1,100 major laws governing the Japanese; including cabinet orders, other rules and regulations, there were about 7000.[7] Thus, it would seem, Japan has at long last become a government of law and not of men. However, the whole post-surrender legal reform stands or falls, as Alfred C. Oppler put it, with an independent judiciary. Japan's courts, in turn, depend on the status of lawyers and jurists in Japan. And these are created from men, not laws.

[7] See Chap. 5, "Government and Political Organization," "Kinds of Present Laws, Regulations, etc.," Japanese UNESCO, *op. cit.,* pp. 142–143.

The Lawyer in Modern Japan

Americans seldom realize that they live under what has sometimes facetiously been called a dictatorship of lawyers. Ever since the time of Chief Justice John Marshall and Associate Justice Samuel Chase[8] our judiciary—and especially the Supreme Court—has enjoyed unique respect and prestige. In American society, the practice of law is still one of the prime means of gaining prestige. Roughly two-thirds of our national legislators regularly come to Congress by way of a law career. In Japan, by way of contrast, only about one in every six members of the lower House of Representatives have been lawyers. The contrast in status stems mainly from basic differences between systems of training for the legal profession in Japan and in the United States.

First of all, it should be noted that there never has been an educational institution in Japan which corresponds precisely to the familiar American law school. In the prewar period, law departments of most universities had a three-year course. Graduates took a national law examination and those who passed with relatively high marks were appointed judicial probationers by the Ministry of Justice. After a further, one-and-one-half-year training course, those who passed another examination were then appointed judges or public procurators. This plan was modeled on the old German *referendar* system.[9] Until 1936, there was no special training program for potential members of the bar. In that year the government instituted a lawyer probationary system but offered no financial support for lawyer-probationary stipends. The system proved unsuccessful. What is even more noteworthy is the fact that, under the prewar system, judges and procurators had different training from that given practicing lawyers.

[8] In 1804, Chase was a member of the Supreme Court which first assumed the power to declare a federal statute or administrative act unconstitutional. He was impeached, triumphantly acquitted, and no subsequent attack of similar nature has ever been made against a Supreme Court Judge. In Japan today, the Diet exercises the important impeachment power over judges. Evidence indicates that it will be used sparingly in Japan too. See Oppler, *op. cit.*, pp. 30–31.

[9] This prewar apprentice system was established under the Court Organization Law (No. 6, 1890). The original draft was drawn by Dr. Otto Rudorff, a German legal scholar then employed by the Ministry of Justice. He took as a model the German Court Organization Act of 1877. See Matsuda Jiro, "The Japanese Legal Training and Research Institute," *The American Journal of Comparative Law*, VII, No. 3 (Summer, 1958).

After Japan's surrender, the legal education system was thoroughly overhauled along lines suggested by Occupation authorities. The American system was not introduced, however. Legal education at the university level was on the whole left untouched. In the revised four-year university program, the initial two or three half years are given over to liberal arts training and the remainder to legal education.[10] The result is that the amount of time devoted to legal education in faculties of law has been shortened.

Moreover, the law department of a Japanese university is obviously quite unlike the American graduate law school. It is organized primarily for the purpose of training those who wish to become civil servants or who wish to enter business, after having received some grounding in general principles of law. A slowly increasing number of graduates of law departments eventually do enter upon legal practice, but they are far fewer than those who follow the traditional legal profession in Japan.

Another major difference from the American pattern is that in Japan a single institution is charged with the task of giving training to those who wish to enter the law in a professional sense. Whereas in the United States, the lawyer must pass a state bar examination after his graduation from law school, in Japan one who wishes to enter the profession must pass the national law examination immediately upon graduation from college. Every year the number of applicants is about 6,000; 250 to 300 are successful.

Those who pass immediately enter the Japanese Legal Training and Research institute, which will be examined in greater detail below. Here suffice it to say the institute differs from the American law school in one significant respect: the latter trains individuals who primarily intend to become practicing lawyers, while the institute trains candidates for the three branches of the Japanese legal profession, the judiciary, the procuracy, and the bar.[11]

In summary, the legal profession in Japan has been and still is divided into three or, more practically, into two separate groups. The overwhelming majority of lawyers enter the judiciary or procuracy; a minority enters the bar. Although there

[10] As of 1957, twenty-five of the 230 universities in Japan had faculties of law; only eleven of the 269 junior colleges (two-year program) taught law; sixty-two universities had *daigakuin* (graduate schools) devoted to advanced academic training rather than training in professional skills.

[11] Matsuda, *loc. cit.*, esp. fn. 4.

has been some contact since the war, under the stimulus of a movement for unification of the profession, interchange between the bar and the other two branches is still exceptional. Such cooperation must of necessity await the strengthening of the new autonomous bar and its transition into an all-inclusive association which includes professors, practitioners, procurators, and judges. With the growth of urbanization and commerce, the demand for practicing lawyers to handle civil cases is growing steadily.[12] Incidentally, an interesting commentary on the connection between law and politics is the fact that most of the lawyers who enter the procuracy and bench by appointment have been affiliated with the ruling Liberal Democratic Party; lawyers with Socialist affiliations have been entering practice in the fields of tax, welfare, and labor law.

Organization of the Courts

In Tokugawa Japan there was no attempt to separate administrative and judicial powers. First, tentative steps awaited the Restoration in 1868, and particularly the establishment of a ministry of justice in 1871. There followed the creation of the Supreme Court in 1875, but only with the Regulation Governing Court Organization, 1886, did Japan gain a distinguishable judicial branch of government. Finally, the Meiji Constitution of 1889 in constitutional theory provided for an independent judicature, established under law. Nevertheless, according to the Japanese doctrine of separation of powers, legislation was drafted by the emperor with the consent of the Diet; the executive power was exercised by the prime minister and cabinet as officials of the emperor; and judicial powers were carried out by the courts as sovereign functions of the emperor. In conclusion, "The spirit of independence of judicature failed for the time being to permeate not only the general public but the government itself." [13]

Under the new constitution (Chap. 6) "the whole judicial power" is assigned to a Supreme Court and various inferior courts (Art. 76). This means that no executive organ partakes of this judicial power. The Supreme Court alone determines the procedure, practices and administration of all courts, including

[12] R. W. Rabinowitz, "Nihon bengoshi no shiteki hatten," a monograph reprint published in Japan, based on Dr. Rabinowitz' Ph.D. dissertation and a briefer summary in English, "The Historical Development of the Japanese Bar," Harvard Law Review, LXX (1956) 27.

[13] Japanese UNESCO, op. cit., p. 160.

the work of the public procurators (Art. 77). The inferior courts prescribed in the constitution have been determined by the Court Organization Law and consist of High, District, Summary and Family courts (Art. 1, Art. 2).[14] The hierarchical arrangement of these courts, their number, location, and branches are illustrated in Figure 7.

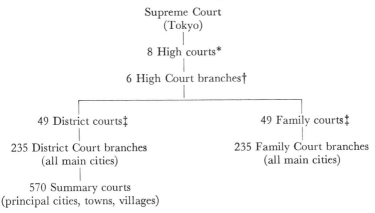

FIGURE 7 *Court organization*

Supreme Court
(Tokyo)

8 High courts*

6 High Court branches†

49 District courts‡

235 District Court branches
(all main cities)

570 Summary courts
(principal cities, towns, villages)

49 Family courts‡

235 Family Court branches
(all main cities)

* Tokyo, Nagoya, Osaka, Hiroshima, Fukuoka, Sendai, Sapporo, Takamatsu.

† Kanazawa, Matsue, Okayama, Akita, Miyazaki, Hakodate.

‡ Tokyo, 1; prefectures, 44; Hokkaido, 4.

SOURCE: "Courts under the New Constitution (as of the end of 1954)," *Recent Developments in the Field of Criminal Justice in Japan* (Tokyo: Supreme Court of Japan, October, 1955).

The Supreme Court is of course the highest court and is by law situated in Tokyo. As a rule the court does not handle cases in the first instance but hears appeals (*jokoku*) and complaints (*kokoku*) appealed from the high courts by reason of unconstitutionality or violation of laws and ordinances.[15] The court sits either as a grand bench, a collegiate body of all fifteen

[14] Law No. 59, April 5, 1947 (hereafter cited as *Law*). Original text of the statute is contained in *The Constitution of Japan and the Court Organization Law, etc.* (Tokyo: Supreme Court, 1958), which also includes the Law for Enforcement, No. 60 (1947) and the Ordinance for Enforcement, Cabinet Order No. 24 (1947), providing for judicial continuity. Fifteen amendments (May 1, 1947—June 8, 1954) are contained in the appendices of *Japanese Judicial System under the New Constitution* (Tokyo: Supreme Court of Japan, 1957).

[15] *Law*, Arts. 6, 7.

justices, or as a petty bench of three or more justices. Except on special occasions, decisions are written and governed by majority opinion. Administration of judicial affairs, previously handled by the minister of justice, are now determined by a judicial assembly of the fifteen justices. The court is aided in this work by a secretary-general, who in turn supervises the work of the secretariat (*jimu sokyoku*). Expenditures for the entire court system are included in the regular national budget.

The eight High courts hear appeals (*koso*) and complaints (*kokoku*) from judgments and rulings of District or Family courts. As courts of first instance they may, in addition, hear appeals from such quasi-judicial tribunals as the Fair Trade commission or Patent bureau. As a rule, these courts use a collegiate system of benches consisting of from three to five judges. They are assisted by six branches, established by the Supreme Court, and also by a secretariat.[16]

District courts are primarily courts of first instance (except for minor offenses) and exercise jurisdiction in each of the forty-nine judicial districts into which the country is divided. They also hear appeals and complaints from the Summary courts. Most cases are heard by one judge; complicated cases, by a collegiate body of three judges. The Supreme Court provides secretariats, branches and local offices in the districts.[17]

It is only natural that modern Japanese judicial procedure would reflect the traditional emphasis on the family as a critical realm of social control and that the present organization of courts would also provide a unique institution for handling family problems.[18] After adoption of the new constitution, provisions of the civil code dealing with family and succession law (Books 4 and 5) were completely revised and, at the same time (1947), the Law for Determination of Family Affairs was enacted. Meanwhile, work was going forward on the revised Juvenile Law (1948) and finally, both major statutes were amended to provide for the creation (January 1, 1949) of a new tribunal called the Family Court (*Katei Saibansho*). Handling of domestic problems thus came to be taken from the administrative and given to the judicial branch.

The general theory of the Family Court can be closely

[16] *Law*, Arts. 16, 18, 21, 22.

[17] *Law*, Arts. 24, 26, 29, 30, 31.

[18] See *Guide to the Family Court of Japan* (Tokyo: Supreme Court, November, 1957), pp. 2–5.

related to the proposals of a famous legal pioneer, Judge Ben B. Lindsey,[19] but the practice of the court is typically Japanese in approach. This court uses not only law but also the community conscience and the latest findings of the social sciences. It applies the casework method, quite different from the normal functions of a judicial tribunal. The procedure of the court is highly informal and readily adjustable to the circumstances of the persons being heard, while its hearings are kept in strict privacy and protected against publicity. The use of judicial laymen, in carrying out its functions, is also a throwback to traditional Japanese usage. The courts not only seek to secure legal rights of individuals but also exercise extensive supervisory functions.

The lowest rung in the formal judicial ladder is the Summary Court. One such court, each with a single judge, is to be found in 570 principal cities, towns and villages. It has authority to try minor civil and criminal cases by summary procedure, and to issue warrants for arrest, seizure and search.[20]

Japanese Judges

In postwar Japan, the status of the judge has been considerably elevated. (Prior to the war even the president of the old Supreme Court, the highest judicial officer, ranked below the minister of justice). The chief justice now ranks with the prime minister and the presidents of both houses of the Diet; justices rank with a minister of state; and judges hold, as a rule, higher status than do administrative officers. The chief justice, after designation by the cabinet, is appointed formally by the emperor. Justices and presidents of the High courts, after appointment by the cabinet, are attested by the emperor. With respect to appointment of judges of lower courts, the influence of the Supreme Court is controlling. While their formal appointment is also vested in the cabinet, the constitution (Art. 80)

[19] Benjamin Barr Lindsey, an American judge and authority on juvenile delinquency, began practice in Denver, Colorado, in 1894. He was instrumental in establishing one of the pioneer juvenile courts in the United States and served as its judge from 1900 to 1927. He reformed the methods of dealing with juvenile offenders and secured legislation making negligent parents and employers responsible.

[20] As of 1957, the Summary Court handled claims not in excess of 100,000 yen and offenses involving lighter penalties. *Law*, Arts. 33 (amendment), 35.

explicitly requires that the candidates be selected from a list submitted by the Supreme Court.[21]

In the spirit of the new independent judiciary the law sets very strict qualifications for judges, as compared with those for administrative officials and others. Supreme Court justices are to be appointed from among "persons of broad vision and extensive knowledge of law"; they must be not less than forty years of age; at least ten must be men who have distinguished themselves for twenty years as judges, procurators or lawyers, and the other five (not necessarily jurists), outstanding citizens of wide experience. Qualifications for inferior judges are relatively as strict.[22]

Although judges are explicitly forbidden to engage in political activities, they have been made independent in the exercise of legal conscience and are bound only by the constitution and laws. They are to receive adequate compensation, not to be decreased during term of office, and cannot be removed except by public impeachment by the Diet or unless judicially declared incompetent to perform official duties. On the other hand, several checks are provided to prevent judges from degrading their positions. Thus appointments of justices are reviewed by the people at the first general election of members of the lower house following the judges' assumption of office and every ten years thereafter. It is doubtful, by the way, that this referendum has constituted an effective check because the business of the courts, although of tremendous social and political significance, is not performed in an atmosphere of dramatic publicity.[23] Nor has there yet been a case where a judge has been called before the Court for the Trial of Impeachment, composed of members of both houses of the Diet. Judges of the lower courts, however, hold office for only ten years (with privilege of reappointment) and this provision can constitute an effective check. Finally, there is a system under which judges who have reached a certain age

---

[21] *Law*, Arts. 39, 40, 41. At first a high-level consultative committee advised the cabinet on the selection of candidates. When this committee, designed to exercise only advisory functions, evolved into an appointing agency, it was abolished by revision of the Court Organization Law. With the eventual emergence of an independent and unified bar, the government will have a logical association with which to consult regarding choice of candidates. See Oppler, *op. cit.*, pp. 28–30.

[22] *Law*, Arts. 41, 42, 44.

[23] One exception was the Supreme Court case involving the Japan-United States security treaty, examined in detail below.

are retired, when they are considered no longer able to perform duties.[24]

The ordinary full judge must first have passed the national law examination and entered the Japanese Legal Training and Research institute, already mentioned above in respect to the training of lawyers. The institute is attached directly to the Supreme Court; its chief, teaching staff and judicial research officials are formally appointed judicial officials; the recruitment of judicial apprentices, their training and examination are all governed by the Supreme Court.[25] It may be of some interest, especially to the American prelaw and law student, to examine the operation of the institute more closely.[26]

The Japanese national law examination is a most rigorous test, administered by a committee attached to the Ministry of Justice. Its required subjects include the constitution, civil law, criminal law, commercial law, criminal procedure and civil procedure. Laws of administrative litigation, bankruptcy, labor, criminology and international private law are electives. An oral examination follows the written stage. Successful applicants pay no tuition and, indeed, receive a monthly stipend equivalent to that paid administrative officials in the government at a similar stage of development. These facts are indicative of the importance attached to training for the legal profession. In 1958, the total number of legal apprentices was 550 (twenty-six women). Their average age was twenty-six.

The apprentices enter an initial training term of four months and are divided into six groups of about fifty members each. The institute's discussion method is in striking contrast with that used by university law faculties, where lectures are primarily used for instruction. Practical aspects of the law, especially developments in case law and fact finding, are emphasized. Another important part of the curriculum is instruction in the drafting of judgments. Inspection tours to prisons, securities exchanges, mental institutions, and large factories round out

[24] *Japanese Judicial System, op. cit.,* pp. 3, 12–13. Provision for review of appointments of justices is contained in the Constitution, Art. 79.

[25] *Law,* Arts. 14, 55, 56, 57, 66, 67.

[26] The author is grateful to Dr. Rabinowitz for his arrangement of an interview with Judge Tanabe Koji of the institute, in his office in Tokyo, in March, 1959. Judge Tanabe, who has pursued advanced comparative law study in the United States, took time out of an extremely busy schedule to describe the work of the institute and to provide the author with numerous original materials on Japanese law and the courts.

the training. Every apprentice attempts some research on one specialized problem.[27]

After the initial training, the apprentices fan out over the country for their sixteen months' field training, with eight months at a District Court (four months on civil cases, four on criminal cases), four months at a public procurator's office, and four months attached to a lawyers' association. During the first of this period, the apprentice is assigned to and actually sits on the bench with a district judge. After field training, apprentices return to the institute for a four-month period of collective training. The final examination is conducted by a special committee whose chairman is the chief justice himself. With rare exceptions, all apprentices jump this last hurdle. Graduates are qualified to become assistant judges and, after ten years' service, full judges. Or they may become public procurators or practicing lawyers. A few enter academic life, some other branch of government or business.

As of 1958, the institute had graduated about 2,000 lawyers: about 600 became assistant judges; about 500, procurators; the others, practicing lawyers. The institute is still young and yet it has begun to exert a discernible effect on the legal profession as a whole. Graduates are better trained, in both practice and theory, than were jurists of the past. There is a growing consciousness of integration of the profession and the former imbalance of training among branches no longer exists. On the side of liabilities, the institute remains almost entirely responsible for professional legal training and there is little impact, as yet, on the universities. The scope of law is widening so rapidly two years are becoming insufficient to hold the institute curriculum. On the other hand, the first year and a half of liberal arts training in the university is also too short.

Nevertheless, the Japanese Legal Training and Research institute has made its mark on Japanese law and not entirely in the training of apprentices. About ten groups of assistant judges, thirty to the group, are given in-service training for one to two weeks each year. Once each year, two months of in-service training are given to newly appointed lay judges of the Summary courts. Finally, the institute administers occasional conferences for judges and a judicial research plan through which judges released from normal duties participate in comparative law studies.

[27] Some of these may be published in the *Shiho Kenshu Shoho,* the law review of the institute. Matsuda, *loc. cit.*

The Judiciary: Powers and Functions

No description of the modern Japanese judiciary would be complete without some estimate of its status, of its present and potential power. The problem is made complex by the fact that, although the Japanese may be familiar with laws, they are less familiar with legal methods for settling disputes; by the fact that Japan is a constitutional monarchy with a parliamentary-cabinet form of government; and finally, by the fact that the new constitution is nevertheless theoretically based on the rather unrealistic doctrine of the separation of powers.

The interconnections between cabinet and Diet, normal in the parliamentary form, have already been described. The statement in the constitution that the Diet "shall be the highest organ of state power" would seem to elevate the legislature to highest rank, but surely such a statement is of more symbolic than legal significance. The development of the postwar government within the context of an Occupation, and the subsequent growth of the administrative state in Japan, as elsewhere, has meant in practice a relatively strong cabinet and particularly a steadily expanding office of the prime minister. In this sense, the Japanese resembles the American Presidential form. Furthermore the third branch, the judiciary, is both subject and object of checks and balances. It is the executive, as we have seen, which designates the chief justice for appointment by the emperor and who appoints associate justices and judges of lower courts. It is the legislature which exercises the important impeachment power.

A delicate issue, involving the relationship between legislative and judicial branches, early arose over the power of investigation. In 1949, the judicial committee of the House of Councillors claimed that under the constitution (Art. 62), the Diet—as "highest organ of state power"—had the right to investigate court decisions, to criticize the wisdom of judgments and to challenge the attitude of judges. The Judicial Assembly of the Supreme Court, in an open letter to the house, promptly protested. It was pointed out that the constitution (Art. 76) vests "the whole judicial power" in the courts. To be sure, in a democracy no branch should remain beyond accountability, but legal experts took heart in the indication that the Supreme Court did not intend to surrender its constitutional powers.[28]

Nevertheless, it was inconceivable that the courts in Japan,

[28] Oppler, *op cit.,* pp. 31–33.

any more than in the United States, could escape controversy entirely. Nowhere was this more clear than in the adoption of an American device, the power of judicial review, which makes the Supreme Court the guardian of the constitution. This was such an unfamiliar concept that the court, in the first four and a half years of its existence, made very cautious use of the power. Even the phrasing in the constitution (Art. 81) had been rendered in roundabout fashion: the court was granted the power to determine whether a law, order, regulation, or official act, literally, ". . . is in conformity with the constitution or not." [29] In determining such a question, the approval of more than eight judges, not a simple majority, is required.

Early in 1948, the Supreme Court faced the question of whether capital punishment violated the constitution, which prohibits (Art. 36) cruel and unusual punishments. Life itself can be taken by due process of law (Art. 31), the court ruled. The court's protection of civil liberties was soon illustrated by a ruling that a conviction resting on a confession after long confinement was invalid. A third dramatic case pitted traditional social norms against due process. In this instance, a public procurator appealed on the basis of the criminal code (Art. 205), which provided heavier punishment for patricide than for injury resulting in death of others. A lower court had applied the constitution (Art. 14), which declared all men equal before the law. The Supreme Court reversed the judgment in this famous patricide case, and held that the principle of equality did not prevent the law from establishing different standards as required by morality, justice, suitability or the relationship between individuals.[30]

A prelude to Japan's most significant constitutional case came in April, 1952, less than six months after the recovery of sovereignty. Chairman Suzuki Mosaburo of the Left Socialist Party filed suit in the Supreme Court seeking dissolution of the National Police Reserve, which had been organized in April, 1951. The reserve, argued Suzuki, constituted war potential, explicitly barred by the constitution (Art. 9). The Court chose

[29] ". . . *Kempo ni tekigo suru ka shinai ka.*"

[30] *Kuni tai Murakami* (State vs. Murakami, 1948); *Kuni tai Imai* (State vs. Imai, 1949); *Kuni tai Yamamoto* (State vs. Yamamoto, 1950). These cases within a general survey of the early history of judicial review were cited by Gokijo Kakiwa (Secretary-General of the Supreme Court), "The Judicial System of New Japan," *The Annals* of the American Academy of Political and Social Science, CCCVIII (November, 1956).

this case to reject suits which were not specific judicial controversies, and further declared that it was not empowered to comment on abstract problems of constitutionality. This was the first, but certainly not the last, attempt to define the boundaries of the court's power, specifically with regard to the controversial Article 9.

The most dramatic, the most significant and, unfortunately, the somewhat inconclusive test of the Supreme Court's power arose out of the so-called Sunakawa case. The long-run effects, at the time of writing of this book, can scarcely be predicted. Nevertheless, a chronological account of the controversy will demonstrate why it was a turning point in post-surrender judicial and political history.

In July, 1957, a horde of demonstrators tried to block surveys designed to expand the American Tachikawa airbase into the area of Sunakawa village, west of Tokyo. In September, the Tokyo Metropolitan Police arrested twenty-five, including seven who were charged with violation of the Special Criminal Law, drawn up to protect facilities assigned to the United States under treaty.[31] It should be noted that the defendants were not ordinary Japanese citizens;[32] the Sunakawa affair soon blossomed into something more than an ordinary judicial case.

The explosive Sunakawa case began its long journey through the judicial process in the Tokyo District Court where, on March 30, 1959, the seven defendants were acquitted by a three-man panel headed by Judge Date Akio. After delivery of the verdict, Judge Date told the press that the court had faithfully followed the constitution, in light of "its original spirit and ideals. Theoretically," he said, "we could not reach any other conclusion." This theoretic conclusion, he emphasized, should not be used

[31] Art. 2 of this law provided for imprisonment of not more than one year and a fine of not more than 2,000 yen "in order to safeguard United States military installations in Japan." Art. 1, Item 32 of the ordinary Minor Offenses Law, governing trespass elsewhere, provided for a shorter term of confinement and smaller fines. At the time of the Sunakawa case, more than seventy cases involving violations of the Special Criminal Law had been heard in District and High courts, where the constitutionality of the statute had always been upheld.

[32] Not ordinary, in the sense that all seven were in the forefront of the political movement dedicated to driving American forces out of Japan. They included, for example, Sakata Shigeru, executive of a major steel labor union, and Tsuchiya Gentaro, Secretary General of the militant students' organization, *Zengakuren*. Unno Shinkichi, a famous criminal attorney, was employed in their defense. See *Mainichi*, March 31, 1959.

for any political purpose.[33] In this somewhat naive hope Judge Date was to be disappointed.

The Tokyo District Court reasoned that, irrespective of the international validity of the security treaty (signed with the United States in 1951), the stationing of American troops in Japan violated the second clause of Art. 9 of the constitution.[34] The court further argued that the security treaty (Art. 1) [35] made arrangements for American forces in Japan not only for the defense of Japan, but also for the maintenance of peace in the Far East. Thus Japan might well become involved, unconstitutionally, in an armed struggle not at all of her own making. Curiously, the court did not deny Japan's inherent right of self-defense but it did hold that Art. 9 forbade war potential, even for defense! The fact that the removal of American troops would obviously leave a vacuum, the court continued, did not constitute a valid legal argument. Finally, since the terms of the security treaty violated the constitution, similarly the implementing administrative agreement and, especially, the Special Criminal Law were also invalid. Protection to the American garrison superior to that accorded the average Japanese thus violated the constitutional provision (Art. 31) that criminal penalty could not be imposed except according to procedure established by law.

The reaction to this ruling was immediate and stormy. The

[33] Noda Minoru, "Supreme Court Facing Nippon-United States Security Pact Case," Part 2, *Mainichi,* May 24, 1959.

[34] The international context of the treaty and agreement are discussed in greater detail below, Chap. 11.

Chapter 2, Art. 9 of the constitution: "Aspiring sincerely to an international peace based on justice and order, the Japanese people forever renounce war as a sovereign right of the nation and the threat or use of force as means of settling international disputes.

"In order to accomplish the aim of the preceding paragraph, land, sea, and air forces, *as well as other war potential,* will never be maintained. The right of belligerency of the state will not be recognized." Italics added.

The circumstances under which the constitution, and specifically Art. 9, were drafted, are described in detail above, Chap. 2.

[35] Security treaty between the United States of America and Japan (September 8, 1951), Art. 1: "Japan grants, and the United States of America accepts the right, upon the coming into force of the treaty of peace and of this treaty, to dispose United States land, air and sea forces in and about Japan. Such forces may be utilized to contribute to the maintenance of international peace and security in the Far East and to the security of Japan against armed attack from without, including assistance given at the express request of the Japanese Government to put down large-scale internal riots and disturbances in Japan, caused by instigation or intervention by an outside power or powers."

government received the news with shock, for Foreign Minister Fujiyama Aiichiro was about to begin negotiations with Ambassador Douglas MacArthur II toward revision and strengthening of the security pact. Narita Tomomi, Chief of the General Affairs Bureau of the Socialist Party, exclaimed in triumph that the ruling justified his party's position. The government, he needled, had been surreptitiously rearming Japan under the guise of defense, and had plans for the introduction of nuclear weapons into Japan.[36]

The political sound and fury all but obscured more fundamental legal issues involved in the judgment. The reader may recall that the constitution is not entirely clear as to the relation between the power of judicial review (Art. 81) and treaties: the court can review laws, orders, regulations or official acts. Elsewhere (Art. 98), the constitution is defined as the supreme law of the nation, and no law, ordinance, imperial rescript or other act of government contrary to the constitution is to have legal force. Immediately thereafter, however, appears the clause that treaties concluded by Japan and established laws of nations shall be faithfully observed. With these provisions in mind, two schools of legal opinion emerged. One, which differed with the District Court, upheld the supremacy or at least equal status of the treaty. The other, which approved the stand of the court, argued for constitutional supremacy and for the right of courts to examine the domestic effects of treaties.[37] In any case, there was sufficient doubt as to the logic of the judgment that the government decided to appeal directly to the Supreme Court, on the grounds of constitutionality, by-passing the Tokyo High Court.

So important was the Sunakawa case to the Kishi government that the Prosecutor-General, Kiyohara Kunikazu, for the first time personally presented the appeal to the Supreme Court. The government's case rested on three essential points: (1) International custom and courtesy demanded special treatment for friendly armed forces and, therefore, the Special Criminal Law. (2) The security pact made up both for the deficiency in UN-supported security and Japanese defense. Japan-based American

[36] *Mainichi*, April 1, 1959.

[37] Okazaki Katsuo, former Foreign Minister, argued that the nation had the inalienable right of self-defense, to be implemented through the treaty-making power. Judge Date had ruled on the spirit of the constitution, and had a suspicion that it had been violated. This was no substitute for a practical legal judgment. Sato Tatsuo, former Cabinet Legislative Bureau Chief, supported the constitutional supremacy doctrine, but he did cast doubt on the logic of the judgment. See *Mainichi,* May 25, 1959.

forces could not engage in unlimited conflict; on the other hand, they were not under Japanese command and, therefore, could not be considered Japanese war potential. (3) Finally, under the constitution (Arts. 81, 98) treaties were political questions outside the purview of the courts.

The defense opened its case unpropitiously by challenging Chief Justice Tanaka Kotaro on his "old-fashioned ideologies admitting war," and thereby his right to hear the case at all. When this gambit failed, the defense presented a 500,000-word argument upholding the ruling of the Tokyo District Court. The hearings began on September 7 and were completed on September 18, 1959. The Supreme Court made its unanimous ruling December 16.

The court accepted the government's argument in part, by interpreting the preamble of the constitution in a fashion diametrically opposite to the reasoning of the District Court. Japan could, the judgment held, offset its defense deficiency by "trusting in the justice and faith of the peace-loving peoples of the world." In this liberal interpretation, American forces became a sort of substitute for United Nations security. Japan had no right of supervision or command over such forces and, therefore, they did not constitute war potential under Art. 9. Judgment as to the validity of the treaty, or revision thereof, was left to the Japanese people as a political matter. In a puzzling *obiter dictum*, Chief Justice Tanaka held that, even if the stationing of American troops in Japan were unconstitutional, the controversial Special Criminal Law was valid. Associate Justices Shima and Kawamura were on sounder ground when they ruled that courts could not study the propriety of policies concerning the maintenance of peace.[38]

The reaction to the Supreme Court judgment was divisive, as had been the response to the lower court ruling. This time, the ruling Liberal-Democratic Party hailed the verdict that "upheld the prestige of the judicature." Yamashita Seiichi, Secretary of the Japan Management association (*Doyukai*), said that businessmen in general welcomed the decision. *The Japan Times* editorialized that the ruling meant that Japan need not give up its right to self-defense. On the other side, former Socialist Prime Minister Katayama Tetsu denounced the decision as a "betrayal of the people's trust in the Supreme Court as a watchdog of the constitution." Socialist Party headquarters announced a nationwide campaign to poll referendum votes against all fifteen jus-

[38] *Tokyo Times,* December 17, 1959.

tices.[39] The Jurists' Council for Research on the Security Treaty, composed of 1,500 judges and practicing lawyers, also criticized the ruling as opportunist.

Despite the exuberance of the Japanese government and the restrained approval of American officials, the ruling in the Sunakawa case may have been a Pyrrhic victory. True, the boundaries of judicial review were clearly marked short of treaties. On the other hand, what everyone hoped would be a clear-cut judicial settlement was turned back into the political arena. The Supreme Court did not pass on what the inherent right of self-defense or war potential is, or should be. There was neither a clear-cut clarification of Art. 9 nor an exhortation to the government forthrightly to amend the constitution, in order to give Japan the power of defense it needs. Put another way, the court chose not to offer an opinion on the security treaty of 1951 nor on its potential successor, the revised treaty (signed in Washington in 1960). Despite the government's enthusiasm with the court's ruling, that decision made a subsequent political judgment of the new treaty by the Japanese people (examined further below, Chap. 11), inevitable, and an eventual judicial ruling on self-defense even more necessary.[40]

Problems of Application and Law Enforcement

At the lower levels of the new court structure, there are gradual and subtle changes in the role of law as a means of social control. The legal issues may be less dramatic than those handled by the Supreme Court in the course of judicial review, but they may be equally significant. Most important, we should not overlook the obvious and yet revolutionary provision of the constitution (Art. 82) to hear cases and pass judgments publicly.[41] This reform, with establishment of the independence of the courts, assures "fundamental rights of the individual, in contrast

[39] The *Sankei Shimbun* commented ruefully that it was peculiar that the Socialists denounced the "political" court for the Sunakawa case, when they had just praised the same "judicial" court for an unbiased ruling in the controversial Matsukawa sabotage case. *The Japan Times,* December 17, 1959.

[40] *Tokyo Shimbun,* December 17, 1959, commented: "As a result, the long-smoldering issue of whether the Self-Defense Forces are constitutional or not remains unsettled. This is a matter for regret."

[41] A court may unanimously decide that publicity is dangerous to public order or morals, but no trial involving political offenses, freedom of the press or civil rights may be tried privately. *Law,* Art. 3.

to the extreme nationalistic and ex-officio action seen in the old system of procedure." [42]

The rights of the individual have been greatly strengthened in both criminal and civil procedures. In modern Japanese courts, as in courts elsewhere, there are now various kinds of disputes: judgments on whether or not the sovereign right to punish exists are criminal in nature; judgments on all other rights and legal relations are civil.[43] Expansion of the legal realm and the power of the courts has resulted, of course, in a tremendous increase in number of cases as compared with prewar days. In 1956, for example, the number had jumped to 50 per cent over the prewar level.

This remarkable increase in number of legal cases can be accounted for in a number of ways. The bulk of civil disputes doubtless reflects the social and economic confusion during and after the end of the war, a turmoil which is now diminishing. On the other hand, the increase in criminal cases is such as to alarm the Japanese. Since 1954, much of it can be accounted for by violations of the Road Traffic Control Law, but there are also serious increases in the number of juvenile cases. Overall, the statistics reflect an increasing use of judicial procedure to settle disputes.

One of the slowest, quietest and yet perhaps most significant legal revolutions is being effected in the courts in connection with the amendments to the civil code, juvenile law and other social legislation. For example, matters newly handled by courts include: (1) abolition of the feudal concept of the house as a legal unit; (2) substantial equality of the sexes; (3) substitution of the court for the family conference, in the role of legal guardian; and (4) court investigation of adoptions. Equally important have been the reforms of civil procedure, whereby the parties examine evidence in place of preliminary investigation by the court; whereby cross-examination replaces examination solely by the judge; and whereby the rights of legal persons are assured. Nevertheless, Japanese courts have retained many traditional, useful and unique features. Thus the trial judge tends to play a more active role than does his counterpart in an American court.

[42] *Japanese Judicial System, op. cit.,* p. 6.

[43] In Japan, both civil and criminal proceedings are usually conducted in open court, judgment being rendered after hearing contentions of both parties. This is called an action. A case which is not primarily a dispute between parties contending—domestic and some juvenile cases—is handled by proceedings, in which the judge examines the documents in chambers. *Ibid.,* p. 5.

There are frequent and informal discussions among the judge and counsels. In a sense, the trial proceeds like an incessant pre-trial conference in the United States.[44]

Without doubt the most unusual development in the Japa-nese court system is the new Family Court. This tribunal is in the forefront of a major social revolution, and yet it manages to operate within the comfortable confines of Japanese traditions. For one thing, it functions as much as a social welfare institution as it does a court. Its most distinctive features are use of a wide variety of formal and informal techniques of adjustment, includ-ing conciliation; and proceedings which involve one judge and two conciliation commissioners (*chotei iin*), one usually a female. Whereas in the Anglo-Saxon tradition the layman appears most often in the jury, in Japan the layman makes his contribution most often in the Family Court. In the first ten years of its evolu-tion, the court went through a remarkable development of organization and activities. It is true that many problems of procedure in the court still await solution. Japanese jurists most often mention the need for a more harmonious relationship between its legal and its social welfare functions. Nevertheless, the Family Court offers the greatest promise of becoming Japan's outstanding court of the people and for the people.[45]

Guarantees of the fundamental rights of the individual are also clearly reflected in the new Code of Criminal Procedure, which dates from January 1, 1949.[46] These alterations came none too soon because postwar economic and social confusion led to a sharp rise in the crime rate. An epoch-making change, establish-ment of a system for rehabilitation of offenders, tried to keep step with the steadily rising crime rate, but offenses involving larceny, gambling and bodily harm have continued to show a marked increase.[47] Most frustrating to the Japanese, as it is to Americans, has been the steady increase in juvenile delinquency.

[44] *Ibid.*, pp. 6–7. Also Judge Tanabe Kohji, "A Brief Comment on Japa-nese Civil Procedure" (mimeographed), January, 1956.

[45] *Family Court, op. cit.*, pp. 18–21.

[46] Main points in reform of the code are as follows: (1) no person is subject to arrest, save in flagrant offenses, without warrant; (2) the old system of preliminary examination, often involving forced confession, is abolished; (3) provisions are made for release on bail; (4) the poor have appointed defense counsels; (5) an accused cannot be convicted solely on a confession; (6) the superior status of the public prosecutor in prewar trials is eliminated. *Japanese Judicial System, op. cit.* p. 7, fn.

[47] *Recent Developments in Criminal Justice, op. cit.*, esp. Table No. 3 and Diagram No. 1, pp. 10–11. Also *Rehabilitation of Offenders in Japan* (Tokyo: Ministry of Justice, 1957).

Statistics on the incidence of juvenile delinquency in modern Japan seem all too familiar in their pattern. Although youth who become involved in crime represent only a little over one per cent of the juvenile population (ages 14–20), nevertheless almost 20 per cent of all offenses against the Penal Code can be attributed to young people. The highest rate, well above that of adults, is in the 18- to 19-year-old group. Japanese juveniles account for about half of all rapes, one of every three robberies, and about one-quarter of all crimes of violence, threats and extortion. The rate of delinquency in metropolitan areas, specifically the six largest cities, is about 1.5 times as high as that in rural areas. The causes of juvenile delinquency in Japan, as in the United States, are complex. Most often mentioned are the turbulence after war, the colonial system of the Occupation, the breakdown of traditional family structure, poor living conditions and the Japanese penchant for organization into gangs. In addition, Japan's situation offers certain peculiar aspects, such as the relation between delinquency and the nature of employment of the father, now under intensive study.[48]

The unprecedented rise of crime and, by Japanese standards, major breakdown of morals have begun to make themselves felt even in the countryside. When apprehended in any of the criminal offenses mentioned, the rural resident is also hailed before one of the courts. In such cases his appearance is, of course, involuntary. Voluntary use of the judicial machine in rural Japan is, however, rare.

In other words, legislative and administrative changes have formally brought law closer to performing the social and political functions familiar to Western states. On the other hand, much of Japanese society is persistently governed by the traditions of many another rural, agrarian Asian society. The Japanese lawyer is on the threshold of, but has not yet quite entered the parlors of the political elite of Japan. The practice of law is still not a major means of gaining prestige. Furthermore in rural Japan, as we have noted, the processes for the settlement of disputes often have little or nothing to do with the law as such and are often effected completely outside the formal court structure. In this sense, the Japanese judicature remains a remote administrative arm of the state, impersonal, alien and suspect.

[48] *Juvenile Delinquency in Japan; Characteristics and Preventive Measures,* 2d ed. (Tokyo: Ministry of Justice, 1958).

9 - The State, the Political Economy and the General Welfare

In the Meiji era (1868–1912) much Western knowledge—including the social science of economics—was imported into Japan. And yet ever since traditional thinking about the political economy has persisted in the depths of Japanese ideology. This phenomenon may be illustrated by the Japanese language itself.

The Japanese word for economics is still *keizaigaku,* consisting of three Chinese ideographs. These were adapted to refer to a new, Western science, presumably with fixed, universal principles somewhat like the laws of physics. The ideographic symbols also call up, however, a set of indigenous impressions, namely:

> *learning,* in the classical Chinese sense and, therefore, linked with the art of government;
> *about statecraft* or political economy in the traditional Japanese sense;
> *for the welfare of the people,* in the ethical, Confucian sense.

Japanese economic thinkers, other than those who have adopted Western economics wholesale, have found it difficult to grasp the assumption (made in the West for laboratory purposes) that economics starts with the individual as an economic unit. True, there appeared in both Meiji and MacArthur Japan brief fads of individualism; but the overriding tradition has been, on the contrary, to assume that it is the moral duty of the state to plan, to regulate and to control the economy for the general welfare.

Paradoxically, the present alien-inspired constitution purported to turn its back on Western concepts of rugged individualism and to embrace some of the most up-to-date concepts of social welfare. As a matter of fact, in so doing it may well have reflected ancient Japanese ideals of livelihood. In any case, the constitution (Chap. III, Art. 25) states:

All people shall have the right to maintain minimum standards of wholesome and cultured living. In all spheres of life the state shall use its endeavors for the protection and extension of social welfare and security, and of public health.

Economic Plans

In order to achieve rapid industrialization, the Japanese government almost from the beginning of the drive toward modernization has assumed the initiative in economic planning. For this reason, for over 100 years there has been no real conflict between government and business interests. Indeed, the Japanese economic climate has produced a type of businessmen (as we shall see, below) who have prospered under the patronage of the state and to whom political contacts have meant the secret to business success. These came to be known as *seisho* (businessmen with political connections).[1]

Increasingly, of course, such businessmen as well as other Japanese became enmeshed in the attempt to solve Japanese economic problems by emigration, military expansion and imperialism. Nevertheless, such efforts were accompanied by active efforts at planning, especially in the decade of the 1930s. Some experts have referred to Japan as the first of the modern neo-mercantilist states. After 1936, especially under the National Mobilization Law, economic planning and control became major governmental activities.[2]

Since World War II, because of the pressing need for basic reconstruction and the shortage of private capital, business and industry have relied mainly on government funds collected by taxation. The preoccupation of the government and political parties as well as business has been predominantly, if not solely, with economic problems. Even today economic planning is mainly in the hands of the state. Various private economic organizations listed below engage conspicuously in economic policy-making, but the initiative is the government's concern.

There is no denying the seriousness of the problem faced by Japanese economic planning (see above, Chap. 3): by the 1970s the population will exceed 100,000,000; even more critical, the pressure of the working age (15–59) population continues to

[1] Chitoshi Yanaga, *Japanese People and Politics* (New York: Wiley, 1956), esp. pp. 326 *ff.*

[2] See Chap. 2, "A Decade of Preparation," in Jerome B. Cohen, *Japan's Economy in War and Reconstruction* (Minneapolis: University of Minnesota, 1949).

build up toward the so-called crisis of 1965.[3] Of the two major factors which play a strategic role in deciding success or failure of Japanese efforts to solve these problems, only one is completely under Japanese control. The rate of capital accumulation perhaps the Japanese can do something about. The international balance of payments situation is something they can do less about.

In late 1957, official planners drew up a blueprint for the growth of the Japanese economy to cover the fiscal years 1958–59 through 1962–63. Even in summary, the plan illustrates the staggering job ahead; (1) to meet a population growth of 0.8 per cent per annum (which, although it is below international levels, does contain a rate of growth in working-age population of 1.9 per cent per annum); (2) to plan expansion of basic industries and to reduce business fluctuations; (3) to provide guiding principles for agricultural production and shifting habits of food consumption; (4) to narrow the gap between large and small enterprises; and (5) to step up the training of scientists and engineers. In short, the principal objectives of this plan are to provide for a steady increase in the standard of living and provide for full employment by accomplishing persistently the maximum rate of economic growth consistent with economic stability.[4]

The Japanese plan sets a goal of long-range economic expansion at 6.5 per cent per annum, computed from a base of fiscal 1956. If this were accomplished, the gross national product in fiscal 1962 would be 40 per cent more than in 1956. Consumption per capita would have increased by some 38 per cent.

This projected rate of growth is admittedly exceedingly high, approximately twice that of most European countries. Indeed, the prewar rate was on the average about 4 per cent annually and was considered remarkable. In the postwar years up to 1956, the economic growth rate steadily rose to a high of about 10 per cent, but this rate could be attributed to the need for almost complete rehabilitation of the economy. In a year of recession, 1958, the rate fell off to about 5.5 per cent.[5]

Turning once again to the major factors in growth, capital accumulation necessary to success means that the Japanese must

[3] *Showa 40 nen no nankyoku torai.*

[4] Japanese government, Economic Planning agency, *New Long-Range Economic Plan of Japan (FY1958–1962)* (Tokyo, December 17, 1957), esp. Part 1, "Basic Ideas"; the quotation is from p. 12.

[5] Kuroda Kazuo, "Blueprint for the Future: Social Welfare is not Luxury but Absolute Necessity for Japan," *The Japan Times,* January 5, 1959.

plow back into the economy some 28 per cent of the gross national product in the form of investments. Under the long-range plan, highest priorities are assigned to transportation and power. Meanwhile, increased freight volume faces a bottleneck because of superannuated rail facilities. Roads and highways will be desperately needed. By 1962, there will be an increase in energy demand of 56 per cent over fiscal 1956. As the economy expands, Japan will feel the pressure for increased imports—foodstuffs, cotton, wool, salt, petroleum and ores—and thus must manage to expand exports as well. In fact, Japan will have to increase exports by 82 per cent—more than double the rate of other countries of the world—between 1956 and 1962.

In 1960, the Japanese government amended the earlier plan with a long-range economic program to be accomplished by year 1970. Key statistics in the new plan are presented in Table 9.

TABLE 9   *Japan's long-range economic plan for 1970*

	*Per cent increase per year**
Gross national product	7.2
Personal consumption	7.1
Industrial production	11.0
Population	0.8

* On basis of 14 years.
SOURCE: *Oriental Economist*, December, 1960, p. 690.

Since the adoption of the long-range plan, in 1957, the Japanese economy has registered some gains and has also suffered some losses. A *White Paper on the People's Livelihood* released by the Economic Planning agency in 1959, for example, revealed that the living standard was indeed rising but that there was an ever-widening gulf between rich and poor. Household incomes of middle and upper classes steadily increased despite the recession of 1958, with a corresponding improvement in quality of food, clothing and dwellings; but the consumer standards of low income workers was increasing at a far slower rate.[6] According to the Economic Planning agency, actual growth of the economy was 6.4 per cent in 1957, 5.3 per cent in 1958, and 10.7 per cent

[6] In 1957, income of workers in the cities rose 6.8 per cent as against income of farmers, 4.7 per cent. High-bracket incomes rose 8 per cent; low-bracket incomes, 3.5 per cent. *Keizai Kikaku Cho hen* (Economic Planning agency, ed.) *Kokumin seikatsu hakusho: Showa 33 nempan* (White paper on people's livelihood, 1958 edition) (Tokyo: Finance Ministry, 1959).

in 1959, for an average economic growth rate of 7.6 per cent for the three years. Much of the gain was made on the basis of strengthened international competitive power: despite sharp increases in import demand, export levels were exceeding world trends.[7]

Machinery for Planning

Originally the basis for the government's efforts to create a viable economy was the general National Resources Development Law, enacted May, 1950. This law laid out a ten-year plan for the development of nine designated areas through the joint efforts of the ministries of international trade and industry, transportation and construction, with half the funds to be provided by the national government. The present economic general headquarters for all such planning is the Economic Planning agency (*Keizai Kikaku cho*). This agency began under the Occupation as the Economic Stabilization board and later became

FIGURE 8 *Economic Planning agency (Keizai Kikaku cho)*

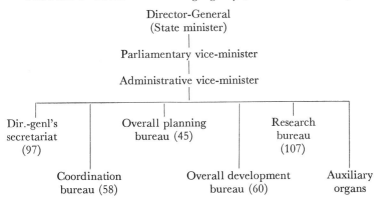

SOURCE: *Government Organization*, pp. 62–64; and *Kiko zu*, p. 28, both previously cited, see above, Chap. 5.

the Economic Policy board. It is attached directly to the office of the prime minister (see above, Chap. 5); its director-general is a state minister and member of the cabinet. Its organization is represented in Figure 8.

[7] "Progress Report on Long-Range Economic Plan," *Japan Report*, New York: Information Office, Consulate General of Japan, Vol. VI, No. 7 (April 1, 1960), p. 4; *Nihon Keizai*, April 9, 1960.

The Economic Planning agency is, in turn, aided by the Economic Deliberation council (*Keizai Shingi kai*), a statutory advisory body also attached to the prime minister's office. The council is a veritable who's who of Japanese finance and industry, including key officers of the government, the shipowners' association, chambers of commerce, major trading companies, Yawata Steel, textile manufacturers' association and the central banks.[8] Both the agency and the council maintain liaison with the more informal Financial Policy Deliberation committee, attached to the Ministry of Finance.[9]

The agency does not of course work alone but with and through the various executive departments and independent agencies. The Bank of Japan is crucial, center of Japan's financial policy formulation. It serves as a go-between in the joint financing of enterprises by commercial banks and as a clearing house for foreign exchange. Moreover, no planning can be effectuated without the cooperation of the Ministry of Finance, with its control over expenditures, appropriations and the budget. The Ministry of International Trade and Industry is entrusted with the execution of policies pertaining to industry, as well as domestic and foreign trade. Both the ministries of Agriculture and Forestry and Transportation assume important roles in planning. To the Ministry of Labor goes planning on wages. One final example is the Hokkaido Development agency, also located in the office of the prime minister. The huge northern island of Hokkaido, traditionally an area of concern on the part of the national government, is the object of a ten-year plan which began in 1952.

Naturally, no long-range plan can shortcut the critical process of successive, year-by-year budget making. For example, the budget for fiscal year 1960 has already been discussed (see Chap. 6). It was supposed to strengthen economic foundations, support small and depressed industries and contribute to the plan to double national income. Public criticism of the process for implementing fiscal policy, however, seemed to identify major weaknesses. A basic issue, familiar in many advanced countries, centered in treasury-central bank relationships. Reports tended to be critical of the Bank of Japan and its lack of independence

[8] A complete roster, with committee assignments, is contained in the EPA, *Long-Range Plan, op. cit.,* pp. 176–194.

[9] This policy-making committee was established in June, 1949, to formulate plans for the Bank of Japan.

and neutrality in the conduct of monetary policy. Another problem was identification of the powers which should be left to the
Finance Ministry. Indeed, others pointed to the plethora of
plans without coordinated control and planning.[10]

Government and Business

The first thing to say about the relations between government and business is that Japan, like many another modern, administrative state, is itself a major manager-operator of key industries.

Part of the program of modernization in the late nineteenth
century, in fact, included nationalization of wide sectors of
Japanese business: the postal service, telephone and telegraph
communications and railways. In addition, tobacco, salt and camphor have traditionally been government monopolies.

Since World War II, these activities have been organized
into public corporations. These are still monopolies, but their
boards do not have the power of final definition of the public interest. This function is placed ultimately in the hands of the
Diet. The three major corporations are the Japan National Railways, the Japan Telegraph & Telephone Corporation, and the
Japan Monopolies Corporation. Finally, there are the Japan
Development Bank, which provides funds for economic development; the Japan Export-Import Bank, the Middle and Small
Scale Enterprises fund, the Agriculture-Forestries-Fisheries fund,
the Home Loan fund, and the National Loan fund.

A simple catalogue of the areas in which the government
actually manages business does not, of course, complete the picture. Mention has already been made (see above, Chap. 3) of
certain unique social characteristics of Japanese industry and
business. These are in turn tied in with management thinking:
Japanese entrepreneurs tend to think in broad national and economic terms and are quite conscious of the interaction between
business policy and national welfare. One reason is the degree to
which both business and the nation are dependent on import-
export exchange for sheer survival. Another is the identical
method of recruitment into government and business, more

---

[10] See the results of nearly two years' intensive research and deliberation
by subcommittees of the Financial Policy Deliberation committee, summarized
in *The Japan Times,* April 16, 1959; also *Asahi Journal,* August 2, 1959.

closely related to education than to any other consideration.[11]

The result is that private economic organizations enter directly and vigorously into national economic planning. The most powerful organization of business and industry is *Keidanren* (abbrevation of *Keizai Dantai Rengo,* the Federation of Economic Organizations). It is also the oldest, having been founded as the Japan Economic Federation in 1922. All nationwide economic organizations were dealt severe blows under the Occupation purges but, as a result of reorganization, this federation of five major industrial and financial groups emerged. So important was its status that its subsidiary, the Japan-United States Cooperation council, provided liaison with SCAP and authorities charged with mutual security in the early 1950s. Membership in the federation is institutional and its work is carried out through nineteen standing committees. The body is interested in the development of the national economy as a whole. The president of *Keidanren* is often referred to as the prime minister of the economic world and the managing director of the financial world. Unwritten law seems to dictate that he come from the industrial sector. In 1960 President Ishizaka Taizo was interviewed on his possible retirement. He stated that his successor should be an outstanding businessman who, equipped with a good grasp of international affairs, could represent Japan in world industrial circles.[12]

In a slightly different category, the Japan Federation of Employers Association (*Nikkeiren*) is an organization complementary to *Keidanren;* it is concerned almost exclusively with labor relations. Whereas *Keidanren* has been more sympathetic with labor and agrarian interests, *Nikkeiren* is far more conservative and resistant to labor's demands.

First established in 1928, the Japan Chamber of Commerce and Industry (*Nisho*) remains a federation of local chambers of commerce. The newcomer in the field is the Management Association of Japan (*Keizai Doyu Kai*). First launched in 1946, it is made up of 700 individual members, organized into four regional units. It is by far the most liberal of the national economic organizations: at its eighth national convention in 1955, for example, it argued that a business enterprise is a public trust. In the autumn of 1959, led by *Keizai Doyu Kai,* all four organizations

[11] James C. Abegglen, *The Japanese Factory; Aspects of its Social Organization* (Glencoe, Ill.: Free Press, 1958), pp. 15–29.

[12] Speculation over the choice of a new president appeared in the *Tokyo Shimbun,* March 15, 1960; see also *Sankei,* March 24, 1960.

planned the establishment of an organ for overall economic surveys to cope with the problems inherent in the program to liberalize Japanese trade.

Now with regard to government control of business, mention has been made of the attempt by the Occupation authorities to democratize the economy by deconcentration of economic power. Holding companies were liquidated, while antitrust and antimonopoly decrees were used to try to break up the huge *zaibatsu*. Despite widespread planning and the use of complex administrative supervision, the program instituted in 1945 was never given an opportunity to become firmly established. In the first place, a basic contradiction in the American New Deal was echoed in Japan. Trust-busting and business fragmentation ran counter to the need for extensive planning in order to achieve rehabilitation of the economy. Second, reform soon gave way to reconstruction in the chill blasts of the cold war. As a result the Japanese Fair Trade commission, established in 1947, has never played the role that its counterpart, the Federal Trade commission, does in the United States. In Japan, the commission of three members nominally has as its tasks the promotion and protection of free competition and the furtherance of the interests of the small and medium business and of the consumer. Although it is the watchdog of the anti-monopoly laws on the books, the commission itself has been a vigorous advocate of relaxation of the legislation.

The Japanese Fair Trade commission is assisted by the Ministry of International Trade and Industry and the Medium and Small Enterprises board. With a counterpart fund, the latter works to utilize effectively the some 2,000,000 workers employed in small-scale industries and to improve the nation's standard of living. Regulation of foreign exchange, currency, and credit lies in the hands of the Ministry of Finance, the Bank of Japan, and the Securities & Exchange commission. Regulation of supply, demand, and prices is shared by the Ministry of International Trade and Industry and the Ministry of Agriculture and Forestry.

As has been indicated, there has long been a tradition in Japan for the government's promotion of business interests by means of special financial privileges, subsidies and loans at low interest rates. Today the Japan Development Bank (established in April, 1951, formerly the Reconstruction Finance Bank), provides long-term credit for reconstruction and development. Through the Export-Import Bank (established in December,

1950), long-term operating funds are supplied for import and export activities.[13] Finally, the government at all levels—national and local—renders technical assistance to the several industries through all sorts of agencies.

Government and Labor

Professor Nakayama Ichiro, Chairman of Japan's Central Labor Relations commission, has said that there are in the world four categories of relationships among governments, management and labor. In the first, the employer—actually, the government—flatly sets down working conditions (this is the situation in the Soviet Union). In the second, management exercises a kind of parental authority (for example, in West Germany). In the third, both government and management are considered enemies of laborers, in persistent class struggle (for example, in Italy and in France). In the fourth, labor and management are on equal footing with the government acting as umpire (for example, in the United States and in Great Britain). Japan offers a conglomeration of the last three categories. This is because, Professor Nakayama concluded, labor organization in Japan has sprung from a social milieu dominated by the myth of the extended family. Labor unions have been organized almost entirely on the basis of individual trades. And finally, in the government-management-labor field there has been only a brief and contrasting experience with legal and administrative machinery for settlement of labor disputes.[14]

The Japanese penchant for informal modes of settlement of disputes and, particularly, for conciliation, is reflected in labor-management relations. On numerous occasions we have noted that social custom seeks to avoid direct confrontation and conflict; this characteristic is especially significant for employer-employee relations. The use of intermediaries has been a time-honored device. Flexibility to suit individual cases and avoidance of adjudication have led to the use of conciliation in labor disputes, a mode highly amenable to traditional indirection in

[13] A useful reference is *Outline of the Financial System in Japan* (Tokyo: Bank of Japan, December, 1953), kindly supplied to the author by Mr. Akashi Kageaki of the Bank of Japan.

[14] Nakayama Ichiro, "Japan's Unique Labor Relations," *The Japan Times,* October 27, 1958; see also *Rodo Sogi Chosa Kai, hen* (Institute for Labor Dispute Study, ed.), *Ro-shi kankei ni okeru kihon mondai* (Basic problems in labor-management relations) (Tokyo: Chuo Koron Sha, 1959), 3 vols., especially Vol. 2.

social relations. Professor Solomon Levine, the outstanding American authority on Japanese industrial relations, has concluded:

It seems reasonable to conclude that the factors which lend emphasis to the heavy reliance upon conciliation in Japanese industrial relations also account for the sparse use of unfair labor practice procedures and the slow development of administrative law in this area.[15]

One of the chief objectives of the Occupation was to reduce, if not entirely to eliminate government supervision of Japanese daily life. Thus an American philosophy of pluralism, which centered on democratically run private institutions, fused with the missionary belief that regimentation of labor had been one of the features of so-called totalitarian government in wartime Japan. With reform in view, labor organization and collective bargaining at first received direct help and were subject to few limitations.

For example, the Occupation-inspired new constitution guaranteed the right of assembly and association (Art. 21), minimum standards of living (Art. 25), the right to work with standards of wages and working conditions to be fixed by law (Art. 27), and the rights to organize, act collectively and bargain (Art. 28). In 1947 these rights were further spelled out in the original Trade Union Law and complementary Labor Relations Adjustment Law, which placed few restrictions on strikes and, indeed, encouraged organization and collective bargaining.

The result, in the first two years of the Occupation, was an amazing growth of labor organization. Growth has continued slowly since, although the percentage of industrial workers who are organized began to decline. This trend is illustrated in Table 10. Furthermore, despite the early mushroom growth, certain unique characteristics left an indelible stamp on postwar labor relations. About half of all unions are independent and unaffiliated with any national federation. The overwhelming majority were small (about half with less than 50 members). Over 90 per cent (with 84 per cent of total union membership) were organized on the basis of an enterprise, rather than on the basis of a trade or industry. Almost two-thirds of all unions included manual and white-collar workers (despite Art. 2 of the Trade Union Law, which made representatives of management ineligi-

[15] Solomon B. Levine, *Industrial Relations in Postwar Japan* (Urbana: University of Illinois, 1958), especially Chap. 6, "Government Regulation of Industrial Relations"; the quotation is from p. 155.

TABLE 10   *Growth and rate of organization in the Japanese labor movement, 1950–1954*

Year	No. unions	No. members	Per cent of industrial workers organized
1950	29,144	5,773,908	46.2
1951	27,644	5,686,774	42.6
1952	27,851	5,719,560	40.3
1953	30,129	5,842,678	40.9
1954	31,456	5,986,168	39.6

SOURCE: *Rodo hakusho* (Labor white paper), 1955, Ministry of Labor, Division of Labor Statistics and Research, p. 248, cited in Okichi, *op. cit.*, Supplement, p. 88.

ble for union membership). In fact, until revision of the laws in 1949, many union officials received their salaries from employers, who also provided the unions with offices! As Professor Okichi Kazuo said, "It cannot be assumed that our postwar labor unions are strong, free, or independent." [16]

Nevertheless, the early postwar Occupation period was marked by the principle of voluntarism whereby government regulation of labor, if any, was conducted by labor relations commissions at both national and local levels, with equal representation of labor, management, and the public. Labor relations adjustment legislation stressed conciliatory methods.[17]

Since those honeymoon days, there has been a steady retreat from voluntary principles, as government intervention in labor affairs has grown in two directions: more and more regulation of the form of collective bargaining, and wider definition of conditions and terms of employment. One result has been a greater emphasis on political aspects of Japanese industrial relations.

The first break-throughs came on the government employment front, where some 2,000,000 public servants had been organized. The gap between public and private workers' pay led to intense political activity on the part of public service unions, increasing embarrassment of the Japanese government and, in turn,

[16] See *Review of Labor Conditions in Japan* (Tokyo: Ministry of Foreign Affairs, 1952).

[17] *Roi junen no nyumi wo kataru* (Looking back on ten years' steps of Labor Relations Commissions) (Tokyo: Chuo Rodo Iinkai [Central Labor Relations Commission], June, 1956), especially Chap. 1, recollections on how the Trade Union Law came into effect; March 1, 1946, establishment of the labor relations commissions; and Chap. 3, local labor relations commissions in the cradle.

outright danger to the functioning of the Occupation itself. Faced with powerful threats by joint struggle committees of government workers, General MacArthur moved swiftly and decisively, on January 31, 1947, to forbid a general strike. Limitations on public employees' rights to organize were the indirect result, in July, 1948. Civil servants then went under a new National Public Service law, administered by the National Personnel authority (see above, Chap. 7). Workers in public corporations were dealt with under what is now known as the Public Corporation and National Enterprise Labor Relations Law. Both classes of workers had their right to organize and act collectively restricted; both were denied the right to strike; and the public corporation law provided compulsory arbitration, in event conciliation or mediation failed to secure agreement. The final effect was to remove one in four unions (and about one in three of all members) from the coverage of the less restrictive Trade Union Law.[18]

Again, in 1949, the Diet began to tighten provisions of labor legislation affecting private employment. To some degree, the purpose—as was the case in the Wagner and Taft-Hartley acts in America—was to make union organization more democratic, but the by-product was increased governmental intervention. As the cold war turned warm, and the Occupation authorities found themselves faced with problems of both the security of Japan and of the Korean conflict, the Japanese government was prodded to reaching into union organization itself, in the famous "Red Purge" of 1950.[19] Meanwhile, amendments to the Labor Relations Adjustment Law increased the power of the government over work stoppages. There was increased emphasis on adjustment, cooling-off periods, and the public interest. The honeymoon was over.

Labor-management relations in Japan have felt the press of governmental intervention ever since. Turning to government-sponsored machinery, of course mention should first be made of the Ministry of Labor, which had been established on September 1, 1947. Strictly speaking, the government still provides only a stage for negotiations between labor and management. Of considerably less significance has been the use of legalistic arrangements, such as adjudication of unfair labor practices. Where me-

[18] *Ibid.*, Chap. 2, formation of joint struggle committees of government workers; January 31, 1947 order by General MacArthur to call off general strike; Chap. 5, July 22, 1948, letter from SCAP to Prime Minister Ashida, urging revision of Public Service Personnel Law.

[19] *Ibid.*, Chap. 7, January-November, 1950, the "Red Purge."

diation procedures have been available, adjustment of disputes has tended to follow the least formal pathways. By far the bulk of the activities of the Central Labor Relations commission has been in the realm of conciliation (of over 10,000 cases handled between 1946 and 1956, almost 80 per cent used conciliation).[20] Similarly, because of the stress on informal approaches to settlement, Japan's labor commissions have not rigorously pursued their quasi-judicial powers.[21]

Paradoxically, as Professor Levine has pointed out, in free nations like Japan where living standards are low and inter-relationships among economic sectors precarious, the growth of the welfare state has led to the reduction of private collective bargaining. Thus, although on the one hand even the Occupation once stood for minimum government regulation, on the other it came to insist upon the government's responsibility for working conditions.

One of the chief debates, ever since, has revolved around the task of bringing Japanese standards into line with those set out in International Labor Office conventions.[22]

Direct governmental measures for labor standards all date from 1947 and Occupation-sponsored labor legislation: the Labor Standards Law, Workmen's Accident Compensation Insurance Law, Employment Security Law, and Unemployment Insurance Law. With all this legislation, the greatest limitation is the fact that two-thirds of all enterprises and one-third the labor force, in small family establishments, continue to remain outside the regulations. Implementation of legislation lies in the hands of the Labor Standards bureau of the Labor Ministry. There is no national minimum wage, as exists on the American labor scene. On the other hand, standards on the books for sanitation and safety are among the most advanced in the world. Enforcement is, of course, another matter.[23]

[20] Levine, *op. cit.*, p. 151.

[21] Institute for Labor Dispute Study (with the Asia Foundation), *Sengo rodo sogi chosei shiroku* (Chronicle of postwar labor dispute adjustment) (Tokyo, August 10-September 20, 1957).

[22] As late as 1960, for example, debate continued to swirl fiercely around the ratification of ILO Convention No. 87. The issue involved the necessity for revision of domestic laws to fit the convention, and particularly the Public Corporation Labor Relations Law (*Koro Ho*) and the Local Public Corporation Labor Relations Law (*Chi Koro Ho*). See *Nihon keizai*, March 16, 1960.

[23] Levine, *op. cit.*, pp. 157–163; see also Nakayama Ichiro, *Japan's Labor Problems* (Tokyo: Ministry of Foreign Affairs, 1956).

Government and Agriculture

An owner-farmer establishment law of 1946, part of the Occupation-sponsored land reform, laid the basic foundation for government policies toward agriculture in post-treaty Japan. Surplus cultivated lands owned by absentee or even resident owners in excess of 2.5 acres (10 acres in Hokkaido) were purchased by the government and then sold to small landholders and tenant farmers. Planning for the purchase and sale was the responsibility of agricultural commissions, organized by the Japanese themselves, down to and including the village level. The commissions, reorganized as permanent agencies in 1951, remained responsible for supervision of land sales and tenancy practices, to insure against reconcentration.[24]

One of the basic problems in Japanese agriculture is suggested by this experience with land reform, that is, the desperate shortage of arable land to begin with. Projects for reclamation and improvement have been carried out continuously by the government since 1899. Nevertheless, year after year acres are lost on the outskirts of cities to encroaching houses and factories; and, since World War II, almost 400,000 acres have been lost as a result of natural disasters. Against these losses, the government has opened up 988,000 acres of reclaimed land.

As a matter of fact, the amount expended by the government on reclamation has been relatively small as compared with total amounts spent on improving yields from existent land. Up to 1957, the government spent 32,500 million yen (about $90,000,-000) on land development projects and, within these reclaimed lands, 2,200 million yen ($6,000,000) on soil improvement.[25] Soon thereafter it began to grant bigger subsidies for land development, with priority given to dairy and mixed farming. Furthermore, the Ministry of Agriculture and Forestry has begun reappraisal of land development (the so-called pioneer farm) projects with an eye on integrated construction within social and economic as well as natural surroundings. In 1956 pilot mechanized farm projects were opened in Kamikita, Aomori Prefecture (14,820 acres), in Nemuro and Kushiro (Hokkaido) with the aid of loans from the International Bank for Reconstruction and Development. These projects revolve around the Farmland Development Machine Corporation (*Nochi Kaihatsu Kikai Kodan*), which was established in October, 1955.[26]

[24] Japan FAO Association, *Agriculture in Japan* (Tokyo, 1958), pp. 54–58.
[25] *The Japan Times*, February 23, 1959.
[26] *Ibid.*; also Japan FAO, *op. cit.*, p. 59.

A second problem in which the government is intensely interested is the use of food produced from scarce land with maximum efficiency. Control is actually effected under a 1942 Food Management Law, passed during wartime to maintain stability through rationing, price control, and the prevention of inflation. Fortunately, the law was continued after the war and helped to alleviate desperate shortages. After rehabilitation of the economy, controls on food products—with the exception of rice—were abolished and shifted to indirect management.

Today all rice produced domestically or imported is purchased by the government and rationed. In 1954, compulsory delivery under quota was shifted to the advance sale contract system. Before harvest, farmers voluntarily declare the amount of rice they will produce and obtain an advance of about 20 per cent of the total price through a cooperative. Producers' price is fixed at parity, calculated from an index of prices paid by farmers for agricultural requirements and household living expenses, with the few preceding years as base. In 1952, wheat was shifted to indirect and voluntary control but most farmers prefer to declare their crop (in 1956, however, 70 per cent of the wheat used in Japan was imported).

Certainly a major factor in the steady advance of agricultural production has thus been the rice and wheat delivery system, a sort of price support plan, once denounced by leftists as an exploitation of farmers. In any case, extreme shortages no longer plague the Japanese economy. On August 15, 1958, the Ministry of Agriculture and Forestry estimated the 1959 rice crop at 12,369,000 tons (the record was 1955, estimated at 12,385,000 tons). The influential *Nihon Keizai* put its estimate at 12,482,000 tons and commented on the fact that so-called bumper years had become normal, with increased productivity attributable to the advancement of agricultural techniques and the use of fertilizers and insecticides.[27]

The age-old technique of intensive rice farming, the persistent social norms of agrarian Japan and, moreover, the most up-to-date schemes for the support of agriculture all dictate the use of the cooperative system at the village level. Indeed, the agricultural cooperative continues to be the pervasive mode of informal-formal government in agrarian Japan. Farm cooperatives as legal units emerged about 1900; by 1920 there were 13,442 coops or at least one in every village. Of course, during

[27] Kuroda Kazuo, "Prosperity on Farms," *The Japan Times,* October 4, 1958.

World War II, they were used as instruments of regimentation of farmers.

Agricultural cooperatives were given a new lease on life in postwar Japan under the Agricultural Cooperative Association Law of 1947, which provided for voluntary membership, one man-one vote, non-profit operations, and dividends in kind. As of March, 1957, there were 32,985, of which 12,839 were general purpose and the rest were specialized cooperatives. The general purpose cooperative markets crops, purchases supplies and household goods for members, processes products, and also receives deposits and makes loans. Specialized coops confine their activities to specific products (reclamation cooperatives are also specialized).[28]

The bulk of agricultural credit in Japan is also handled through the hierarchy of cooperatives. Loans are made by the Central Cooperative Bank to cooperative federations and thence to local coops. In 1957, there were over 12,000 general purpose cooperatives, which were members of 47 prefectural credit federations and which served as banking and credit institutions. In addition, in 1948 an agricultural bill system was established to provide short-term credit for the purchase of fertilizers, insecticides, implements, and seeds. Under this system the farmer signs a promissory note, which is accepted by the local cooperative, which in turn obtains a loan from the prefectural federation. The federation discounts the note with the Central Cooperative Bank. Finally, the Bank of Japan can accept the note as collateral against a loan, if the Central Cooperative Bank requires it.[29]

Over on the mainland, across from Japan, the People's Republic of China is in the throes of a gigantic social revolution, which entails the disruption of traditional life of 500,000,000 peasants and their regimentation in the communes. This is the self-styled "great agrarian leap forward." In quiet contrast, Japan's continued effort toward agrarian reform involves voluntary and persuasive methods of the familiar Extension Service. This new service, modeled after the American system, rests upon the Agricultural Improvement and Promotion Law of 1948 and its object is to teach 25,000,000 farmers to produce more and to work more efficiently. Extension Service is a function of the Agricultural Development bureau, established in 1950. It works directly with agricultural improvement bureaus in each of the forty-seven prefectural governments. The nation's agricultural

[28] Japan FAO, *op. cit.,* pp. 65–66.
[29] *Ibid.,* pp. 71–72.

area is organized into 1,586 districts of 4–5 villages each (covering about 6,300 acres, 2,820 farm families on the average). Each district has an Extension Service headquarters, with five farm technologists, and one home economist who works with farm wives on the problems of home management. This service does not, unfortunately, have top budget priority (its budget, in 1959, of 2,310 million yen contrasts sharply with the 100,000 million yen spent that year on U.S.-made jet aircraft). The development bureau is also responsible for administration and coordination of agricultural research.[30]

Equally important, the statistical and survey division of the ministry serves as the center for Japanese agricultural data. Significant publications include an agricultural census (every five years); statistics on production (crop reporting); surveys of farm household economics (a sample of 5,500 families monthly); cost of production (10,736 households); and the Agricultural Outlook service.

The Ministry of Agriculture and Forestry is the executive branch principally responsible for these various agricultural programs and, specifically, for the food control program assigned under the Food Management Law.

The national government, meanwhile, all too often continues the old feudal tradition of paying high respect to agriculture and neglecting agriculturalists. In 1958, for example, Prime Minister Kishi stated:

I wish to pay my tribute to the farming population on their labors, and pledge further efforts of the government to contribute to an uninterrupted advance of the productivity of agriculture, forestry and fishing industries, which are major factors in the expansion of national economy.[31]

There can be little doubt that agriculture has always played a major role in Japan's economic development. Despite efforts of the government, described above, and despite the 50 per cent increase in income of the farming population over prewar levels, however, this sector of the economy representing 40 per cent of the labor force still receives only 20 per cent of the national income. Productivity is still low, and Japan's modern economic body still has feet of clay.

According to Fukuda Takeo, former Minister of Agriculture

[30] The Extension Service was the subject of a full-page article in *The Japan Times,* February 23, 1959; see also Japan FAO, *op. cit.,* pp. 77–79.
[31] *The Japan Times,* October 4, 1958.

and Forestry, agriculture and agricultural administration are approaching a critical turning point. Agricultural production is lagging behind the general rate of growth of the national economy. The demand for foodstuffs and farm products has been slackening since 1953. Technical progress on the small farms is slowing down. Increasing demand for manufactures is causing a continued outflow of labor force from farming districts. The Japanese government faces monumental tasks in the readjustment of agricultural industries, namely, to continue to supply products economically and elevate living standards of farmers; to use land, labor and resources effectively and to expand domestic markets; to help save scarce foreign currencies by decreasing imports; and to contribute to the growth of a well-balanced national economy. Minister Fukuda continued:

> I am convinced that the principal objective of agricultural administration is to encourage the constitutional improvement of our backward agriculture by reducing the difference in living standard and income between farmers and workers of other industries.[32]

Government and Social Welfare

In the immediate postwar era, Japan inherited one of the most serious sets of social problems the world has ever seen: an estimated 8,000,000 persons—war victims, repatriates and those with critical needs. An Occupation memorandum of February, 1946, concerning public relief, set down the fundamental rules for subsequent social work administration. For the first time the state was made responsible for protection of the needy. This responsibility was not to be delegated to semi-governmental or private institutions. The needy were to be protected equally, without discrimination, and expenditures for need were not to be limited by law. There soon followed the basic codes for the welfare state: the Daily Life Security Law (October, 1946), legislation covering child welfare, public health, rehabilitation for handicapped persons, disaster relief and other problems.[33]

Even to the present day, lack of popular interest in public social security can be explained in two ways. Until Occupation

[32] "My View of Agricultural Administration," interview with Fukuda Takeo, Minister of Agriculture and Forestry, in *Diamond,* February 27, 1960.

[33] Japanese Joint Organizing Committee, *Social Welfare Services in Japan* (Tokyo: Kenkyusha, 1958). This, plus many of the other publications listed hereinafter, were issued for the Ninth International Conference of Social Work, which met in Tokyo in 1958. See pp. 39–40.

reforms, security was provided traditionally within the extended, largely rural family. Naturally, this family was rapidly being disrupted under the blows of mobilization, war, and defeat. The second reason for continued apathy is that public responsibility for social security was first thrust upon the nation by the Occupation, that is, without vigorous effort on the part of the Japanese themselves.[34]

In fact, it was the Occupation which, in November, 1948, also suggested the so-called Six Principles of Social Work, a code for administration used to the present time: (1) a system of welfare administration districts; (2) reorganization of welfare administration in city governments; (3) advice and practical supervision by the Ministry of Health and Welfare; (4) clarification of responsibilities undertaken by public and private agencies; (5) establishment of social welfare councils; and (6) in-service training of professional staff. In 1951, the Social Welfare Service Law carried these six points into effect; from that time there has been strict supervision of private agencies established under law.[35]

The immediate post-surrender crisis has, of course, long since disappeared. Social problems have not, however, but have merely taken different shape. Almost all are tied to Japan's population and its qualitative shift—the familiar aging population of Western countries—the nature of the economy, and the so-called crisis of 1965, already amply described. In this last category, the most critical problem is the provision of sufficient social security to exclude the post-59-year-old group from the labor force. Statistics show that in Japan, over half those over sixty-five are still working (in the United States, in 1954, 41 per cent). Such data highlights the inadequacy of the present pension system in Japan.[36]

Social welfare white papers continually refer to the dual economy of Japan, with great, modernized industries at the top and older, small enterprises and small family farms at the bottom. The direct result is the related low wage structure. Then there is the ever-widening gap between standards of living of the rich and the poor. The Welfare Ministry itself has warned that welfare policy must be treated as an essential part of economic planning. Japan's present program has been unfavorably

[34] Kuroda Kazuo, "Blueprint for the Future; Social Welfare," *loc. cit.*

[35] Japanese Joint Committee, *Social Welfare Services, op. cit.*, p. 41.

[36] Payment of dues for forty years' (between age twenty and fifty-nine) results, after reaching age sixty-five, in payment of only 3,500 yen (less than $10) per month; without payment of dues, 1,000 yen a month, after age seventy (and yet life expectancy for the male is sixty-five and sixty-nine for the female). Kuroda, "Blueprint," *loc. cit.*

compared with the 1954 Vanomi plan, in Italy, which set about reducing unemployment and correcting the imbalance in Italian economic life.[37]

The Welfare Ministry's white paper on national welfare, issued at the end of the fiscal year 1958, revealed similar gains and losses. For example, health insurance then covered some 80 per cent of Japan's total population. The death rate was at a record low of 7.4 per 1,000; the average life span for males was 64.9 and for females 69.6 years. On the other hand, the average Japanese had to spend 5 per cent more for livelihood in 1958, as against 1957. The national diet was steadily improving, but almost three-fourths of total calories consumed were still supplied by grain (chiefly rice). Despite general economic advances, 580,000 households had come under the Daily Life Security Law; a wide gap continued to grow between workers in big industries and those in small enterprises and on farms. Japan had the highest rate of suicide in the world for youths between the ages of 15 and 24.[38]

Public social welfare service, designed to tackle these problems, is administered by the Ministry of Welfare.

Special mention of one or two of the welfare bureaus and their work will illustrate operations of the ministry. The Social Affairs bureau handles all research in social services, public assistance, in-service training of specialized personnel, disaster relief, and rehabilitation services. Also very important is the Children's bureau, which is responsible for administration of the Child Welfare Law.[39] This statute places under the jurisdiction of the state all children with special needs, fatherless families, expectant and nursing mothers and juvenile delinquents (in co-operation with the courts). The bureau also supervises child welfare centers and other welfare agencies at the local level.

Among programs closely related to the operations of the Welfare Ministry, perhaps those of the National Health administration are most important. Administration centers in the Public

[37] *Kosei sho, Daijin kambo, kikaku shitsu hen* (Welfare Ministry, Minister's secretariat, planning room, ed.), *Kosei hakusho* (Social welfare white paper, 1958 edition, issued in commemoration of the 20th anniversary of the establishment of the Welfare Ministry) (Tokyo: Finance Ministry, 1958).

[38] See the summary in *The Japan Times*, December 11, 1959.

[39] Ministry of Welfare, Children's Bureau, *Child Welfare Laws of Japan* (Tokyo, 1958). See especially "The Children's Charter," proclaimed on May 5, 1951 (Children's Day) which codifies the following general principles: the child shall be respected as a human being; the child shall be given due regard as a member of society; the child should be brought up in a good environment; p. 2.

Sanitation bureau, Medical Affairs bureau, and Children's bureau. With the statistical services provided by the ministry, these bureaus direct the health programs of forty-six local prefectural governments.[40]

Although public social services occupy an increasing part of total social welfare activities in Japan, the heaviest burden is still shouldered by voluntary agencies. Councils for social welfare coordinate the public and private activities carried on by such organizations as the local community chest ("Red Feather") campaigns, the Japanese Red Cross Volunteer service, and others. Nevertheless, the total expended on social welfare services in Japan remains small: the proportion of the appropriations for the welfare budget to the total national budget was, for example, only about 8.2 per cent in 1958.

One of the acid tests of the success of newfound welfare activities in post-treaty Japan, as well as of protection of civil liberties and rights, is to be found in the legal and, more importantly, social status of women. The patriarchal system of family life, so often regarded as unique to Japan, has actually existed in the history of most nations. Nevertheless, the system has lived on longer in Japan (legally, to 1947 and the new constitution) and particularly in the ideological concept of the household, or *ie,* in rural Japanese villages. To this concept are linked primogenitive attitudes.

Japanese women traditionally and literally have become *yome-iri* (joining of the daughter-in-law by marriage to the husband's household). Not until 1873 was divorce from the wife's initiative even countenanced legally, and it is still rare in rural Japan. The new constitution and revision of the civil code, in 1947, formally eliminated such concepts. Those over forty years of age still find it difficult, however, to adjust to the new freedoms.[41]

Civil Liberties and Rights

Indeed, much of postwar Japanese democracy revolves around constitutional rights, legally granted, and their effectua-

[40] Ministry of Welfare, minister's secretariat, *A Brief Report on Health Administration in Japan* (Tokyo, September 1, 1958).

[41] *The Status of Women in Postwar Japan* (Tokyo: Ministry of Labor, Women's & Minors' bureau, 1956). One of the serious problems mentioned is the great disproportion of men to women in the 30–34 age group, with 80.8 men to 100 women, leaving a large number of women unmarried. See p. 21.

tion in daily, social life. Even a cursory glance at the new constitution reveals that the bill of rights is the crux of the new political system. To such rights are devoted thirty-one of 104 articles
in the organic law. The enumeration is more detailed and
specific than can be found in constitutions of older democracies
like the United States.

Problems have arisen out of the fact that far greater emphasis has been placed on rights than on duties of citizenship, in
a society famed for its discipline and order. Nevertheless, as a
legacy of a long authoritarian tradition, people still demonstrate
a fear of officialdom. There is still a general reluctance on the
part of individual Japanese to challenge administrative actions,
to question the wisdom of executive judgments and, most important, to participate in shaping administration as a duty of citizenship. According to cases referred to the Civil Liberties bureau of
the Justice Ministry, there have been increases in the abuse of
authority by public servants, in ostracism as a private sanction,
and in cases of physical violence. During Human Rights Week,
December 4–14, 1956, 6,000 cases of infringement of rights were
reported in Tokyo alone; the total rose to 7,000 in 1957; and it
was estimated the total would reach 9,000 in 1958. There was a
wide range of offenses: white slavery, abuse of official power,
violence, rape and slander.[42] These are doubtless, as the older
generation is quick to point out, symptoms of a society in political and economic revolution.

As against individual rights, there has been a constant fear
on the part of the government that it will soon be unable to
cope with subversive activities. The Subversive Activities Prevention Law, passed in 1952, was one of the most controversial pieces
of legislation to be enacted in postwar Japan. The potential
threat to civil liberties, as it was widely interpreted by leftists,
labor unions, students and liberal groups, was later followed by
the abortive Police Duties Revision Law, which completely tied
up orderly government in 1958. As mutual security, military obligations shared with the United States, and covert rearmament
(discussed below, Chap. 11) take hold in Japan, opposition forces
fear further rapid steps in what they regard as a reverse course.
In 1960, for example, the director-general of the Defense agency
stated that a new law protecting military secrets might become
necessary about 1965. Thus coincidentally, in the minds of many
Japanese, basic problems of social welfare, civil liberties, and the

[42] *The Japan Times,* December 18, 1958.

specter of rearmament may reach a climax in that particular
year.[43] The crisis of 1965 may prove fateful for the entire future
of Japanese democracy.

10 - Local Government in Japan

Far north on the western coast, facing the Japan Sea, Korea
and Siberia, a liaison officer from the Welfare Ministry in Tokyo
has just arrived in the port of Niigata to consult with prefectural
officials concerning the ticklish problem involved in the repatria-
tion of Korean residents to the jurisdiction of North Korea. To
the east in Yamagata, capital of a basin prefecture tucked in
among mountain ranges, a local welfare officer has just completed
an inspection tour of dormitories housing Japanese recently repa-
triated from mainland China. Farther south, in the great, sprawl-
ing, noisy city of Tokyo, between 7 a.m. and 7 p.m. of a given
day, close to 100,000 vehicles have passed through Imperial
Plaza; nearly 90,000 cars, trucks, and buses have made the tortuous turn around Shimbashi Station. (Metropolitan police have
estimated that, for maximum efficiency and safety, no more than
30,000 vehicles should pass a point on a four-lane highway in a
12-hour period.) Also in Tokyo, at Hirakawa-*cho*, Chiyoda-*ku*,
Prince Takamatsu, Director-General of the Autonomy agency
(now a ministry), the governor of Tokyo, and representatives of
some 550 municipalities throughout Japan have just completed
a ceremony dedicating the $2,000,000 ultra-modern six-storied
ferro-concrete municipal center, the handsome headquarters for
the National Mayors Society.

Six hours by limited express farther south in the great industrial complex of the Kansai, the mayor of Osaka is preparing
to leave for Tokyo, to negotiate details of grants-in-aid to his
urban prefecture. Even farther south in the rural prefecture of
Okayama, on the storied and beautiful shores of the Inland Sea,
officials have just completed a meeting devoted to the rehabilita-

---

[43] The potential military secrets law was discussed, in the climate of
controversy surrounding revision of the Japanese-American security treaty, in
Sankei, March 5, 1960.

tion of prostitutes and the search for new employment for brothel-keepers, whose ancient vocation has just been outlawed by national decree. A little farther south on the same Inland Sea, the mayor of Kure has just adjourned a labor liaison conference made up of representatives of his city, the local shipbuilding industry and labor unions. Several hours away, by modern rail-ferry across the Inland Sea and by bus into a remote valley, a township clerk in the records office (*yakuba*) is pouring over statistics: within this tax jurisdiction there are 4,215 Japanese grouped in thirty-seven small hamlets (*buraku*), which contain 848 households with, on the average, 1.23 acres cultivated per household.

In the circumstances described above, the locale, the subdivisions of government and the personnel vary, but they share one thing in common: they are all illustrative of the complex and varied functions involved in intergovernmental relations and in the business of Japanese local government.

The Structure of Local Government

Japan emerged as a modern state, as we have seen, after the Meiji Restoration in 1868. The establishment of institutions of local government came along a little later: a system of cities, towns, and villages, in 1888; a system of prefectures and counties, in 1890. At the time there was, it is true, a transfer of power from the higher to the lower ranks of the *samurai*, but this development had long been under way in both domain (*han*) and feudal headquarters (*bakufu*) politics.

The powers of local government were gradually broadened and units came to be rationalized. In 1922, for example, the old counties (*gun*) were abolished.[1] Nevertheless, local administrative organization under the Meiji Constitution was extensively controlled by the central government. Only nominally could the system be described as one characterized by local autonomy. Finally, during World War II local institutions were even more centralized and bureaucratized in the attempt to consolidate Japan's national power.

The general tendency, after the end of the war, toward decentralization and local self-government was firmly buttressed in the new constitution. Chapter 8 provides for local public entities organized and operated in accordance with the principle of

[1] *Gun* boundaries are in use today only to indicate postal zones and to establish the jurisdiction of some local courts.

local autonomy (Art. 92), with chief executive officers and assemblies elected by direct popular vote within the communities (Art. 93). The organization and functions of local government were then voluminously spelled out in the 300-article Local Autonomy Law, enacted in 1947. The major points in this statute may be summarized as follows:

(1) the responsibility for the management of local entities belongs to local residents;

(2) the presidential form is adopted for local bodies (in contrast with the parliamentary-cabinet form at the national level);

(3) direct democracy, including referendum, initiative and recall, is prescribed for local institutions;

(4) a commission system is introduced for the first time in Japan, with executive as well as quasi-judicial and quasi-legislative powers;

(5) a standing committee system is introduced into the large assemblies.[2]

The other major statute which provides a framework for local government is the Local Public Service Law, enacted in the same spirit as was the national law (1947), to secure democratic as well as efficient administration. The following will offer some indication of the scope of local personnel:

TABLE 11 *Local government employees (in thousands)*

Type of personnel	1950	1955	1957*
General	604	572	613
Prefecture (*fu, ken*)	250	232	215
City, town, village			
(*shi, machi, mura*)	354	340	398
Educational†	685	622	662
Police†	105	146	137
Fire†	26	32	31
TOTAL	1,420	1,372	1,443

* Average fixed number, budget year.
† Includes office personnel.
SOURCE: Ministry of Finance statistics, *ibid.*, Table 3, p. 12.

As we shall notice later, the key to the postwar fate of local autonomy has been public finance. The record has both encourag-

[2] The Japan Local Self-Government institute, *Guide to Local Government in Japan* (Tokyo: *Shisei Kaikan*, 1959). pp. 2–3 (the author was privileged to edit the English version of this pamphlet, on the request of Mr. Tanabe Sadayoshi, Director, Tokyo Institute for Municipal Research).

ing and discouraging features. Here it will suffice simply to note the steady growth in level of expenditures on local, as compared with national government operations.

TABLE 12   *National and local finances compared*

	Fiscal total, general accounts			General administration expenses		
Year	*National* (A)	*Local* (B)	% (B/A)	*National* (A)	*Local* (B)	% (B/A)
1945	21,496	5,014	23	17,136	4,463	26
1950	633,295	522,564	83	402,447	511,442	127
1952	873,942	804,180	92	571,826	779,824	136
1954	1,040,761	1,129,002	108	818,654	1,061,804	130
1956	1,069,205	1,248,495	117	885,279	1,131,113	128

Figures in millions of yen. 360 yen = $1.00.
SOURCE: *Chiho Zaisei Tokei Nempo* (Local Finance Statistical Yearbook) (Tokyo: Autonomy agency, 1956), *ibid.*, Table 4, p. 13.

Legally, local public entities in Japan consist of two types. Ordinary public bodies include: one capital prefecture (*to*), Tokyo-*to*; one province (*do*), Hokkaido-*do*; two urban prefectures (*fu*), Kyoto-*fu* and Osaka-*fu*; 43 rural prefectures (*ken*), including Okinawa, still under U.S. occupation; and the municipalities categorized according to population, commercial and industrial activities into cities (*shi*), towns (*machi*) and villages (*mura*), all of which have the same structure and legal status. Special local public bodies include: special cities (none established as yet); 23 special wards (*ku*), in the former City of Tokyo, and associations of local public bodies. Structurally, Japan has two tiers below the central government, consisting of the prefectures and the municipalities. The total area can thus be illustrated in simple diagram as in Figure 9 on the opposite page.

Under severe pressure in the late stages of the war, Japan proper was briefly subdivided into nine administrative regions. After surrender, these were disbanded but, paradoxically, the Occupation also found it convenient to think of the nation in terms of regional headquarters for military government. Today one of the most often heard proposals is to enlarge the major administrative areas, the prefectures which descend from the semi-self-sufficient feudal domains. Mayor Nakai Mitsuji of Osaka summed up the criticism in this fashion: "The present 46 prefectures are glaringly unbalanced in their social, economic and cul-

FIGURE 9   *Local government structure*

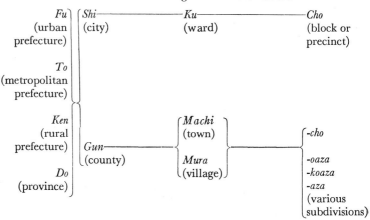

tural progress to be a suitable geographical division for modern local self-government." [3]

TOKYO-TO. The great metropolis of Tokyo is something like the elephant whose various parts could feel so different to the blind men. It is inconceivable that such an animal exists!

On October 1, 1957, Tokyo had a population estimated at 8,534,993—the largest city in the world—distributed among twenty-three wards, ten cities, twenty-three towns, ten villages, and a number of offshore islands. Its total area was 789.2 square miles. Tokyo's growth rate, like Japan's birth rate, is leveling off at about 250,000 persons per year, most of them migrants from the provinces. Within the city, the center of population has shifted steadily westward out of the central, downtown wards. In population structure, it is a city of the young: its fir-tree population graph flares out in the twenty-year-old age group. This bulge is more pronounced on the male side of the graph: at ages 22–24, there are close to 150 men for every 100 women. (Welfare officials explain this is why the problem of prostitution is worse in Tokyo than anywhere else.)

With only one-tenth of the total Japanese population (1957), Tokyo nevertheless has 17 per cent of all Japanese automobiles, 15 per cent of the crimes, 15 per cent of all traffic accidents in Japan, 15 per cent of the income, and 60 per cent of all firms capitalized at 1000 million yen or over. Tokyo has 15,300,000

[3] Nakai Mitsuji, Mayor, Osaka, "Local Autonomy," in the column, "Kansai Speaks," *The Japan Times,* December 10, 1958.

lights, probably more neon lights than any city in the world, and consumes 5,600,000,000 kilowatt-hours of electricity per year. It has twice as many movie theaters as New York has. One in every six restaurants in all Japan is located in Tokyo. Its residents, hordes of businessmen on expense accounts, and tourists drink 15 per cent of all the *sake* consumed in Japan. Between April, 1952, and September, 1957, the number of vehicles using Tokyo streets nearly quadrupled. Streets in the city occupy only 9.2 per cent of the total (only Nagoya boasts a 22 per cent area; New York has 35 per cent; Washington, 43 per cent). Tokyo has less than one square yard of park per capita (Washington, sixty square yards). In 1955, the housing space per capita had risen to only three-fourths the prewar level. In January, 1956, an estimated average of 107 tons of soot fell on each square kilometer of central Chiyoda Ward.[4]

The metropolitan government of Tokyo is the major unit of local government in the metropolis. The difference between Tokyo-*to* and other urban or rural prefectures lies in the fact that the metropolis combines the powers of the capital, those of a prefecture, and those of a large city. Fig. 10 presents a simplified outline of the metropolitan government offices. The operations of a more typical prefecture will be examined in greater detail, below, but in the case of Tokyo it may be noted that government is centered in three major organs. The chief executive, the governor (*to chiji*), is popularly elected for a four-year term. The deliberative organ is the popularly elected Metropolitan Assembly (*To Gikai*) with its assembly-elected speaker and vice-speaker, all serving four-year terms. Finally, there is a set of commissions which aid the governor and assembly in handling education, elections, public service, police, labor and inspection of local government.

The status of the governor of Tokyo-*to*, like that of the mayor of New York City, is sufficiently important to allow him to rank alongside his neighbors, national government cabinet members. The gubernatorial and assembly elections for Tokyo, in April, 1959, for example, attracted widespread attention and both major parties injected national issues into the race. Through something less than a coincidence, the Liberal-Democrats supported Azuma Ryutaro, a member of the Japanese Olym-

---

[4] These, and many other fascinating statistics and data, are contained in one of the most thorough studies of the city ever undertaken—a best seller in Japan—Shibata Tokue, *Tokyo; sono keizai to shakai* (Tokyo; its economy and society) (Tokyo: Iwanami, 1959), on which Fig. 10 is also based.

FIGURE 10 *Tokyo metropolitan government*

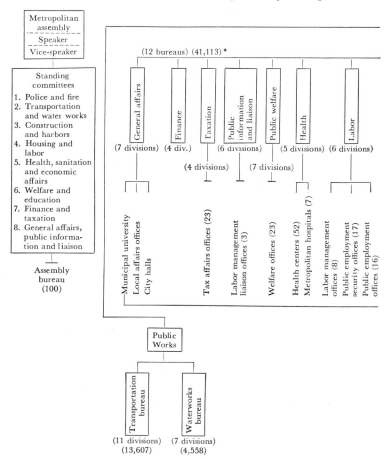

pic Committee (Tokyo hoped for and later, in July, won the honor of being host to the Olympic Games for 1964). Azuma won against the veteran Socialist Arita Hachiro, whose identification with the left wing of his party frightened many of the capital's businessmen.[5]

The Tokyo governor coordinates the work of the various commissions and directs the business of the metropolitan government office (*Tokyo Tocho*). The latter consists of a chief treasur-

[5] Douglas H. Mendel, Jr., "Behind the 1959 Japanese Elections," (in "Notes and Comment") *Pacific Affairs*, XXXII, No. 3 (September, 1959).

(*Tokyo-tocho*) (*1957, revised to Sept. 1, 1959*)

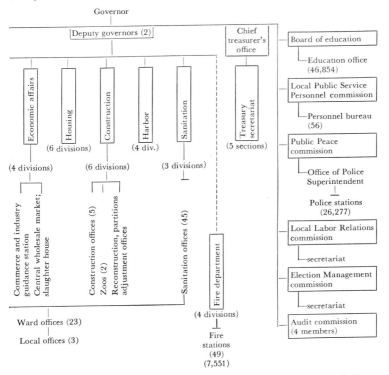

* Numbers in parentheses indicate approximate number of personnel, where available, as of 1957.

sources: Shibata, Tokue, *Tokyo: sono keizai to shakai* (Tokyo; its economy and society) (Tokyo: Iwanami, 1959), chart, pp. 160–61; Revised Japanese & English language listing of *The Government Organization of Japan* (based on publications of the Administrative Management agency, other government agencies), mimeographed (Tokyo: American Embassy, September 1, 1959).

er's office and two deputy governors who, in turn, direct twelve bureaus, sixty-two divisions, a number of branch offices and institutions, twenty-three ward offices and three local offices. The main offices embrace over 40,000 public service personnel; in addition, there are about 25,000 employed in public works—transportation and water—and in the fire department. The general account budget of Tokyo (1952–53) ran to about 69 billion yen ($191,000,000): about 60 per cent of revenue was derived from municipal taxes and about 17 per cent, from national grants-in-aid; 23 per cent of expenditures went to education; 13

per cent, to administration; 13 per cent, to police; and 10 per cent, to public works.[6]

It is not clear, at time of writing, whether the recommendations of the Local Government Research committee of the central government—to reorganize the prefectural areas into 7–9 regions—will soon be adopted. It is safe to say, however, that considerable progress has already been made toward fulfilling the promises of the Greater Tokyo plan. In June, 1956, the National Capital Region Development Law was enacted by the Diet and various construction plans based on the law have since been devised. In essence, plans call for a region centered on Tokyo Central Station and covering a radius of about sixty-five miles. This region is divided into three areas: the inner urban belt, the green belt, and the peripheral area. To implement the plan, the government established as an external organ of the prime minister's office, the National Capital Region Development commission, with a state minister as chairman, two full-time and two part-time members. As an advisory body, a council of forty-three members was also established, with three members each from the House of Representatives and House of Councillors, twelve specialists, nine government officials and eight chairmen of prefectural assemblies. It is of interest to note that Greater Tokyo eventually will cover not only Tokyo but also adjacent Kanagawa, Saitama and Chiba, and even parts of Tochigi, Gumma, Ibaragi, and Yamanashi prefectures. It is estimated that the inner urban belt alone, if left undisturbed, would increase to a population of almost 14,500,000 by 1975. The suitable maximum is estimated at about 11,500,000; the remainder is to be decentralized over the next two decades.[7]

THE PREFECTURES (FU AND KEN). Tokyo-*to* is, of course, neither by name nor by structure typical of local government at the prefectural level in Japan. Also somewhat unusual in size and scope of activities are the two urban prefectures, Osaka-*fu* and Kyoto-*fu*. Legally, however, there is little difference from the rural prefectures (*ken*) or even from the other municipalities. All are ordinary local, public bodies by statute.

The chief executive officer of the prefecture, the governor (*chiji*), is popularly elected for a four-year term. Although directly responsible to the assembly (*gikai,* ranging in size from 40 to 120 members depending on size of population) for the execu-

---

[6] "Better Service for 7 Million Citizens" (extra number), *Tokyo Municipal News* (Tokyo: Metropolitan Government, August, 1953).

[7] *Japan Report,* V, No. 4 (February 15, 1959).

tion of legislation, the governor is, in addition, closely supervised by the national Autonomy Ministry, in carrying out duties delegated to him by the central government. He works closely with the Prefectural Assembly which, with its standing committees and secretariat, is the legislative organ of the prefecture. Between the executive and legislature stand many commissions. Members of the Board of Education, Public Peace commission, Audit commission and most of the others are—together with the vice-governor and chief treasurer—appointed by the governor with the consent of the assembly for four-year terms. The third branch of government, in this essentially presidential form, consists of the local courts. A simplified chart of all these branches is presented in Fig. 11, which uses Okayama-*ken* as an illustration.

The work of some of the commissions will be described in more detail, under powers and functions, below. Here we might take note of the Election Management commission which, unlike the others, is elected for a term of three years. There are four members, with an equal number of alternates; no more than two active members may be affiliated with the same political party or organization. None is permitted to engage in current election campaigns. Prefectural commissions take charge of elections of members of the House of Councillors (local constituencies), of the House of Representatives, as well as governors and assemblymen. The Autonomy Ministry supervises the commissions on election matters, excluding the election of upper house members (national constituency) and the review of Supreme Court justices. Commissions on the prefectural level supervise commissions on the local level.[8]

The prefecture, like Japan itself and most other modern nation-states of the world, has very definitely entered the era of the administrative state. This means the bulk of day-to-day operations are carried out in the prefectural government office (the *kencho*). In prefecture after prefecture, such functions are today performed in startlingly modern multi-storied steel-concerete-and-glass buildings erected since the war. The reason, in most cases, is simple: the old prefectural offices were often clustered around the castle in the center of the city, usually Point 0 in the devastating fire raids which reduced city after city to ashes during World War II. Although generalization from the specific case may prove dangerous, it will perhaps be useful to describe the structure and, later, the operations of one *kencho,* that of

[8] For the central election management commission, see Chap. 4, above. *Ibid.*, V, No. 8 (April 20, 1959).

FIGURE 11 *Okayama prefectural government (December, 1958, revised to June, 1959)*

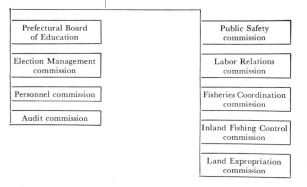

Okayama prefecture, with which the author is thoroughly familiar.

The chief administrator of the Okayama *kencho* was (1961) governor Miki Yukiharu, representative of many of the new, younger faces which made their appearance at the local level in the postwar era. Originally elected in 1951 as an independent, Governor Miki was reelected for a third term in the prefectural poll of 1959. He brought to his task considerable administrative experience gained in the central government, particularly in social welfare matters. He has since added political acumen and a talent for inspiring sweeping plans for the large-scale development of his prefecture. He has traveled widely, both throughout Japan and, in 1958, to North and South America where, in Brazil, he inspected the new communities of immigrants from his own Okayama prefecture. In 1960, he visited Southeast Asia, to promote exports from his prefecture.

In Okayama (1961), there was no vice-governor, the affairs of the prefecture being administered by the governor, the chief treasurer, and a conference of six department chiefs, served by the Planning section of the General Affairs department. This department, with its eight sections and twenty-seven divisions, is the heart of the *kencho*. Its secretariat serves the governor directly and manages problems of publicity and public opinion. The Personnel section handles all matters concerning public service employees, including the training institute and liaison with the Personnel commission; it is also charged with duties connected with court decorations and visits of the imperial family. Liaison with the Prefectural Assembly, as well as with the Tokyo Office of the Prefecture, is the responsibility of the Finance section (because it drafts the prefectural budget). The law drafting office is, however, the Document and Education section. Its Foreign Affairs division supervises alien registration for the central government and makes arrangements for citizens traveling abroad. The Local Affairs section is the liaison agent with the Election Management commission, as well as with cities, towns and villages. The duties of the Taxation and Statistics sections are apparent from their names.

Duties of the Civil and Labor Affairs department can best be understood by a simple listing of section names: social welfare, women and minors, insurance, veterans' affairs, labor policy, employment security and unemployment insurance. Similarly, the Health department and its three sections handle medical affairs, public health, pharmaceuticals and problems of sanitation.

Okayama, bordering on the Inland Sea National Park, is getting an increasing share of the tourist trade in spring and summer. Its northern mountainous regions offer ski slopes and hot springs in close proximity. Tourist affairs and trade promotion are handled by a section of the Commerce and Industry department. The Industry, Mining and Textiles section works closely with laboratories, training institutes, and local industries to improve prefectural products. Two of the prefecture's most famous products have been known since before history was recorded: the *i*-grass mats, which serve as floor covering in traditional Japanese houses; and *Imbe* ware, a famous folk pottery. One of the prefecture's most modern products is uranium. In 1958, reserves estimated at 3,000,000 tons were discovered in the villages of Kamo and Awa.

Next to the General Affairs department, and equal in size, the most important office in the *kencho* is Agriculture and Forestry. Its eight sections supervise agricultural administration, village development and cooperatives; improvement of soils, crops, fertilizers, farm homes; livestock; land engineering and improvement, including the vast Kojima Bay reclamation project, described below; fisheries, both Inland Sea and rivers; and forests. Working closely with the agricultural experts are personnel of the Civil Engineering department. They too are concerned with land surveys, multi-purpose development projects, the construction of roads and the control of rivers and erosion. The department is concerned, in addition, with ports and harbors, city planning and construction.

Alongside the General Affairs department, the other major housekeeping office of the *kencho* is the Treasury secretariat. Its Accounts section handles receipts and disbursements of prefectural and national monies, staff salaries and liaison functions with the Audit commission. The Prefectural Printing office is under the Supplies section. Finally, there are two major external organs: the Land Transportation office and the Electricity bureau. The latter coordinates those hydroelectric stations previously mentioned (in Chap. 3), generator plants located within the prefecture.

The six departments and the Treasury secretariat employ over 1,600 public service personnel, not including the seventy-two in external offices. The Personnel commission holds a qualification examination every year, in February, to recruit applicants for prefectural posts from among graduates of the senior high schools. Recently the competitive rate has been running at about 1:15. Those who qualify are engaged in order of merit as vacancies arise. Occasionally, the Governor requests the Autonomy Ministry in Tokyo to transfer necessary and suitable personnel to the prefectural service.

Prefectural personnel are divided into two classifications: senior employees (*shuji*) and all others. Important positions— department, section and division chiefs—are chosen by the governor. Monthly pay scales range from 6,100 yen ($17) to 57,000 yen ($160), with increases of 1000 yen every year of satisfactory service. The promotion waiting period is longer in proportion to monthly pay, 12, 18, 21 and 24 months. There is, in fact, no age limit for public service, but personnel are expected to retire at about fifty. There is a lump separation allowance, in addition to retirement benefits figured at about one-third pay at retirement (after seventeen years satisfactory service).[9]

MUNICIPALITIES. Elsewhere (Chap. 3) a rather detailed description of the two different ways of life—rural, agrarian Japan and urban, industrial Japan—has been presented and their effects on the economy and political behavior underlined. The steady growth of a complex metropolitan, if not urban, culture is one of the outstanding characteristics of modern Japan. The recent balance in area and population is illustrated in Table 13.

TABLE 13   *Urban and rural area and population*

Area (km²)		*Population (October, 1955)*	
		Total	89,275,529
Total	369,765.89	(Male)	43,855,764
		Urban	50,288,026
Urban	67,722.62	(Male)	24,769,739
		Rural	38,987,503
Rural	300,869.46	(Male)	19,086,025

No. persons per sq. km.: 241.4

SOURCE: *Japan Statistical Yearbook 1957* and other data presented by Japan Local Self-Government institute, *op. cit.*, Table 1, p. 9.

Formerly, the minimum standard of population for a city (*shi*) was 30,000, but this was later raised to 50,000 under the new Local Autonomy Law. In addition, over 60 per cent of the total population must be engaged in commerce and industry. Furthermore, over 60 per cent of the total number of households must be concentrated in the central sections of the city. Finally, the number of educational institutions, government offices and other establishments in the city must be large enough to satisfy conditions laid down under prefectural regulations. A town

[9] This description, the charts (above) and the summary of functions (below) are based on the chart (in Japanese), *Kikaku Chosa ka* (Planning & Projects section), *Okayama-ken Gyosei Soshiki* (Administrative Organization of Okayama), revised to June, 1959 (Okayama: *Kencho*, November, 1958); and (in English) "Organization of Okayama Prefectural Government, as of December, 1958," typescript supplied the author by the Foreign Affairs division, Document & Education section, General Affairs department.

(*machi*) is a generally urbanized municipality and must also satisfy conditions laid down under prefectural regulations. All the rest of the prefecture, aside from areas embraced in cities and towns, is subdivided into what legally are called villages (*mura*). As a matter of fact, as we shall see later, the *mura* (sometimes, *son*) is an artificial amalgamation of the extra-legal units, the face-to-face living groups, the hamlets (*buraku*).

The most striking event in Japan's local government in recent years has been the amalgamation (*gappei*) of small towns and villages across the country. As a result of the first basic reorganization of local institutions made after the surrender, the scope of functions of towns and villages was widely expanded. Their area and financial resources, however, were not broadened. Therefore, it soon became necessary to merge smaller towns and villages in order to give them sufficient administrative and fiscal powers and to raise their standards of management. The Law for the Acceleration of Amalgamation of Towns and Villages, enacted in October, 1953, set out to accomplish these purposes. At that time, Japan had 9,582 towns and villages, but this number has since been reduced to about 3,000.[10]

Traditionally, the mayor (unlike the prefectural governor who had before the surrender been an instrument of the central government) has always had a great deal of power at the municipal level. Even today, he serves as coordinator of the administration in the city hall (*shi yakusho*) and also as the city's ceremonial head. In the 1950s, for example, there was a fad for Japanese cities to affiliate with foreign cities—Tokyo with New York, Kyoto with Boston (and Paris), Kobe with Seattle, Osaka with San Francisco, Okayama with San José—and out of this the mayors gained considerable mileage, both of the geographic and publicity varieties. The mayor is assisted in the carrying out of his responsibilities by an assistant mayor, a treasurer, and various commissions which handle matters relative to education, public safety, elections and others. Once again, a specific case will better serve to illustrate the structure of a typical city. Figure 12 diagrams the administrative organization of the city hall of Okayama-*shi*.[11]

Under the Local Autonomy Law, an attempt was made to check the power of the mayor by giving the City Council author-

[10] *Ibid.,* p. 6.
[11] *Okayama-shi Shisei Yoran* (Handbook of Okayama Municipal Functions) (Okayama: *Shi Yakusho,* 1957); and *Gaikan Okayama-shi Shi* (General History of Okayama) (Okayama: *Shi Yakusho,* 1958).

ity to pass a vote of nonconfidence, in which case the mayor must resign or dissolve the council and call for a new election. Each municipality has a popularly elected council, ranging in size from twelve members in the smaller up to 120 members in larger areas. The term of office of the members, and of the chairman they elect, is four years. Although in some instances the chairman of the council, or the chairman of its most important standing committee, is the chief political rival of the mayor, seldom do differences reach the breaking point.

The administrative structure of a town is, of course, a simplified version of that of the city. And at the lowest rung of the administrative hierarchy is the village. In one sense, this last is one of the most fascinating and, perhaps, important levels of local government. As such, its structure and politics will be discussed at the end of this chapter.

Functions and Powers of Local Government

The legal foundation for local government in postwar Japan lies, as we have noted, in Chap. 8 of the new constitution: specifically, in the regulations of operations fixed by law "in accordance with the principle of local autonomy" (Art. 92); in the right of local units to manage their own property, affairs and administration (Art. 94); and in the protection that the Diet cannot enact a law, without the consent of the public entity concerned, which is applicable to only one local area (Art. 95). Beyond these constitutional provisions, the prefectures must rely on national laws for administrative action; most important are the Local Autonomy Law and the Local Finance Law.

Many of the functions of prefectural government are related to the fact that it serves as the local agency of the state. Thus, so far as delegated duties are concerned, the prefecture directs and supervises the activities on an area-wide level, and serves as a liaison organ between the national and local government units. The governor, for example, often acts as a state organ, as well as chief executive officer of an ordinary local public body. Similarly, the mayor is also responsible for carrying out certain duties entrusted to him by the central government and other public organizations and, in these tasks, direct supervision comes down from the state.

With regard to local powers of legislation, both the assembly and the governor may submit bills for consideration (the budget excepted). These are then referred to the appropriate standing

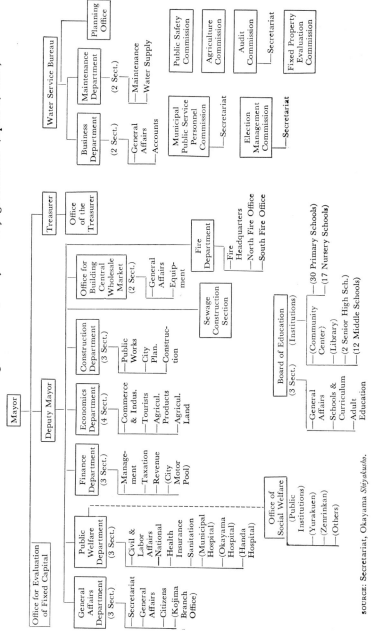

FIGURE 12 *The administrative organization of Okayama City government (April 1, 1959)*

SOURCE: Secretariat, Okayama *Shiyakusho.*

committee. The committee reports out the bill to a plenary session, which accepts or rejects the legislation by majority vote. Ordinarily the relations between the assembly and the governor are very close, but the former does retain the right to vote nonconfidence in the governor.

The governor, in turn, convokes the assembly and may dissolve it (in case of a vote of nonconfidence). He can also suspend enforcement of legislation or veto bills. The various commissions act independently of both assembly and governor (their finances are, however, provided in the prefectural budget). In the broader sense, the governor supervises and coordinates their activities. To take one example, in the immediate postwar period boards of education were established as popularly elected bodies (following the American model). In 1956, however, the boards became appointive and all members are now selected by governors or mayors, with the consent of prefectural assemblies and municipal councils. Educational personnel are paid out of national and prefectural budgets; senior high school buildings and equipment are supported by the prefectures; and those of junior high and elementary schools by the cities, towns and villages.[12]

Judicial affairs are of course independent. But prefectural police are closely related to the courts and to the offices of the public procurators. In the area of police affairs, as in the case of education, the postwar era saw a rather drastic decentralization. At first, municipal police were organized in the urban areas and separate national local police in the rural areas. In 1954, these two forces were unified into a prefectural police and centralized to some extent as regards personnel administration. The force is under the supervision of the Prefectural Public Safety commission. Some degree of centralization is provided by making prefectural police subject to the supervision of the National Police agency, by making senior superintendents national public officials, and by disbursement of some funds out of the national treasury. There exists no control by the National Fire Defense board or by governors over fire departments of cities, towns and villages. The director of the national board may, however, give advice to prefectures and municipalities, and governors to municipalities, in matters pertaining to fire defense.

The major exception to the ordinary legislative process of the prefecture, described above, has to do with the budget. Budget bills are always initiated by the governor. The very first estimates

[12] "Organization of Okayama Prefectural Government," *op. cit.*

are drawn up by the Finance section of the General Affairs department, the chief of which may amend the draft budget on the way up. After the governor has approved, the bill proceeds to a plenary session of the Assembly, where the governor faces interpellation on his administrative policies. The bill is then broken down among committees and then the budget is reported out again. Adoption requires a majority vote. This is the procedure in Okayama prefecture, at least, and a resultant budget is presented below.

TABLE 14   *Outline of a prefectural budget (Okayama, 1958–1959)*

Income		Expenditure	
Prefectural taxes	¥2,864,560	Assembly expenses	¥40,208
Locally conceded taxes*	583,849	Prefectural government (*Kencho*)	1,266,348
Locally granted taxes†	3,500,000	Police expenses	813,382
		Civil engineering	899,987
Public enterprises & prefectural prop.	21,271	Education	4,865,186
Allotment & apportionment‡	133,063	Social welfare, labor	681,306
		Health and sanitation	259,103
Rents & fees	487,436	Industry and economics	818,385
Payment from national treasury§	3,502,794	Property	11,501
		Statistical surveys	8,412
Contributions	5,982	Election expenses	70,843
Miscellaneous	273,450	Public loans**	1,087,796
Others	4,739	Miscellaneous	614,785
Prefectural loans	70,000	Reserve fund	10,000
TOTAL	¥11,447,245	TOTAL	¥11,447,245

Figures in thousands of yen. 360 yen = $1.00.
* Portion of admission, road taxes conceded to the prefecture.
† Portion of income, *sake*, tobacco taxes.
‡ Localities especially benefited by prefectural facilities bear this share.
§ Compensation for nationally entrusted business.
** For redemption of prefectural loans.
SOURCE: "Organization of Okayama Prefectural Government," *op. cit.*

In many senses, problems of local public finance reflect accurately the Japanese search, in the postwar years, for a viable system of local autonomy. It is quite clear that, prior to the war, local public entities had no financial autonomy except nominally. The turning point after the surrender came in 1949 with the Japanese Taxation Mission led by Professor Carl S. Shoup. The final, complex recommendations of the Shoup mission occupied four sizable volumes. The aims, on the other hand, were simply stated, "to draw up a plan of a permanent tax system for Japan"; and to outline a series of interconnected steps, "not a number of isolated measures having no connections with one another." [13] These, in turn, were to fulfill what the new constitution had promised, the financial foundations for true local autonomy.

The short-range effects of the Shoup proposals were: (1) basically to replace the prefectural tax system by those of the cities, towns and villages; (2) to limit the prefectural tax power to a direct enterprise tax and such indirect taxes as are levied on amusements and admissions; and (3) to replace the old system of tax distribution to prefectures by a new system of equalization grants. With benefit of hindsight, it is now possible to say that there were a number of defects in the application of the proposals. First, actual conditions in Japan—not sufficiently democratized for Shoup's lofty recommendations—threw prefectural finance into trouble and caused unnecessary friction between the local and national governments. Second, to be fair to the proposals, they were of little use unless effected as a whole, whereas, as late as 1952 no fundamental reform had been carried out but only temporizing steps taken.[14] Third, and perhaps most important, it is doubtful whether a compact and relatively poor country like Japan could ever enjoy the degree of federal autonomy envisioned in the earlier reforms.

Ever since the Shoup proposals there has been steady pressure for a wider base for prefectural taxes, increases in the equalization grants and a larger authorization for prefectural loans. Too often, it is true, local governments tend to depend upon the grants, while neglecting their own fiscal planning. On the other hand, in some prefectures tax revenues are a mere 20 per cent of total revenues. As Mayor Nakai Mitsuji of Osaka put it, "One of the basic problems is financial stringency which plagues many prefectures and cities—much to the detriment of the wholesome growth of local autonomy." [15]

The remarkable thing, however, is that the prefectures have accomplished so much, rather than so little, under such handi-

[13] *Report on Japanese Taxation by the Shoup Mission* (Tokyo, Japan: SCAP, September, 1949), 4 vols.; 1, pp. 1–4.

[14] Araki Eietsu, "*Fu-Ken Zaiseisei Seido no Mondai ten to Kaikaku no hoko wo Ronzu.*" (Problems of finance and tax systems of prefectures and their reform) *Jiji Tsuchin,* November 18, 1952, pp. 6143–45; November 19, 1952, pp. 6152–54.

[15] Nakai, "Local Autonomy," *loc. cit.*

caps. One last time, illustrations may best be drawn from the experience of Okayama prefecture in a given year. In calendar 1958, for example, the prefecture completed a three-year study by specialists in various fields, for the five-year development (1960–1965) of Okayama. This plan included proposals to rationalize prefectural administration, first, in order to realize most efficient results from limited financial resources. It covered exploitation of all natural resources in the region and economic development on a broad front.

During the same year, a dream which had once been reduced to blueprints by a feudal lord and his advisers was brought out to reality. South of Okayama City, a great arm of rock embraces Kojima Bay and holds it up against the bosom of the land. At the eastern extremity of this peninsula, Kinkozan, like a thumb thrust up into the air, offers a magnificent panorama of what is now the largest artificial lake in the world. More vital, this lake irrigates 12,500 acres of paddy fields reclaimed from the sea. In May, 1959, the national government issued a commemorative postage stamp to celebrate the final closing of the dike joining the peninsula to the mainland. On the eastern side of the prefecture during that same year, the dike at Kinkai Bay was completed. This made possible the reclamation of a 1,250-acre salt farm, which will soon provide one-sixth of the total salt production of Japan.

To the south and west near the city of Kurashiki, meanwhile, work was well under way on the giant Mizushima Industrial Center. This is a joint project undertaken by the prefecture and the Mitsubishi Oil Company, in cooperation with an American oil consortium. The plans make use of an older reclamation, dating from World War II and started by an aircraft company. The oil companies have pledged an expenditure of $55,000,000 in the first stage of construction, but eventually three times that amount will be spent.

The prefecture's task is to provide temporary housing for some 30,000 construction workers and, later, the foundations for an entirely new city. New concrete roads are in sharp contrast to the twisting old dirt roads through the rural areas. A small harbor, originally used for fishing craft, is being dredged to a depth of fifty-seven feet and expanded sufficiently so that it can take mammoth oil tankers of the 100,000-ton class.[16]

To the north, in the mountain fastnesses of the prefecture,

[16] *Okayama-ken Kogyo Kichi* (Bases for the industrialization of Okayama prefecture) (Okayama: Planning & Projects section, 1957.

in 1958 work had been completed on the Asahi River hydro-electric dam; surveys were already started on the multiple development of the Takahashi River and the Komoto Dam; and a special committee was formed to plan for the multiple development of the Yoshii River.

On an entirely different plane of prefectural activities, in 1958 the famous *No* dance stage in Korakuen—one of Japan's three most famous feudal, now public, parks—was reconstructed in its original form. It had been destroyed in the wartime bombing. On the northern edge of Okayama City, the prefecture was completing the Tsushima Sports Park, in preparation for the national athletic meet to be held there in 1962.

Local government experts aided in the modernization of twenty-two cities, towns, and villages. Also in 1958 welfare officials formed an intergovernmental committee for the study and prevention of juvenile delinquency. And finally, by way of illustration of the prefecture's multifold activities, a health boat began visiting remote islands of the Inland Sea where there were no local public health centers.[17]

Japanese Intergovernmental Relations

Enough has been said to illustrate clearly the fact that intergovernmental relations at all levels remain important in Japan despite the determined attempt, beginning with the Occupation, to guarantee local autonomy and even a kind of federalism. Of course, intergovernmental relations are significant in a unitary or in a federal state, but in Japan such relations merge more and more into dominance by the central government. In theory, the amount of control varies, as we have seen, according to whether a function is being performed by the municipality as an autonomous entity or as an organ of the state. In practice, this fine distinction breaks down, mainly in the financial area, where there is a great deal of central control. When prefectures and municipalities receive subsidies from the national government—and universally they do—guidance and supervision works its way down from the competent state minister, who has authority to inspect, instruct and direct; through the prefectural governor, who supervises the municipality; to the municipality itself which,

---

[17] These were some of the prefectural activities selected for publicity purposes; *"Okayama-ken Niyusu," Eiga Fuirumu Mokuroku* (A list of motion-picture films, "Okayama Prefectural News"), Okayama, Secretariat & Public Information Section, No. 1 (1958).

like the prefecture, must submit to financial inspection by the central Board of Audit.[18]

In national-local relations, no doubt the most important force is the Autonomy Ministry in Tokyo. Next in order of importance are the Agriculture and Forestry, Construction, Welfare and Education ministries. In prefectural-municipal relations, the Local Affairs section carries the advice of the governor to the town and village mayors.

The gradual shift of the center of gravity back toward the central government is illustrated by six national associations, which act as federations of local government groups. These have no legal power, but they do try to exercise political influence on the national government and on the Diet. Three are executive organizations: the National Association of Governors, the Japan Association of City Mayors, and the National Association of Towns and Villages. The other three are legislative: the National Association of Chairmen of Prefectural Assemblies, the National Association of Chairmen of City Assemblies, and the National Association of Chairmen of Town and Village Assemblies. The Japan Local Self-Government institute, together with the Tokyo Institute for Municipal Research, located in Hibiya Park, Tokyo, serve as independent research organizations or a sort of collective secretariat for the national associations.[19]

Towns and villages constitute the lowest legal rungs in the ladder of government. As a matter of fact, the town (*machi*) is a somewhat more built-up village (*mura* or *son*) and both are treated alike in laws and decrees: both are, from one point of view, somewhat artificial products of the amalgamation of older, smaller social groupings. Legally, the town or village has a dual character: on the one hand it is "an autonomous local entity"; on the other, it carries out a number of national functions fed down through the prefecture by way of "entity delegation." [20] And actually, this distinction also breaks down under the impact of the extensive guidance offered by the branch office of the prefectural government (*chiho jimusho*), of the constant liaison provided by the (county-based) association of town and village

[18] Japan Local Self-Government institute, *op. cit.,* p. 5.

[19] The Tokyo Institute for Municipal Research was founded in 1922 by Viscount Goto Shimpei, assisted by the late Professor Charles A. Beard. See *The Tokyo Institute for Municipal Research and its Work,* Hibiya Park, Tokyo, 1948.

[20] Kurt Steiner, "The Japanese Village and Its Government," *The Far Eastern Quarterly,* XV, No. 2 (February, 1956), p. 190. Professor Steiner was (1961) about to publish a full-length study of local government.

mayors (*choson chokai*), and of the steady stream of model by-laws passed on by the prefectural governments from the Autonomy Ministry and various ministries in Tokyo. These relations, in other words, remain stubbornly characteristic of the paternalism and hierarchy which continue to permeate Japanese life.

In post-surrender Japan under the Occupation, the village too felt the effects of the determined attempt to democratize, to create out of whole cloth a system of local autonomy. The result is a curiously semiparliamentary system, wherein the village assembly has legal power to force the mayor out of office on nonconfidence, unless he decides to dissolve the assembly and take the issue to the people in a new election. In fact, members of the assembly discuss and approve.[21] Indeed, the village reflects to a remarkable degree the persistence of a traditional decision-making process so characteristic of smaller social units. In the first place, members owe their seats to a quite informal but rigid system of election constituencies based on the face-to-face living groups, the hamlets, rather than to selection by the village at large. Second, assembly-mayor relations are governed by characteristic "negative consensus," or recommendation without objection. Often the mayor's role is to get a law passed exactly as is demanded by higher authority, but with informal, careful assurances of application according to the consensus.[22]

The governmental structure of a village is quite simple. Let us take that of Tokoi-*mura* in Okayama prefecture as an example. Under the mayor, who is elected to office for four years, serve a vice-mayor and a treasurer, nominated by the mayor and approved by the Village Assembly. There are twelve village clerks—in charge of taxation, family records and census, public welfare and statistics, land and requisition, general affairs, and finance sections—all appointed by the mayor. The sixteen assemblymen are elected for a term of four years. There are, in addition, members of the Board of Education, Election Management commission, Agricultural commission, and the Firefighting headquarters (a cooperative endeavor involving all men between the ages of seventeen and thirty-five). In Tokoi, as in most nearby villages, there are also a number of other committees, boards,

[21] Robert E. Ward, "Some Observations on Local Autonomy at the Village Level in Present-Day Japan," *ibid.*, XII, No. 2 (February, 1953), p. 192.

[22] Beardsley, Hall and Ward, *Village Japan*, previously cited, is one of the most recent and one of the best treatments ever offered in English. See especially Chapters 12, 13 (research by Professor Ward).

cooperatives and informal groups.[23] Most important of these is the Agricultural Co-operative association (*Nogyo Kyodo kumiai*), which performs at the same time certain local banking and loan functions. Until 1950, the agricultural commission handled the problem of redistribution under land reform. Now it manages rice, the only crop requisitioned by government. There are, finally, some sixteen other high-sounding but largely inactive committees.

It is quite clear that the village's future in the fiscal and, therefore, political field of autonomy is dim. To the extent that the villages are under steady pressure to amalgamate, their numbers are constantly decreasing. To the extent that their financial affairs are increasingly dictated at high levels, their autonomy becomes more and more nominal. Nevertheless, even today the village remains significant, but only as "a transitional unit of organization occupying a point midway between the traditional world of the *buraku* and the legally oriented world of formal politics and government." [24]

The Rice Roots of Local Government

This brings us, at long last, to the very rice roots of politics in Japan, the hamlet (*buraku*) and the household (*ie*), the basic social components where—to paraphrase Robert M. MacIver—the habits of government are early bred. The importance of the Japanese household is not surprising, for the family is a conditioner for politics everywhere. The *buraku* was, however, completely proscribed in 1947. It continued as a vehicle for decision-making beneath the law, and by 1952–53 the decree outlawing the hamlet began to lose its force. Today it is an extra-legal (not an illegal) grouping and still possibly one of the most important in Japan. In the *buraku* are enshrined all the traditional Japanese values: the family as constituent unit, status determined by family, social norms set within the family, hierarchy (rather than equality), diffuse loyalties (rather than specific rights), and harmony (rather than justice). This value pattern strongly influences the operations of the smallest legal unit, the rural village. And it reaches into the city too. Japan is, as we have seen, rapidly becoming a metropolitan, if not an urban

[23] "Organization of Okayama Prefectural Government," *loc. cit.* Described in detail by Paul S. Dull, "The Political Structure of a Japanese Village," *The Far Eastern Quarterly*, XIII, No. 1 (February, 1954), pp. 182–6.

[24] Beardsley, Hall, Ward, *op. cit.*, p. 358.

nation. Yet, in the sense in which Max Weber meant the term, Japan is still a rural society.

In the *buraku,* as Professor Ward has ably described it, the world of formal legal relationships is left behind. Even the local residents do not think in terms of constituted authority, the rule of law, or government in the Western sense, but of community functions in the traditional sense. Decisions, when they have to be made, are arrived at in a monthly religious meeting (the *kanki*) or in an ordinary meeting (the *jokai*). Seldom is a divisive vote taken; rather, issues are settled by recommendation and consensus. Membership is based on household units and each family has a single vote. They select the *buraku* officers, a headman, a vice-headman and a treasurer.[25]

Politics at the *buraku* level provides once again a sharp contrast with politics as we understand it at the local government level in the West. Indeed, the contrast is apparent in Japan itself, for example, between interest groups in Osaka and those in the villages of Okayama.

In the latter environment interest groups are few, and tend to be of the latent, inarticulate, ephemeral, *ad hoc,* local-focused and unorganized variety. In Osaka, they are numerous, very vocal, continuous, programmatic, and of expansive focus, and well organized. This would seem to be one of the most dramatic and significant of the differences between rural and urban Japan.[26]

The *buraku* is significant for another reason. There has been a slow collapse of the traditional way of life, it is true, as individualism has invaded the hamlet and has eroded the hierarchy of familism. Land reform struck powerful blows at the foundations of agrarian conservatism. It is not argued here that such invasions are upsetting an older, ideal bucolic democracy, a disguised political *laissez-faire.* The old-fashioned mode of politics involved little or no participation by the ordinary farmer, no real sense of citizenship; and it often camouflaged injustice, bitter secret opposition, and festering distrust of all politics.

On the other hand, the drive for local autonomy has not succeeded in producing the elusive treasure of participation

[25] Robert E. Ward, "The Socio-Political Role of the Buraku (Hamlet) in Japan," *American Political Science Review,* XLV (December, 1951), p. 1025; also Beardsley, Hall, and Ward, *op. cit.,* pp. 350–358.

[26] Robert E. Ward, "Urban-Rural Differences and the Process of Political Modernization in Japan: A Case Study," *Economic Development and Cultural Change,* IX, No. 1, Part 25 (October, 1960), p. 152.

either. If anything, the well-meant reforms probably have sharpened the gap between the persistent, traditional rural way of life in the hamlets and the modern, dynamic, urban way of life in the cities. The adjustment of these two Japans may provide the clue to the problem, whether Japan will develop an indigenous, viable democracy.

11 - The Foreign Relations of Japan

Perhaps no country in the world offers the bewildering variety of diplomatic experience which Japan has enjoyed (or suffered) since it became a nation-state, Western style. The rapid and often urgent shifts in international stature have left profound impressions on the Japanese image of the outer world.

Patterns of Contact

Prior to the earliest Western impact, Japan had no real tradition of inter-state contact. The only model of international relations, as modern jargon puts it, was the venerable Confucian family of nations. Within this family of unequals—not sovereign and equal states—Japan had always been a kind of distant, younger cousin of the great Middle Kingdom of China.[1] In modern times there have been echoes of the older Sinic system. The Greater East Asia Co-Prosperity Sphere was, on its more idealistic side, an attempt to reject the secular Western nation-state system and to build a new order for Asia, in which Japan was to play the self-appointed role of elder brother.

The Portuguese first arrived in Japan in the 1540s, soon to be followed by the Spanish, Dutch and English. For about 150 years Japan was in contact with Europe. One of the effects of this experience was, however, to frighten the Japanese into isolation against all foreign ideas. Nevertheless, this same experience

[1] The best reconstruction of this system is by M. Frederick Nelson in *Korea and the Old Order in Eastern Asia* (Baton Rouge, Louisiana State University, 1945).

meant that, from the sixteenth century on, change in Japan as in all Asia was to be paced by the remote and then proximate pressure of the Western world.[2]

From the early 1600s to the 1850s, Japan lived in what we in the West call backwardness and isolation under the protective tent of Tokugawa autarchy. During this long period Japan did, as we have seen, begin to develop many functions of the modern state. Two, however, were almost completely lacking: the conduct of foreign relations and diplomacy as we have known them in the Western nation-state system since the Treaty of Westphalia, 1648; before that, in the Italian city-states; and even before that, in the ancient Greek model of an international world.

And yet, during the two and a half centuries of isolation, Japan did enjoy security and peace.

From the 1850s to the 1950s, Japan was opened to what we of the West call enlightenment. And yet, for the Japanese, this century was distinguished by successive crises and wars.

One hundred years of American-Japanese relations, for example, began in 1854 with the arrival in Japan of men-of-war. (Since 1954, the annual Black Ships Festival has been held every May 17 at the tiny port of Shimoda on the Izu Peninsula[3]).

In 1860, Japan's first diplomatic mission journeyed to Washington: its task, to exchange ratifications of the Treaty of Amity and Commerce which had been negotiated between the shogunate and American Consul-General Townsend Harris. (In 1960, Americans celebrated the centennial of diplomatic and commercial relations between the two nations.[4])

In the late nineteenth century, contacts with America were marked by the gentle tutelage of men of peace: missionaries, educators, agricultural experts, literary figures and diplomats who aided the Japanese in their process of rapid modernization.[5]

In the mid-1940s the skies over Japan, the seas around Japan

[2] A sophisticated analysis of the central problem of intercultural penetration (with Japan as the major case study) is offered by Sir George Sansom, *The Western World and Japan: A Study in the Interaction of European and Asiatic Cultures* (New York: Knopf, 1950).

[3] "Black Ship Festival Held at Shimoda," *Japan Report*, New York, IV, No. 11 (June 1, 1958); the original visit was best described by Arthur C. Walworth, *Black Ships Off Japan: the Story of Commodore Perry's Expedition* (New York: Knopf, 1946).

[4] *The First Japanese Embassy; Japan-U.S. Centennial, 1860–1960*, Consulate General of Japan, New York, 1960.

[5] The best account is contained in Robert S. Schwantes, *Japanese and Americans; A Century of Cultural Relations* (New York: Harper [for the Council on Foreign Relations], 1955).

and, finally, the land of Japan itself were once again visited by American men-of-war. The occasion for surrender was marked by the use of the newest weapon of war, the atomic bomb, and one of the oldest instruments of political security, the imperial command.

From 1945 to 1948 Japan was prepared, largely under American auspices, for a peaceful life. From 1950 and the beginning of the Korean conflict to 1960 and the revised security treaty between Japan and the United States, the Japanese were reintroduced to the harsh realities of diplomacy and force.

The major disaster of war had, however, led the Japanese to believe conclusively in the idea, even before it became incorporated in Art. 9 of their new constitution, that they should renounce force as an instrument of national policy. Today, in Japan—once regarded as congenitally warlike—pacifism is perhaps the only religion in which the bulk of Japanese have faith.[6]

The post-peace treaty foreign policy of Japan, which often seems paradoxical, is at least partially a product of these previous patterns of contact. Because of deep-rooted traits of national character and historical experience, Japanese are psychologically attuned to relationships marked by hierarchy and inequality, rather than to legal fictions of sovereign equality. Few factors in the experience of reemergence into the family of nations tend to offset such a Japanese reaction.

For one thing, despite or because of the technological conquest of space, Japan's geographical location must of necessity play a dominant role in the formulation of its foreign policy. For another, Japan's dependence on foreign trade makes it imperative to stay on good terms with as many nations as possible and, in any case, with the United States.

To the outsider, the path seems simple: if Japan were only to rearm, at least to some extent, then to that extent the country could direct its own destiny in relative independence. One can never forget, however, the close connection between domestic politics and foreign policy in any country. To many Japanese, the path to rearmament points only to the danger of revived military predominance. In this respect, the Socialists' position seems closer to that of the Japanese public at large. Even conservatives, who argue for security pacts and eventual rearmament, must face the cost: the deliberate sacrifice of the rapidly spreading benefits of

[6] See the article by the author, "Ideological Issues Facing Japan Today," *SAIS Review*, Washington, School of Advanced International Studies, III, No. 4 (Summer, 1959).

rising production, the intoxication of the consumer boom and the unprecedented luxuries, all of which provide the foundations for the new popular culture.

It is, then, not altogether out of idealism that the Japanese have experimented with a diplomacy without force, have hoped to enjoy security without cost, have offered to co-exist with those who are still legally enemies, and have looked to international organization for a solution to mankind's dilemma.

Post-treaty Posture

Neither the feudal isolation nor the modern emergence of Japan as a nation-state, neither the disaster of defeat nor the reforms of the Occupation, could basically change Japan's geographic and strategic location off the coast of Asia. Thus, aside from the legal and diplomatic niceties, Japan's outlook is primarily toward the North and West, to nearby Russia; toward the West, to the two Koreas; and toward the West and Southwest, toward the two Chinas and what we call Southeast Asia. Today, Japan remains an Asian power.[7]

Japan's post-treaty position is also an end result of the truly amazing process whereby Japan moved from war through defeat to surrender, and from Occupation by the Allied powers through a majority peace treaty to the exercise, once again, of its sovereignty.[8] It is sufficient to repeat here the major factors involved:

The international juridical aspects of the Occupation differed sharply from the structure imposed on any other Axis power.

Japan was not divided into zones as was Germany.

Japan was not placed under direct military government by foreign military forces, as was Italy.

Japan did not collapse into political chaos, as did much of Europe.

The Occupation of Japan, although nominally international in scope, was qualified by the unquestionable primacy of the United States among the victors.

[7] For the Japanese public, these geopolitical relationships were explained in a little booklet, *Gaimusho, hen., Ajia tokuhon* (A primer on Asia) (Tokyo: Ministry of Finance, 1958), especially Introduction, which described the shift in center of gravity of world politics to the Afro-Asian world and the significance to Japan of this historic transition.

[8] A recent reflective, inside view of this experience is contained in Kazuo Kawai, *Japan's American Interlude* (Chicago: University of Chicago, 1960). The author, now Professor of Political Science, Ohio State University, was editor-in-chief of the *Nippon Times* (now *The Japan Times*) between 1946 and 1949.

The paradox in these developments can be simply stated: the Japanese thus won important conditions within the so-called unconditional surrender of 1945; however, there were also important conditions attached to what might otherwise be regarded as the unconditional return to Japan of the exercise of sovereignty in the peace treaty of 1952.

As early as March 17, 1947, when he held a press conference in Tokyo, General MacArthur advocated a prompt end to the Occupation and an early peace treaty. Governmentally, Japan was already preparing for re-entry into the Western family of nations. This fact is surprising and, in fact, a tribute to Japanese ingenuity for, early in the Occupation, Japan had been as cut off from international intercourse as the nation had been under the Tokugawa regime. The Supreme Commander for the Allied Powers, technically the exerciser of Japan's sovereignty between 1945 and 1952, had insisted upon receiving all chiefs of mission —including American diplomats—in Tokyo. Behind this new screen of insulation Japanese nevertheless managed to keep abreast of diplomatic developments. Trained and experienced diplomatic personnel were simply transferred to the significant if subdued agency called the Central Liaison office (CLO; *Shusen Renraku Chuo jimukyoko*). The work of this office forecast, as the peace treaty approached, the reemergence of the Foreign Ministry.

Obstacles to the peace treaty, then, were not put up either by SCAP or by the Japanese government. Delay was rather occasioned by maneuvers in the growing cold war, Soviet intransigence, and the appearance of a new power, the Chinese People's Republic. In Washington too, Defense department officials, harassed by responsibilities arising out of the Korean conflict, continued to oppose the MacArthur-State department plan for an early Japanese peace treaty. Late in 1950, an interdepartmental agreement to retain bases in Japan cleared the way in the United States. Then President Truman assigned the treaty problem to Special Adviser (later, Secretary of State) John Foster Dulles.[9]

Among the former enemies of Japan invited to attend the peace conference, held in San Francisco in September, 1951, only

[9] A detailed analysis of the peace treaty issue on the American scene is contained in Bernard C. Cohen, *The Political Process and Foreign Policy: the Making of the Japanese Peace Settlement* (Princeton: Princeton University Press, 1957).

three—India, Burma and Yugoslavia—declined. The emerging dispute over the two Chinas was avoided by seating neither the Nationalist regime, on Taiwan (Formosa), nor the Communist, on the mainland.[10] Forty-nine nations, including of course the United States and Japan, signed the treaty on September 8, 1951. Only the Communist nations, the Soviet Union, Poland and Czechoslovakia, refused. The treaty went into effect on April 2, 1952.[11]

To most Americans ever since, both the Occupation and the eventual peace treaty have been symbols of the generous treatment accorded a former enemy. Honest Japanese too will admit that the terms of the treaty were indeed mild. On the other hand, from the Japanese point of view it is doubtful that Japan would have regained its sovereignty had it not met certain conditions accompanying the treaty. In fact, the peace treaty itself (in Art. 6) specifically recognized a right not yet clear under Japan's own postwar constitution (in Art. 9), the right of self-defense mentioned in the United Nations Charter. To make sure, the treaty recognized Japan's right to have foreign troops stationed in Japanese territory for the defense of Japan. Whereupon Japan then concluded two basic pacts with the United States—a security treaty signed along with the peace treaty on September 9, 1951, and an administrative agreement signed February 28, 1952.[12] The latter was supplemented, in March, 1954, by Japan-United States Mutual Defense Assistance agreements.[13]

The long-range effects of this complex set of treaties and agreements on Japanese international and domestic politics will be examined further below, under the heading of United States-Japanese relations. For the present, key implications of the

[10] The text of the peace treaty between the Republic of China and Japan, signed in Taipeh, April 28, 1952, is included in "Documentary Material," *Contemporary Japan*, XXI, Nos. 1–3 (1952), pp. 160–163.

[11] See *Conference for the Conclusion and Signature of the Treaty of Peace with Japan: Record of Proceedings* (Washington: [Publication 4392, International Organization and Conference Series 2, Far Eastern 3] 1951).

[12] For the text of the security treaty, see *Department of State Bulletin*, September 17, 1951; the text of the administrative agreement was included in *Contemporary Japan*, XXI, Nos. 1–3 (1952).

[13] These so-called MSA agreements consisted of four parts: (1) Japan-U.S. Mutual Defense Assistance agreement; (2) Agreement regarding purchase of agricultural commodities; (3) Agreement on economic arrangements; and (4) Agreement regarding the guarantee of investments. See "MSA Agreements," pp. 31–32, *Political Handbook of Japan, 1958* (Tokyo: Tokyo News Service, 1958).

arrangements will be singled out for comment. In an official statement of defense policy issued in 1957, the Japanese government declared its intention to develop gradually a military establishment of its own. Until such forces could be developed, however, the Japanese had to continue to base its security on the American pacts. In other words, the Japanese posture was to lean in the direction of the United States and the free world. On the other hand, one can understand why, for example, the director of *The Japan Times,* Fukushima Shintaro, claimed that Japan therefore has come to enjoy something less than sovereign independence. Japan has not been in a position to regularize its relationships with near-neighbors, Communist China and the Soviet Union. "The national interest," concluded Mr. Fukushima, "must become the basis for Japan's foreign policy." [14]

If Japan, in its post-peace treaty posture, could not exactly achieve equality in one direction, it could seek a much-desired legal recognition of its re-entry into the family of nations in another. Up through 1955, Japan's hopes for admission to the United Nations were caught in a tangle of cold war politics: a paired veto of Outer Mongolia (by the Nationalist Chinese), Soviet demands for admission of its ally (Communist China), and outright Soviet blackmail (a Russo-Japanese peace treaty as a price of admission). By October, 1956, Japan still had not achieved agreement with the Russians on a peace treaty, but Premier Hatoyama Ichiro, in Moscow, had succeeded in wringing out of the Soviet Union a joint declaration providing for termination of the state of war and support of Japan's application for United Nations membership. On December 18, 1956, Japan became the eightieth member of the United Nations. On January 1, 1958, Japan was seated as a non-permanent member of the Security Council, and its delegation could pretend, at least, once again to play the role of a great power.[15]

With this overview of Japan's post-treaty international posture, it can therefore be concluded that the Japanese government is engaging in something more than rhetoric when it states that:

[14] "Ideological Issues Facing Japan Today," *op. cit.,* p. 11.

[15] Termination of the state of war with Russia and subsequent developments are discussed below, under the heading of Japanese relations with the U.S.S.R. Japan's role in the U.N. is also summarized below. For a chronicle of events leading to Japan's admission to membership, see the author's contributions titled "Japan," *Britannica Book of the Year* (Chicago: Encyclopaedia Britannica, 1957, 1958, 1959).

The three main principles underlying Japanese diplomacy are support of the United Nations, cooperation with the free nations of the world, and retention of Japan's position as an Asian nation.[16]

These principles constitute not only Japanese hopes. They also make up, in very broad terms, Japanese political commitments. Sometimes these commitments tend to run to cross-purposes. More important, however, a nation's posture unfortunately cannot consist solely of commitments (as Americans themselves have discovered). They must be matched by capabilities. Here, once again, post-treaty Japan offers a unique case study.

Diplomacy without Force

Diplomacy has been realistically defined as public international negotiation, with the alternative instrument of force components in the background.[17] Now it would obviously be erroneous to state that Japan's post-treaty posture has been buttressed by no force whatsoever. Indeed, the irony of Japan's post-surrender history lies in the fact that Japan has enjoyed military security to an extent undreamed of in the days of the Imperial Japanese Army and Navy. These force components have been largely supplied, however, by the United States, and they have remained under American direction. In addition, Japan has gradually built up—against bitter opposition—a small, paramilitary force.

It is precisely at this point in the description of Japan's posture where the definition of national interest becomes confused with domestic Japanese politics and the outside observer cannot possibly identify the players without a program. Even with a guide, he finds the Japanese scene replete with ironies and paradoxes.

Looking in from the outside, Americans now tend to be impatient with the constitutional block to the rearmament of Japan provided by Art. 9 of the new organic law. This article, as we have seen, renounces war as an instrument of policy and forever foreswears war potential. Yet there is little doubt that

[16] *Gaimu Sho hen* (Foreign Ministry, ed.) *Waga gaiko no kinkyo* (Present state of our foreign relations) (Tokyo: Ministry of Finance, October 15, 1957); this "Diplomatic Blue Book," Part I, was followed by Part II (same title), April 1, 1958.

[17] This is not a cynical but rather a technical definition. See Quincy Wright, *The Study of International Relations* (New York: Appleton-Century-Crofts, 1955), especially the chapter on the art of diplomacy.

Americans originally concurred in the writing of this very provision. And to this day, the article expresses the popular sentiment of Japan, which is strongly and emotionally pacifistic. Moreover, if antinuclear armament in Japan is not a religion of a most fanatical sort, it is at least an emotional response which has had a powerful effect on the definition of national interest. In its very first appearance in the United Nations, before the 12th General Assembly, 1957, Japan offered a draft resolution calling for suspension of all atomic and hydrogen tests.

Before Japan's new constitution had gone into effect, as we have seen, the Supreme Commander for the Allied Powers revised his view of Americans' handiwork. Self-defense is an inherent right, he argued. Japanese were understandably puzzled. Then came the long-awaited treaty of peace but with a *quid pro quo:* the security treaty and administrative agreement, which provided for the presence of war potential in the form of American bases, troops and arms. Meanwhile, the surreptitious rearmament of Japan itself began.

Further details concerning Japanese-American security relations are presented in a later section of this chapter. Suffice it to say here that precisely in constitutional and foreign policy questions lie the greatest differences between the present conservative party and administration of Japan and the opposition Socialist parties. Conservatives, who generally favor revision of the American-inspired constitution, argue for continuation of United States-Japanese security arrangements for the time being, until Japan can develop its own defense capabilities. The opposition, which generally favors retention of the American-inspired constitution intact, bitterly opposes United States-Japanese security arrangements as well as the further expansion of Japan's own defense capabilities. It is they who wish to revert to a unique experiment, an idealistic attempt to engage in diplomacy without force.

It has been said that the operations of various foreign offices differ not so much because of their respective administrative structures, but because of the varying constitutional frameworks within which they must work. Japan does not provide an exception.

Since Japan is in its structure a parliamentary-cabinet form of government, final responsibility for management of foreign affairs rests with the prime minister under the constitution (Art. 73). Similarly, the treaty-making power is vested in the cabinet, within which the prime minister usually entrusts the foreign minister with diplomatic negotiations conducted under his direction, after approval by the cabinet. Of course, the cabinet, prime minister and foreign minister are all accountable to the Diet. Treaties must be submitted to the Diet for approval. Once approved, treaties become supreme law of the land (Art. 98).[18]

Beneath this formal, symmetrical structure, there are, of course, numerous cross pressures to reconcile among the cabinet, the bureaucracy and the political parties. The practice of diplomacy at home is chiefly the job of the minister of foreign affairs, who thus has the second most difficult assignment in the cabinet.[19]

Movement toward the revival of a normal Ministry of Foreign Affairs actually began in February, 1950, with the establishment of Japanese overseas agencies in major cities of the world. These were not, of course, accredited to the governments of the countries since each office required the formal approval of SCAP and, through SCAP, of the host governments. Until the signature of the peace treaty, this was as far as Japan could go toward achieving normal diplomatic relations. On May 27, 1960, the Foreign Ministry moved into its new $3,500,000 building situated in Chiyoda Ward, downtown Tokyo.

The administrative structure of the Ministry of Foreign Affairs (*Gaimu Sho*) is generally organized very much like the familiar British Foreign Office or the United States Department of State. Unlike the American department, however, there are no positions corresponding to the under secretaries and assistant secretaries. Career officers fill all positions up to the second highest rank; in other words, political clearance affects only the minister and the parliamentary vice-minister.[20]

[18] Treaties therefore enjoy a legal status different from ordinary laws, which must be pursuant to the constitution. For a discussion of the Supreme Court's ruling on the status of treaties, see above, Chapter 8, p. 168.

[19] Kosaka Zentaro was appointed Minister of Foreign Affairs in the Ikeda Cabinet on July 19, 1960. At forty-eight, he was the youngest person to hold the position in postwar Japan. He had behind him a distinguished political career: first elected to the lower house in 1946, he was serving his seventh term; in 1949 he led a budget survey mission to the United States; in 1953 he held the Labor portfolio in the fifth Yoshida Cabinet. On the occasion of his visit to the United States in September, 1960, the Japanese Consulate General issued a "Special Supplement" on the Foreign Minister, *Japan Report* (September 8, 1960).

[20] This description of the *Gaimu Sho* is based on the following materials: *Gaimusho List* (Tokyo: Ministry of Foreign Affairs, October, 1958); *Gaimu Sho soshiki rei* (Ordinance for the organization of the Foreign Ministery), mimeo-

Moreover, the internal structure of the ministry is far simpler than that of the American State Department. The *Gaimu Sho* is directed by a permanent careerist, the administrative vice-minister. It is subdivided into a secretariat and eight bureaus, with a director in charge of each. Three of the bureaus are politico-geographic in scope; the remaining five are functional in nature and deal with economic affairs, treaties, United Nations affairs, information and cultural affairs, and passports.

Perhaps the most important and largest of all the bureaus of the Foreign Ministry is that which handles economic affairs. Its size is a tribute to the important role economic problems play in Japanese foreign affairs. The organization of the Economic Affairs bureau is somewhat different from that of the others, in that it combines geographic and functional affairs.

Military Capabilities

Let us now turn to the other side of the coin, Japan's own military capabilities. Japan's military policy too, like its post-treaty diplomacy, is profoundly affected by the previous policies of the Occupation, which led the Japanese into what Professor Royama Masamichi has called "an atmosphere of negative peace." [21] It is severely limited by Art. 9 and the constitutional barrier to rearmament; and it has been inversely influenced by the manner in which American force components have been used to fill Japan's defensive vacuum.

With the advent of the cold war, the shift in American policies toward Japan beginning about 1947–48, and the Korean conflict, even Japanese began the long, agonizing reappraisal of self-defense, a problem which hitherto had been almost taboo. In June, 1950, many American troops based in Japan were transferred to Korea. At that point, General MacArthur authorized the creation of a National Police Reserve of 75,000 men.[22] The

graphed, No. 385, August 30, 1947 as amended to No. 87, March 31, 1959, 26 pp.; *Zaigai kokan no meisho oyobi ichi wo sadameru horitsu* (Law establishing the location and title of Japanese missions abroad), mimeographed, No. 85, April 12, 1947 as amended to No. 31, March 24, 1959, 10 pp. The official manual is *Sori Fu* (Office of the Prime Minister), *Gaimu Sho* (The Foreign Ministry) (Tokyo: Ministry of Finance, 1958) 196 pp.

[21] Royama Masamichi, "Problems in Self-Defense," *The Annals, loc. cit.,* p. 167.

[22] The letter of authorization from General MacArthur to Prime Minister Yoshida was dated July 8, 1950. On August 10, the Japanese Government responded with the National Police Reserve Force Order. Masuhara Keikichi, *A Review of Japan's Defense Strength* (Tokyo: Ministry of Foreign Affairs, 1956), p. 3.

primary mission of the reserve was, in truth, to maintain internal security; its establishment can be regarded, however, as the beginning of Japan's self-defense program. Responsibility for defense began to shift toward Japan with the previously described United States-Japan security treaty of 1951. Under this arrangement, American troops were to be withdrawn contingent upon "such alternative individual or collective security dispositions" as to assure the security of Japan.

In May, 1952, the National Police Reserve was increased in authorized strength to 110,000 men. At the same time a new Maritime Safety Force of 7,590 men was organized. On October 15, 1952, six months after the recovery of Japan's independence, the old reserve was reorganized into the National Safety Force, which combined land and sea components, under the jurisdiction of the National Safety agency (the forerunner of today's Defense agency). The agency was originally under direct control of the prime minister, but later was headed by a director-general. Self-defense had now achieved cabinet rank. Another milestone was reached the same year, when Japanese officers activated the first postwar (northern) regional corps and took over the defense of the island of Hokkaido. As they were transferred, some veterans of the famous American First Cavalry Division must have shaken their heads in disbelief to see units of the Japanese army reactivated just seven years after the surrender.

Formal approval by Japan of the Mutual Defense Assistance agreement with the United States, in 1954, marked the further transformation of Japanese forces into a full-fledged defense army. Up to that point, responsibility for defense against direct outside aggression remained with American forces. On the other hand, the United States was aiding the Japanese defense effort in both organization and equipment. Beginning in 1954, Japan's defense-share contribution to the United States amounted to about $155,000,000 annually. Further implications for Japan's rearmament were contained in the provision whereby increases in allocations to Japan's own forces would result in a decrease in defense-share contributions.[23] The Japanese government was clearly moving to fulfill pledges in the security treaty, that Japan would gradually increase its ability to defend itself.

[23] Article 25, paragraph 2,b (defense-share) of the U.S.-Japanese agreement provided that Japan would make available to the United States Japanese currency for procurement of transportation and other military services in Japan. By 1959 the equivalent fell off to $115,000,000. *The Japan Times,* June 24, 1959.

In the spring of 1954 the National Safety agency drew up plans for the expansion of land, sea and air power to a combined strength of 152,000 men. On July 1, 1954, two laws further entrenched the self-defense forces and created, in effect, a ministry of defense. The first was the Defense Agency Establishment Law, which set up the present defense organ under the office of the prime minister. This law also outlined the mission of the new agency:

The purpose of the Defense Agency is to protect the peace and independence of our country and to safeguard its security. For this purpose it has as its mission to supervise, manage and handle all matters concerning the Ground Self-Defense Force, the Maritime Self-Defense Force and the Air Self-Defense Force.[24]

The second statute was the Self-Defense Forces Law which, as is apparent, reorganized the land and sea components and added a new air force. Their mission was in turn defined as follows:

The Self-Defense Forces, in order to protect the peace and independence of our own country and to safeguard its security, shall have as its principal mission to defend our country against both direct and indirect aggression (which includes large-scale internal disturbances and sedition breaking out as a result of instigation or intervention of a foreign country), and to take steps whenever necessary to maintain public order.[25]

The budget for fiscal year 1955 allotted 87,000 million yen (about $241 million) for an authorized force of 195,810 men, including 179,767 in uniform and 16,041 civilians.

Meanwhile, the government was planning the establishment of a national defense council, with the duty of advising on long-range defense policy and the relation of rearmament to industry. In May, 1955, the Hatoyama government drew up a bill for such a council but ran into intracabinet problems, a nonconfidence motion against the director-general of the Defense agency, and aroused public feeling over the sudden arrival in Japan of Honest John rockets. Instead of the statutory council, a provisional cabinet ministers' council was established. In 1956, the bill setting up the Defense Council again went to the Diet and this time it passed.

[24] Masuhara Keikichi, op. cit., p. 5. Mr. Masuhara had been first director-general of the NPR headquarters; he became vice-director-general of the new Defense agency.

[25] Ibid., p. 5.

At this point in its development, Japan's self-defense forces reached a plateau. Inspired by repeated successes, the Defense agency drew up for its own use a Six-Year Defense plan, which projected a total force of about 260,000 men by 1960.[26] This plan was never fully published because of pending negotiations on security with the United States and growing opposition to rearmament within Japan.

Although mention has frequently been made of elevating the status of the agency to that of a ministry, it has remained (in 1961) an external organ of the office of the prime minister. The Defense agency is headed by the director-general, who is a cabinet minister, assisted by his deputy (the administrative vice-minister), and a parliamentary vice-minister. The structure of the agency is simple, with seven bureaus: the secretariat, defense, education, personnel, health, finance and equipment. The Joint Staff Council has a chairman (the highest ranking career officer), and chiefs of the ground, maritime, and air staff; its secretariat is composed of sections, J-1 (administration), J-2 (intelligence), J-3 (operations and training), and J-4 (logistics).

The Ground Self-Defense Force is composed of six divisions (consisting of 12,700 men each), combined brigades (about 6,000 men each), and supporting units.

The Maritime Self-Defense Force consists of the Self-Defense Fleet, one training squadron, and one minesweeping squadron. There are five regional districts centering on the traditional ports of Yokosuka, Kure, Sasebo, Maizuru and Ominato. On August 1, 1958, the Force had 408 vessels with a total tonnage of 96,797.

In 1958, the Air Self-Defense Force had about 890 airplanes, including trainers, transports and jet fighters. In January, 1960 the Defense Council approved a 96,800 million yen program for domestic production of Lockheed F104J Starfighter jets (of the sum to be spent, the United States agreed to share 27,000 million yen [about $75,000,000] of the total cost).[27]

[26] The Six-Year Defense plan was first summarized in the semi-official *Boei Nenkan Kanko Kai hen* (Committee for the publication of Defense yearbook, ed.) *Boei Nenkan,* 1956 (Defense yearbook, 1956) (Tokyo: Ito, Chikan, 1956). Issues of the yearbook up to and including 1959 have been consulted by the author. This yearly compendium contains an up-to-date military estimate of the worldwide situation; detailed description of the work of the Defense Council, Defense agency, and Self-Defense forces; and comparative charts and data on major armies, navies and air forces of the world.

[27] *Defense Strength of Japan* (Tokyo: Defense agency, August 1, 1948); see also the brief history and organization of Japan's defense forces in *The Japan Times,* June 24, 1959. See also *The Japan Times,* January 27, 1960.

Japan's Self-Defense forces grew steadily, then, until in 1959 they counted 210,000 personnel, 1,300 aircraft, and over 400 vessels. Personnel in the Ground Self-Defense Force numbered 170,000, which was 10,000 less than the target for that year. Recruitment showed an upward trend, because of improved public relations and especially the disaster relief work carried out by the men in uniform. The rate of enlistment competition for private second class slots had risen to 4.3, for the first time topping the number (four) thought necessary to improve the quality of recruits. Competition for the Defense University stood at 14.5 (7,689 applicants for 530 places), about the same as that for Tokyo University.[28]

The total defense budget for the 1959–60 fiscal year came to 136,040 million yen (about $380 million). In the Diet, Finance Minister Sato Eisaku denied Socialist allegations that national defense was burdening the people's livelihood. In fact, he claimed that defense expenditures were declining in weight and, to prove it, gave these figures: in 1953, defense took 12 per cent of the national budget and 1.2 per cent of national income; in 1958, 11.1 per cent and 1.7 per cent; and in 1959, 10.8 per cent and 1.7 per cent.[29]

The year 1960 was doubtless a turning point in the development of Japan's military capabilities, for in that year the Defense agency laid down plans for a second phase build-up, revolving around the construction of missile units. *Keidanren* (Federation of Economic Organizations) had already blueprinted a ten-year development program. Three groups were frequently mentioned: the Mitsubishi Heavy Industries, Reorganized, Ltd., Kawasaki Aircraft Company, and Fuji Precision Industry.[30] Publicity for such a program had to be muted, however, for the famous U-2 incident involving the United States and the Soviet Union and the controversy over revision of the American security treaty had aroused fanatical opposition to even the mention of missiles and nuclear arms.

Indeed, there were only a few who dared, in Japan's atomic climate, to look even further ahead. One of these was Hattori Takushiro, a brilliant former colonel in the Imperial Japanese Army. At the head of a private research group, Hattori argued that Japan would, sooner or later, have to jump from conven-

[28] "Outline of Japan's Growing Defense Program," *Mainichi,* March 17, 1959.

[29] *The Japan Times,* June 24, 1959; July 6, 1959.

[30] "Missile Industries to Start," *Diamond,* January 23, 1960.

tional to nuclear arms for both purposes of efficiency and economy. He advocated the dispatch of personnel to America to learn
missilry; use of the Nike or other defensive missiles with a
range up to 200 miles; procurement of nuclear weapons; and the
creation of a missile staff.[31] Until such plans were realized, however, Japan continued to rely mainly upon American support for
its defense. Paradoxically, the continuation of this support has
been the central issue in the treaty revision struggle which has
dominated recent Japanese foreign policy.

Recent Foreign Policy

SECURITY AND INSECURITY: RELATIONS WITH THE UNITED STATES.
By 1960, a "Japan boom" in the United States had risen to such
a crescendo that even the Japanese were taking note of it. Grand
Kabuki, the traditional Japanese dance-theater, fortuitously
opened in New York during an actors' strike, which had dark-
ened all other major houses. During 1959 almost 200,000 tourists
visited Japan, the vast majority Americans. In May and June,
1959, the imperial household *Gagaku* musicians and dancers
performed before intrigued Americans in six leading American
cities. The American image of Japan, once etched in horror,
was becoming definitely pleasant, if blurred, once again. Some
critics in Japan may be excused for having puzzled over the long-
range effects of the American fad; and, on occasion, for having
questioned "Fujiyama diplomacy," the denomination standing
both for the name of the foreign minister and the identification
of Japan solely with Mt. Fuji as a mecca for tourists.[32]

In 1960, the Japanese image of America was becoming even
more blurred. It is true that most Americans in Japan encountered little or no anti-Americanism on a personal level. Crowds
of eager music lovers jammed provincial halls to hear the Boston
Symphony Orchestra; a few were mildly disappointed that this
great ensemble did not try at least one piece of *avant garde*
Japanese music. The most widely read foreign magazines in
Japan were *Time, Life* and *Newsweek.*[33]

One professor of the author's acquaintance bought a TV set

[31] Murata Kiyoaki, "Nuclear Armament and Japan," *The Japan Times,*
March 5, 1959.

[32] The term "Fujiyama diplomacy" was coined by the widely-read Professor of Tokyo University (Director of American Studies), critic, and TV commentator Nakaya Kenichi; see *Shukan Koron,* March 22, 1960.

[33] "Foreign Magazines Read by Japanese," *Japan Report,* VI, No. 4 (February 15, 1960), p. 7.

in order to watch the wedding celebrations for the crown prince, baseball, and the weekly "Alfred Hitchcock Presents" mystery series, imported direct from the United States and skillfully rendered into Japanese! In all too few American cultural centers scattered throughout Japan, dedicated U.S.I.S. directors tried to offset the impression being left by imported American movies with English conversation classes, lectures on Lincoln and John Dewey, and discussion groups concerned with American elections. Serious Japanese friends of America recognized the need for equality in the cultural exchange area.[34] They also realized the necessity, after two decades of alternating anti- and pro-American propaganda, for a sound, objective, Japanese-initiated, Japanese-directed, private program of American studies. The fate of the two countries had become so inextricably intertwined, it had become absolutely essential that Japanese, in their own national interest, come to study and understand the United States.

The primary difficulty, however, has been that wittingly or unwittingly the image of the United States projected to Japanese was of a government almost solely concerned with matters of military security. Not that the United States has had any difficulty with the succession of conservative governments which have led Japan since the peace treaty. On the contrary, the Japanese Foreign Office, under both external and internal pressure, has unequivocally rejected neutralism as a viable policy for Japan:

This is why our nation, while building up the defense capacity, plans to safeguard its security by maintaining security arrangement system with the United States. This is, indeed, the keynote of our nation's diplomacy predicated on the present world situation and our position therein.[35]

The "security arrangement" with the United States was, as we have seen, incorporated in the original security treaty signed with the peace pact in 1951, a treaty which sowed the seeds

[34] In 1959, the Exchange Student Association in Tokyo celebrated the tenth anniversary of GARIOA, and the seventh anniversary of Fulbright fellowship grants. It is significant that these useful grants provided, however, for an imbalance of Japanese scholars over teachers sent to the United States, and a parallel imbalance of teachers over scholars among Americans sent to Japan. See *Pacific Bridge*, Tokyo, American Embassy, III, No. 5 (May 31, 1959).

[35] Gaimu Sho hen (Foreign Ministry, ed.), *Waga gaiko no kinkyo, op. cit.,* Part 3 (March, 1959). Chap. 2, "Recent Foreign Relations," pp. 8–34.

of its own revision. Withdrawal of American forces has always been contingent upon alternative methods of assuring peace and security in the area "in and about Japan" and, indeed, "in the Far East" (Art. 1).

Ever since 1951, there have been at least six problems connected with the security treaty and its suggested revision. First, even the most flexible interpretation of Japan's constitution (Art. 9) and of the right to station foreign troops in the nation would permit such war potential only for the defense of Japan. In the 1951 treaty there was no clear stipulation obligating American security forces to defend Japan; on the other hand, such forces could be "utilized to contribute to the maintenance of international peace and security in the Far East" (Art. 1). Second, there was almost immediately a demand to delete the clause (Art. 1) providing for use of American forces "to put down large-scale internal riots and disturbances in Japan." Third, Japan relinquished the right (Art. 3) to grant any bases to a third power without the prior consent of the United States. Fourth, both countries soon ran into snags in the administration agreements (Art. 3) on disposition of armed forces in and about Japan; and no prior consultation was provided in case American forces based in Japan were used outside the country. Fifth, Japanese wanted a clearer definition of compatibility between the treaty and the United Nations Charter. Sixth, and finally, there was no effective treaty term stated.[36]

These, then, were the legal problems. There were also public emotional attitudes involved (just as in the question of Japanese rearmament). As the revision controversy gradually built up to a climax, there was an unfortunate tendency on the part of United States officials, and even of private American press coverage, to attribute opposition to the security arrangements only to left-wing political elements. As a matter of fact, all the evidence pointed to a deep-rooted, ambivalent attitude on the part of the Japanese people toward American military bases on Japanese soil. This attitude has been fed by a lack of administrative efficiency on the part of Japanese-American committees charged with handling delicate problems of conflicting jurisdiction (in a country historically famous for its sensitivity to so-called unequal treaties). There has been inevitable friction with inhab-

[36] These problematical points were freely admitted by the Foreign Ministry in its Diplomatic Blue Book, Part 3, *Waga gaiko no kinkyo, op. cit.* (March, 1959).

itants close to American bases. And there has been, of course, organized left-wing political pressure. This last factor should not, however, obscure the basic trend of opinion.

One of the most careful American observers, Professor Douglas Mendel, Jr. of the University of California at Los Angeles, has been studying Japanese attitudes on such questions since Japan achieved its independence. His conclusions, based on personal field study and Japanese surveys, were that the American presence has never enjoyed majority support; the trend ever since 1950 has been in the opposite direction; only a minority, even of Liberal-Democratic voters, favored the continuation of bases, much less introduction of missiles or nuclear weapons; and, in fact, as early as 1957 a plurality of voters thought that such bases endangered Japan's security.[37]

In any case, in the opinion of Professor Royama Masamichi (with whom Dr. Mendel has worked), the treaty revision question has been the gravest problem facing Japan since the war's end and might well decide the future course of parliamentary politics in Japan.[38]

The Mutual Defense Assistance Agreement of 1954 had, as a usual condition, that the nation receiving aid was prepared to defend itself against outside aggression (the so-called Vandenberg Resolution). In September, 1955, when Foreign Minister Shigemitsu visited Washington, it was clearly restated that treaty revision would follow Japan's becoming strong in defense. The Japanese-American communique also implied that Japanese forces might have to be used overseas.

The next step along the path toward revision came in June, 1957, when Prime Minister Kishi first visited the United States. He and President Eisenhower issued a joint communique, defining the continuing threat of communism, and recognizing need to review the treaty of 1951 so as to place relations on a "foundation of sovereign equality." The United States promised to reduce forces based in Japan.[39]

From the Japanese point of view, these developments came

[37] Douglas H. Mendel, Jr., "Japanese Attitudes toward American Military Bases," *Far Eastern Survey*, XXVIII, No. 9 (September, 1959). He is preparing a more comprehensive report under the title, *The Japanese People and Foreign Policy*.

[38] Quoted from *Sekai*, "Trend of Magazines" (February, 1960): *Summaries of Selected Japanese Magazines,* mimeographed (Tokyo: American Embassy, March 14, 1960).

[39] *Japan Report*, III, No. 11 (special supplement, "Prime Minister Kishi's Visit to the United States," July 10, 1957).

none too soon, for 1957 was the year when both Japanese and American tempers were aroused by the complex Girard case.[40] Fortunately—for both Girard and relations between the two countries—the American government agreed to waive jurisdiction over this Army Specialist, and the United States Supreme Court refused to review the status of forces agreement. After intense political pressure had built up in both the Japanese Diet and the American Congress, on the very eve of Premier Kishi's visit, Girard was tried by a Japanese court, convicted, then the sentence was suspended, and he was released. It was doubtful whether the Japanese-American alliance could stand another such case.

When Fujiyama Aiichiro was reappointed Foreign Minister in the second Kishi Cabinet, in June, 1958, he publicly resolved to seek a change in the security treaty. That fall, with rising tensions in Taiwan Strait, Socialists pressed Mr. Fujiyama hard on the fact that Japan exercised no control over American forces based in the country, forces which might be used to reinforce the United States Seventh Fleet. The foreign minister again promised to seek amendment of the seven-year-old treaty, so as to provide prior consultation with Japan over disposition of American forces. He then flew to Washington to hold conversations with Secretary of State Dulles, on September 11 and 12, 1958. Fujiyama returned to Japan full of hope, leaving the impression that two or three meetings with Ambassador Douglas MacArthur II would be sufficient to iron out difficulties. First conversations with the ambassador began October 4.

Meanwhile, the Japanese government began to encounter dissidence not only from the opposition Socialists, but also from an anti-main current faction of the ruling Liberal-Democratic Party. Introduction of the Police Duties Revision Law, inevitably linked in the Japanese mind to the rearmament of Japan, led to total domestic confusion and a cautious attitude on the part of Ambassador MacArthur. No further conversations were held in November, and those conducted in December were only for the purpose of keeping negotiations open.[41]

In 1959, Japanese politics were dominated by the issue of revision of Japanese-American security arrangements. Both in official parleys with the American ambassador, which began again, and in unofficial negotiations between the government

[40] For a detailed summary, see the author's contribution, "Japan," *Britannica Book of the Year, 1958* (Chicago, 1959).

[41] "Review of Japanese Diplomacy in 1958," *The Japan Times,* December 29, 1958.

and the Liberal-Democratic Party, a number of problems arose. For example, would Okinawa and the Bonins, not yet returned to Japanese jurisdiction, be included in the new defense area?

In March, in the midst of these delicate negotiations, Japan (and the United States) were jolted by the Tokyo District Court decision, basing acquittal of seven trespassers on an American air base on the assumption that the security treaty was unconstitutional.[42] Not only the whole treaty structure, but also Art. 9 of the constitution, became subject to review. Eventually in December, as we have noted, the Japanese Supreme Court ruled that the presence of United States troops and bases did not violate the constitution. The Japanese court refused, however, to review the treaty, and thus revision inevitably was turned back to become a political issue.

In July and August, the Liberal-Democrats were preparing for a nationwide campaign to win wider support for revision of the treaty. They distributed pamphlets like, "Why We Propose Pact Revision" and "Questions and Answers on the Security Treaty." Socialists began to drum up opposition to revision, in fact, to retaining any security pact whatsoever. It was then that Asanuma Inejiro, Socialist Secretary-General, proposed instead a collective security arrangement among Japan, Communist China, the Soviet Union and the United States. This course Socialist Nishio Suehiro denounced as impractical and, in the end, led the Democratic-Socialist bolt from the party. Two Rightist united front groups planned a struggle against Socialist opposition. The battle lines were drawn.[43]

Japan's vigorous free press swung into action. Between September, 1958, when Foreign Minister Fujiyama opened negotiations, and January, 1960, when the revised treaty was signed, Japan's big three newspapers, *Asahi*, *Mainichi*, and *Yomiuri*, carried a total of sixty editorials of comment. All three originally welcomed revision in principle, in order to convert a unilateral into a bilateral pact. In October, the joint defense area (specifically, Okinawa and the Bonins) evoked controversy, but this died down when Fujiyama withdrew island areas outside of Japan from consideration. By April, 1959, newspapers centered on prior consultation, the implications of the Vandenberg Resolution and the term of the treaty. During the summer and early autumn,

[42] For details of this, the Sunakawa case, see above, Chap. 8.
[43] "Weekly News Review," *The Japan Times*, July 27, August 3, August 19, 1959.

public opinion surveys conducted by the newspapers and the Government, revealed that the Japanese people's understanding of the treaty issues was inadequate. Nonetheless, the public "felt uneasy"; few felt the need for revision (*Mainichi*, August 27). Another poll (*Asahi*, January 18, 1960) demonstrated that the government's publicity had not been effective. Most often cited was the belief that revision ran counter to the principle of co-existence, after Khrushchev's visit to the United States. Finally, *Asahi* came up with its own revision plan: replacement of "prior consultation" with "prior agreement," limiting the purpose of the treaty strictly to "the security of Japan," deletion of all clauses which raised constitutional doubts and drastic reduction of the treaty term.[44]

Issues which had long lay imbedded in the Japanese-American security treaty relationship were now being chipped out by the sharp chisel of public debate. Ouchi Hyoe, former President of Hosei University, challenged the Kishi government: if it could not achieve approval of an amendment to the no-war constitution, then the security pact should be dropped entirely. Ironically, the American-drafted constitution was referred to as an organ of "everlasting peace" (Art. 9), as a manifesto of "complete non-armament," the San Francisco peace treaty itself as "unconstitutional," the security treaty as a "renunciation of peace and neutrality." [45]

The government had argued that treaty revision would put Japan on an equal footing and obligate the United States to defend Japan. Actually, responded the critics, there has been a discrepancy in expectations: Japan properly places priority on defense, but America is solely interested in Japan as a base for its military operations in the Far East. The area might include the maritime provinces of the Soviet Union! "Prior consultation" raises doubts: a major change in American equipment might never be discussed, and Mr. Kishi might allow the United States the right to bring in hydrogen bombs.[46] The debate was beginning to touch exposed Japanese nerve ends.

By March, 1960, one public opinion poll showed that only about 25 per cent of those questioned were in favor of revision while 36 per cent were opposed (proponents were steadily de-

---

[44] Press trends surveyed by staff, *Asahi Journal*, February 7, 1960.

[45] *Sekai*, Sept., 1959.

[46] Such was the skillfully designed line of attack by Mori Motojiri, Socialist member of the House of Councillors. *Sekai Orai*, April, 1960.

creasing and the opposition, increasing). The *Asahi Shimbun* poll showed that 38 per cent of those questioned about revision feared that Japan might be dragged into a war.

Americans seemed to be losing every contest: when Khrushchev smiled before American TV cameras, Japanese argued that security pacts were out of date in the warm climate of coexistence and summitry; when Mr. Khrushchev loosed his tirade in Paris over the spy-in-the-sky incident, Japanese glanced nervously at American U-2's parked on Japanese runways. Even Americans were quoted in the growing clamor.[47]

Government determination to forge ahead was matched by equal determination on the part of the opposition to block all further consideration of revision. Seldom were the real, serious issues in Japanese security policy debated. Friends of Japan gravely wondered if the tender transplanted rice roots of democratic procedure could withstand the typhoon of emotion. Opposition swirled up in the streets before the powerful gusts. Students scarcely old enough to vote beat in waves against the official residence of the prime minister. Members of the premier's own unstable Liberal-Democratic coalition opportunistically watched to see if his structure of leadership could be washed away. Succession to the premiership, in some political leaders' minds, became more important than the issues of security.

After Prime Minister Kishi was given an unusual *mi-okuri,* a farewell party, at Haneda International Airport (made possible by cordons of police), the revised United States-Japan security treaty was signed in Washington, January 19, 1960. The text could scarcely have been expected to placate the opposition. After recognizing the right of self-defense affirmed in the United Nations Charter, the new treaty defined the common concern of the two parties "in the maintenance of international peace and security in the Far East" (preamble). This was a key and, in Japan, a controversial clause. Both parties undertook to refrain "from the threat or use of force" against any other state (Art. 1), an action which would be, in any case, unconstitutional on the part of Japan. They were "to consult together" when the security of Japan or in the Far East was threatened (Art. 4). For the pur-

[47] For example, Professor Frederick L. Schuman of Williams College (a distinguished contributor to the series of which this volume is a part) was quoted as saying the treaty was anachronistic in an age of nuclear weapons; Professor Hans Morgenthau of the University of Chicago, that Japan was justified in preparing defenses against Communist China, but that Japan should minimize the dangers of an outright military alliance. *Sekai,* April, 1960.

poses of the treaty, the United States was granted continued use of facilities and areas in Japan (Art. 6). Of almost equal importance to the Japanese was the joint communique issued by Kishi and Eisenhower. The major provision read:

> In this connection, the Prime Minister discussed with the President the question of prior consultation under the new treaty. The President assured him that the United States Government has no intention of acting in a manner contrary to the wishes of the Japanese Government with respect to the matters involving prior consultation under the treaty.[48]

Back in Japan, the treaty went to the Diet in an unusual night session on February 1, 1960. After prolonged debate, Liberal-Democrats approved the treaty over the protest of Socialists, who boycotted the Diet. Tension continued to rise as the House of Councillors discussed the pact, again in the absence of Socialist colleagues; and as the Kishi government prepared to welcome President Eisenhower on a state visit to Japan, June 19, 1960.

The crescendo of protest and organized opposition reached a peak on June 12, when mob pressure interfered with the arrival of White House Press Secretary James A. Hagerty at Tokyo International Airport; and on June 15, when a bloody clash took place between policemen and students on Diet premises. Finally on June 16, after an extraordinary cabinet meeting, the Japanese government was forced to ask the United States to postpone the visit of President Eisenhower. Premier Kishi announced that "present events force us to the conclusion that this is not an appropriate time to receive an important state guest, greatly to our regret." [49]

Although exchange of ratifications of the new Treaty of Mutual Cooperation and Security took place in Tokyo, June 23, 1960, the whole episode was widely interpreted as a diplomatic defeat of the United States. Shortly thereafter, Premier Kishi announced his intention to resign. The day before his retirement, in an ominous revival of violence typical of Japan of the 1930s, Mr. Kishi was assaulted by a knife-wielding fanatic Rightist, who barely failed in his attempt to assassinate the Prime Minister.

The climate, if not the real substance, of Japanese-American relations began to change in late 1960. In 1961, it was too early to

[48] *Japan Report* (special supplement, January 25, 1960).
[49] "Prime Minister's Statement on Postponement of President Eisenhower's Visit"; "Statement of Foreign Minister on Security Treaty Ratification," *Japan Report,* VI, No. 12 (June 25, 1960); see also *The Japan Times,* June 17, 1960.

predict how far actual changes would go. There is no doubt, however, that these were important factors in the altered attitudes: the retirement of the unpopular Premier Kishi, the election of John F. Kennedy, and the subsequent election of Premier Ikeda. Between June, 1960 and June, 1961, both countries paused and took a deep breath.

The Japanese press and all major political parties, intent on their own campaign in November, 1960, unanimously agreed that Mr. Kennedy's election did not signify any radical change in American foreign policy. Nevertheless, it was noted that the president-elect paid "greater attention to non-military factors" and aimed at countering Soviet influence "by strengthening the economic and psychological, as well as military, ties with other free nations." One newspaper said flatly that Mr. Kennedy's election was "a victory of American intelligence." Hirawawa Kazushige (NHK news commentator) reflected on a previous meeting with Mr. Kennedy: "He has stronger concern for Far Eastern affairs than any other American political leader I have met." In a panel discussion, Tokyo University Professor Nakaya welcomed an expected change in American diplomacy. "In my opinion," he said, "it will become much more flexible than at present." [50]

After an unfortunate delay (caused by the need for routine security checks) and considerable stir of rumor in Japan, Edwin O. Reischauer (born-in-Japan Harvard professor of Far Eastern history and bi-lingual in English and Japanese) arrived as ambassador in the spring of 1961. For the first time since the war, many Japanese felt—rightly or not—they were receiving one who truly understood them. It was only a matter of time, however, before some Japanese intellectuals would discover that Ambassador Reischauer was not in agreement with their neutralist position.

REACTION: THE SOVIET UNION. If at first one were to reflect upon the historical background and the postwar status of formal legal relationships between the Soviet Union and Japan, one might conclude that Japan's relations with Russia have been far worse than those with the United States. Japanese have always demonstrated an ambivalent attitude toward Russia, compounded of respect and fear. Respect springs, as it does throughout Asia, from a practical recognition of the enormous strides the people of Russia have taken from agrarian backwardness to industrial and military might. Marxism, particularly when it is

[50] For these successive comments, see *Tokyo Shimbun,* November 10; *Yomiuri,* November 10; *Sankei,* November 10, 1960.

re-interpreted as anti-Western imperialism, still proves so persuasive as to obscure the gross naiveté inherent in this self-styled science of history. When these kinds of respect fail, Japanese still have reason to fear the Soviet Union.

And yet, in the post-war era the Russians have enjoyed one advantage over Americans. The major American instrument of persuasion in the Japanese theatre has been armed force wielded by military men, from General MacArthur down to Mr. Girard. In contrast, most Japanese (except a few on tiny islands to the north) have yet to see a Russian or Chinese Communist soldier.[51] We should not be too surprised, then, when some Japanese credit the Communist bloc with peaceful intentions, while suspecting us of war-mindedness.

Moreover, Russia (between 1945 and 1957) and China (today) have never allowed the wretched status of diplomatic affairs to stand in the way of efforts to influence through ideas, propaganda, enticements, pressures, cultural interchange, sports or even trade. Here Communist states practice what we preach: they work on several planes of international politics and never neglect peoples-to-peoples contacts.[52]

Nevertheless, it is cause for wonder that contacts between Japan and Russia and particularly, with Communist China, are as good as they are. Legally, Japan is still defined by the Communist bloc as the unregenerate fascist enemy of World War II, the aggressor suspect and, recently, the lackey of American imperialism. Neither Russia nor, of course, Communist China signed the San Francisco peace treaty. Both still regard Japan as at least a hypothetical enemy and, behind Japan, the United States as the real enemy.[53] In the Sino-Soviet Treaty of Friendship, signed on February 14, 1950, the two powers agreed "jointly to prevent the re-birth of Japanese imperialism and the repetition of aggression on the part of Japan, or any state which directly or indirectly would unite in any form with Japan in acts of aggression." This was a thinly veiled threat to the United States. On occasion, both countries have offered completely to normalize diplomatic relations with Japan, but the price has always been the severing of security arrangements with the United States.

[51] This was the point made by the Hon. Ernest A. Gross in the Foreword of *Japan between East and West* (New York: Harper, 1957).

[52] This was the theme of the author's article, "Japan's Relations with the Communist World," *Current History*, XXXIV, No. 200 (April, 1958).

[53] Tajiri Akiyoshi, diplomatic commentator, in *Gaiko Jiho*, May, 1960.

In 1955–1956, the Japanese tried their best to have their cake and eat it too. After Soviet overtures and Hatoyama's promise to re-establish normal relations, negotiations began in London and dragged their weary way to Moscow. Two issues seemed insurmountable: the return of Japanese prisoners of war and disposition of the Southern Kurils, especially Habomais and Shikotan, just off Hokkaido's Nemuro peninsula.[54] By September, 1956, it was obvious that the most Japan could obtain was an agreement to sidestep territorial issues and a full peace treaty, and to restore diplomatic contact. In Tokyo, December 12, 1956, eleven years and four months after the actual end of the war, Russia and Japan exchanged ratifications of an agreement.

Despite the normalization of relations, Japanese have been given cause to wonder ever since if there has been any profit in coming to agreement with the Soviet Union. Closely related to the sensitive territorial issue, fisheries agreements have been fought out year after year, since the first Northwest Pacific Agreement in 1957, and never to the satisfaction of Japanese needs. At first, Japan fared little better in trade negotiations. A primary trade agreement signed in December, 1957, provided for exports from Japan to Russia of only $20–25,000,000 annually, and imports from Russia estimated at $20–23,000,000. Nevertheless, even conservative financial papers like *Nihon Keizai* argued that too great dependence on the United States was dangerous, and that Japan should try to expand trade with the Soviet Union, regardless of its political structure and ideology.

In fact, this question of trade was one of the few blandishments the Soviet Union could offer Japan. Finally, in March, 1960, Japan and Russia signed their first long-range trade agreement, retroactive to December, 1959 and designed to run to December, 1962. Under this agreement, Japan was to export $230,000,000 and import $210,000,000 worth of goods from the Soviet Union in a three-year period. Soviet spokesmen in Tokyo spoke glowingly of their seven-year economic plan, under which development of Siberia was expected to be at a faster rate than the average for the entire country. Russia offered Japan much-needed coking coal, iron ore, Ural oil, and timber; for the devel-

---

[54] In summary, the Japanese claimed that at no time in history have Shikotan and the Habomai islands been foreign territory; Kunashiri and Etorofu have never been held by Russia; Karafuto (Sakhalin) has changed several times. *The Northern Islands; Background of Territorial Problems in the Japanese-Soviet Negotiations* (Tokyo: Foreign Ministry, 1955).

opment of Soviet Far East industry Japanese machinery was in demand.[55]

Japanese-Russian relations came to revolve, nevertheless, around the explosive issue of United States-Japan security arrangements. The Russian response to Japanese signature of the revised security treaty in Washington, in January, 1960, was prompt. In the words of Takagi Sokichi, a military commentator, "The Slav's age-old tradition has been to smile at the strong and threaten the weak." [56]

The Russian attitude was contained in the Gromyko Memorandum of January 28, 1960, which denounced the American treaty as "a military alliance against the Communist bloc." After having promised, in 1956, to reconsider the status of the Southern Kurils, the Soviet Union now refused to return Habomais and Shikotan so long as they might be used by Japan and the United States for aggressive purposes. Many Japanese felt that Soviet interference in domestic Japanese affairs was most clearly revealed by gratuitous Soviet comments on the constitutionality of the treaty, and by the real intention of the Gromyko Memorandum, which was to strengthen the antitreaty camp within Japan. This move, some Japanese said, was a culmination of the unilateral scrapping of the Soviet-Japanese Non-Aggression Treaty, in 1945. It trampled on the much heralded Khrushchev co-existence principle. Critics of the Kishi government responded that it was to blame for failing to conclude a peace treaty with the Soviet Union, promised in the negotiations of 1956.

REACTION: COMMUNIST CHINA. If Japan's formal relations with the Soviet Union have been difficult, diplomatic relations with the People's Republic of China have been impossible. Although Japanese statesmen have tried to ignore them, the barriers have been formidable: a treaty relationship, established of Japan's own free will and stubbornly continued, with the Republic of China on Taiwan; close (the Chinese say, semicolonial) relationship with the hated United States, and the curious Japanese penchant for departmentalized thinking. In this wishful thinking, Japanese intimacy with America can somehow be separated from establishment of relations with mainland China; and, if

[55] *The Japan Times,* March 3, 1960; also, interview with Dmitri Petrov, Chief of the Tokyo Office, *Izvestia,* by Harada Unji, Editor-in-Chief of *Toyo Keizai Shimpo,* in the latter magazine, April 9, 1960.

[56] See the extensive symposium on the Gromyko Memorandum in *Keizai Orai,* March, 1960.

not, Japanese trade with China can be separated from political relations with the People's Republic of China.[57]

As a matter of fact, Communist China's policy—without any diplomatic contact with Japan—nevertheless illustrates the strength of ceaseless and adroit propaganda designed on the mainland. This studied campaign naturally profits from 2,000 years of geographic proximity, historical community and cultural homogeneity between China and Japan. The author can testify, from personal experience in the Japanese academic world, that an insatiable curiosity about the emergent People's Republic is ably met by a load of printed and spoken material which, in terms of sheer weight, is incredible.[58]

At least until the collapse of summitry, in 1960, the Japanese were indeed ahead of the United States in predicting that eventually even America would have to swing to a two-China policy. In October, 1959, the Japanese press carried lively commentary on Representative Charles Porter's advocacy of an international trusteeship for Taiwan. As elections in the United States approached, and the American public determinedly pursued an ostrich-like head-in-the-sand approach to the existence of Communist China, Japanese observers pounced on the highly publicized (in Japan) Conlon report.[59] They read into this sober projection a shift in the climate of American China policy.[60]

Once again, however, revision of the Japanese security arrangement with the United States proved critical. As the great debate progressed, three schools of thought emerged in Japan. One, the anti-revised treaty group, was linked to demands for normalization of relations with Communist China. Another, closest to the official government policy, was anticommunist and at most, even schemed to use the United States alliance against Communist China. At the least, this school assumed that settlement of outstanding issues with China was impossible. A third assumed that, even with a revised American treaty, the deadlock

[57] See Jerome B. Cohen, "International Aspects of Japan's Economic Situation," *Japan between East and West, op. cit.*, pp. 137–144.

[58] Professor Martin Wilbur, a China expert, believes that direction of this ceaseless propaganda campaign emanates from the very top of the Chinese Communist hierarchy, from the Japan Problem committee which includes Liu Shao-ch'i, Kuo Mo-jo (who was educated in Japan) and others. "Japan and the Rise of Communist China," *ibid.*, p. 205.

[59] This significant report was published as U.S. Senate, Committee on Foreign Relations, *United States Foreign Policy; Asia* (Study No. 5, prepared by Conlon Associates, Ltd.), Washington, November 1, 1959.

[60] *Asahi Journal*, February 7, 1960; *Economist*, February 2, 1960.

with China could eventually be broken, providing the Kishi government could be forced to resign.[61]

In any case, much of the debate revealed a discrepancy between Japanese thinking and the views of Communist China's leaders. The basic Chinese attitude was that Japan was not a free agent. In October, 1954, a Khrushchev-Mao communique had bluntly stated: "Nine years after the end of the war, Japan is not yet independent, placed in the status of a semi-occupied country." [62] Peking's official posture was taken by the Foreign department, on January 14, 1960, before the revised treaty was signed in Washington. The "U.S.-Japanese military alliance" marked the revival of Japanese militarism, an aggressive expansion in Southeast Asia, and an attempted reconstruction of the ill-fated Greater East Asia Co-Prosperity Sphere, the Chinese claimed. On January 23, in Peking, Kuo Mo-jo, President of the Chinese Peace Committee, set the tactical tone:

> We know that there was a dispute in Japan on which to choose, a road to independence and peace or a road to militarism and imperialism. The Japanese people preferred the former. . . . We, therefore, draw a distinct line between the Japanese people and Japanese militarists and have tried to establish friendly relations with the Japanese people.[63]

Foreign Minister Chen Yi, speaking at a celebration of the tenth anniversary of the Sino-Soviet treaty, warned openly of the revival of neo-Hitler and neo-Tojo forces. The virulence of the Chinese attack may have startled even Khrushchev, preparing for the summit. Certainly, Chinese intransigence, so well illustrated in this response to the new security treaty, played a large role in persuading the Soviet leader to change his tune.

Early in 1961, severe cuts by the United States in its spending abroad, in order to save scarce dollars, led to renewed interest among Japanese businessmen and others in the possibility of reviving trade with Communist China. The interest became

---

[61] A report by Saionji Kikazu, from Peking, to *Sekai*, April, 1960; and analysis by Iwamura Michio, Director, Chinese Affairs Research institute, *Sekai Orai*, April, 1960. With regard to the third school of thought mentioned, at one stage the Liberal-Democratic Party threatened to expel former Premier Ishibashi Tanzan for his suggestion to shelve the security treaty temporarily, to seek a territorial settlement with the U.S.S.R., and to try to normalize relations with the People's Republic. Opposing views on this plan aired by Shigemori Tadashi and Utsunomiya Tokuma were carried in *Nippon Shuho*, March 25, 1960.

[62] *Sekai*, May, 1960.

[63] Saionji Kikazu, from Peking, to *Sekai*, April, 1960.

translated into pressure on the Ikeda Government to explore the China problem. Normalization of relations became one of the priority study projects in the hands of Foreign Minister Kosaka.

THE REST OF ASIA. One of the charges which the Chinese hurled at the Japanese during negotiation of the new American security treaty was that the pact symbolized the gradual emergence of a hostile alliance among America, Japan, South Korea, and Taiwan, a NEATO directed against the mainland regime. The history of Japanese relations with the Republic of Korea, at least until the retirement of President Syngman Rhee, rendered this claim patently ridiculous.

Like the apocryphal domestic instability of the husband and wife who were not merely incompatible—they hated each other —the hostility between Japan and Korea has been unlike the relationship between any other two allies of the United States in the world. For some reason, the United States has chosen to pursue a policy of noninterference in this deep-seated quarrel, urging Japan and the Republic of Korea to work out their problems through direct negotiations.

It is entirely possible to arrive at the sociologist's view of Japanese-Korean relations, that some conflicts rest on entirely unrealistic and yet unchanging foundations.[64] Thus Japanese, particularly in their shameful treatment of Koreans resident in Japan and the resultant guilt complex, have scarcely been able to regard their neighbors on an equal level of humanity. Negotiation under such circumstances is made most difficult. In turn Koreans, suddenly released into an orgy of nationalism, still regard Japan as poised to reinstitute a system of brutal colonial rule. Conversations directed toward restoring normal relations, from the first phase (October, 1951-April, 1952) through the second (April 14-July 23, 1953), third (October 6–21, 1953), and fourth (April 15-December 21, 1958), have all been dominated by mutual suspicion and have come to naught.

Not that there are no real issues involved in Japan-Republic of Korea relations. The list can be gloomily recounted: claims and counterclaims to property, arising out of the dismantled colonial system; fishing zones extending onto the high seas, the so-called Rhee line and MacArthur line, forcibly implemented by both sides; and a territorial dispute over an island with, naturally, two names (in Japanese, Takeshima; in Korean, Tockdo). Into these various raw spots, salt was rubbed when the Japanese

[64] International Sociological Association, *The Nature of Conflict* (Studies on Sociological Aspects of International Tensions for UNESCO), Paris, 1957.

government announced plans, in 1959, to repatriate as many of the Korean minority in Japan who wished to go, to North Korea. All further contact between the Republic of Korea and Japan thereupon broke down. With the student deposition of the militantly anti-Japanese President Rhee, there began to be a faint hope of reestablishing some degree of normal relations.

With regard to the rest of Asia, Japanese leaders appear to feel that they, representing an Asian nation, have a complete understanding of the problems faced by the region in formulating and executing policies of economic development and modernization. On occasion, Japan has tried to explain the case of the underdeveloped, to the developed nations. This explanation has also led Japan to deal with Asian nationalism and non-commitment.

For Japan, the problems of political diplomacy are thus mingled with the economics in working out policy toward Southeast Asia. It was the desire for unity with Asia that prompted Japan to send a delegation to the Afro-Asian Conference, held in Bandung in April, 1955. This was the first time since the war that Japan sent a delegation to a conference of such a size (twenty-nine nations). To a large extent, the delegation revealed the humble objective of persuading Asia to take Japan back into the fraternity of nations.

Symbolic diplomatic apology was followed by concrete steps to settle problems of reparations for war damage to Southeast Asian countries. Of the four countries having claims on Japan for reparations—Burma, the Philippines, Indonesia, and Viet Nam—Burma was the first with which Japan settled accounts, on April 16, 1955. The agreement set a pattern for the direct method of payment, whereby the claimant obtains goods directly from manufacturers, by-passing the Japanese government. Payment was to be made in both goods and services. With signature of the agreement with Viet Nam, in Saigon, May 13, 1959, the last page in reparations was written.[65]

As a matter of fact, was it finally written? Already, by 1960 it was apparent that there was a subtle economic significance to these reparations agreements not at first apparent on the surface. Beyond doubt, they established a long-range pattern of trade relations, a flow of goods and skilled Japanese services which would be difficult to eliminate. In a limited sense, Japan—in apologetic peace-making—was reconstructing a minor greater

[65] "Japan's Reparations Summarized," *Japan Report,* V, No. 14 (July 15, 1959).

East Asia prosperity sphere, a project at which the nation had
failed in war.

The strategy for the development of Southeast Asia, in
which Japan has retained a burning interest, took on new significance with shifts in American-Japanese trade relations. In
1960, Japanese economic journals were vigorously discussing
aspects of Undersecretary of State Douglas Dillon's plans for
allies of the United States, including Japan, to take on a greater
share of the task of development of underdeveloped areas. Space
does not permit a detailed examination of all the ramifications
of Japanese-American trade relations. At the time of writing, the
campaign for liberalization of Japanese trade was receiving close
attention.[66]

JAPAN AND THE UNITED NATIONS. Even before Japan recovered
its independence, economic relations within the Asian area were
furthered through certain specialized functions of the United
Nations, especially in ECAFE, GATT, and the United Nations
Special Fund.[67] The chronology of Japan's movement to full
membership in the United Nations has already been given. In
January, 1959, Foreign Minister Fujiyama underlined Japan's
policy as implemented through the world organization:

> Of the three principles [of diplomacy], I think that the diplomacy
> centering on the United Nations is by far the most important and is
> different from the other two. Questions frequently arise when the other
> two principles—Japan as a member of the Asian family of nations
> and Japan's position in the free and democratic camp—are applied
> parallel with each other.[68]

There is, of course, an element of idealism in this phase of
Japanese policy. The intent is to develop the support of the
United Nations into an effective agency for the maintenance of
peace and the prevention of aggression. Were this ideal achieved,
Japan could begin realistic engagement in diplomacy without
force. It would fulfill the policy first propounded by Japan, when
it entered the General Assembly, relating to the expediting of
disarmament talks and the ultimate suspension of nuclear tests.

---

[66] See, for example, the articles by Matsui Kiyoshi on liberalization and
prosperity, *Economist,* April 19, 1960; and on Japan's international balance of
payments, *Toyo Keizai Shimpo,* April 23, 1960.

[67] These three, signifying the major areas of economic cooperation for
Japan, are the Economic Commission for Asia and the Far East, the General
Agreement on Tariffs and Trade, and the Special Fund (proposed as SUN-
FED).

[68] Interview with Hosokawa Ryugen, in *Gaiko Jiho,* January, 1959.

Make no mistake, Japanese leaders feel this line is in the national interest and no postwar leadership has been in a position to deny public pressure in this direction. Japan considers itself the natural leader in this movement, being so far the only country to have experienced the terrors of atomic warfare.[69]

Japanese political and legal organizations have shown great interest in analyzing and criticizing weak points in the United Nations Charter.[70] A study group of the Japanese branch of the International Law Association has declared that revision of the charter is essential. The group asserted that "the Charter was created by its framers on the assumption that the member states of the United Nations would be integrated into one universal community under the united authority of the major powers associated in mutual trust and common responsibility." Japanese, in the postwar world, have slowly begun to discover that such assumptions, made both in the charter and in the Japanese constitution, must unfortunately be revised.

12 - The Japanese Political System: An Overview

There are at least two dangers in the attempt made in this book to contribute to our knowledge in the field of foreign governments. If political science (or if you prefer, study of the art of politics) must approach all governments as institutions sprung from the roots of cultures, then the author must write for an average American still largely uninformed about non-Western cultures and institutions. That is to say, both author and reader

[69] See various speeches by Japanese delegations, carried in *Japan Report,* III, No. 16 (September 25, 1957); IV, No. 2 (January 2, 1958). During 1958–59, the author verified the deep-rooted interest in activities of the UN, by following closely publications like *Kokuren Kyoto,* the U.N. Association of Japan, Kyoto branch (monthly).

[70] For a more detailed account, see Japan Association of International Law, *Japan and the United Nations* (New York: Manhattan Publishing, 1958).

run the risk that Japanese government will be judged only in light of familiar Western cultures.

Meanwhile the author himself runs perhaps an even greater danger in his attempt to provide the links between a culture and political institutions so subject to dynamic change as are Japanese society and politics. And yet the attempt must here be made, if only to bring the reader at long last to the end of the book! Furthermore a bold try may serve some purpose at that, not so much in providing answers and predictions, but in identifying some of the key questions about the relevance of Japanese experience to a general theory of politics.

Modernization Theory and Japan

The timing of Western scholarship concerned with Japan, like the timing of the modernization of Japan itself, has been crucial. Gradually analysis of Japanese political behavior has been driven down to the level of culture, and back to the critical process of modernization, which was accelerated during the Meiji era. A thorough understanding of the Meiji transformation rested in turn upon more than generalized treatment of what was strangely called the centralized feudalism of the Tokugawa epoch. To some extent we are still awaiting more thorough analysis of the central problem of modernization, answers to which are relevant to the experience of any culture or any state.[1]

The difficulty with the term, modernization, is that this word—like some others, Westernization, industrialization or development—may suggest value judgments. Perhaps the chief advantage of the word modernization lies in the fact that it obviously stands for an extremely broad concept. Modernization seems to have no definable beginning, no foreseeable terminal point. In other words, it is a dynamic and not a static idea. There are no absolutely modern societies; in every society the process is more or less advanced.

If modernization is, first of all, broadly conceived as culture change, it can also be thought of as a product of culture contact. Indeed, Westerners with characteristic lack of humility usually think of the process as one of Westernization. The danger lies in

[1] In this section I am particularly grateful to my colleagues in the New Jersey Seminar on Asian Studies, faculty members from Rutgers, the six state colleges, Princeton, Farleigh-Dickinson and Seton Hall. Late in 1960, they added a number of dimensions to my working paper, "The Problem of Transition: 'Modernization' in Asia" (Working Paper No. 1, mimeographed), prepared for undergraduates and summarized here.

superficially assuming that the complex process of modernization is solely a matter of exposure to the products of Western cultures. As has been pointed out, in Japan the process of modernization has been marked as much by the Japanizations of imports from the West as by a Westernization of Japanese life.

Both words, modernization and Westernization, suggest that familiar classifications of governments have inherent weaknesses when applied for comparative purposes to various countries in Asia and, specifically, to Japan. Stereotypes such as totalitarian-democratic, federal-unitary, presidential-parliamentary, monarchical-republican, and so forth, seem hopelessly inadequate for describing the dynamic process of change in Japan. Some more meaningful categories which call to mind, for example, the distinction drawn by Sir Henry Maine, between societies resting on status and those resting on contract, will prove far more useful to an understanding of the variety of political behavior. The continued interaction between rural, agrarian, village-centered Japan and urban, industrial, metropolitan Japan has been a major theme of this book.

Recent attempts to identify the characteristics of a modernized society have singled out the following: urbanization and a relatively high degree of commercialization and industrialization within the economy, coupled with a relatively high per capita income; extensive geographic and social mobility; widespread literacy, coupled with a penetrative network of mass communication media; widespread participation and involvement by members of the society in modern social, economic, and political processes.[2]

In considering the progress of modernization in Asia according to the criteria listed, Japan offers the case study *par excellence*. As such it is viewed with interest and some envy by nations just embarking on the twentieth century's unpredictable voyage of discovery. It is also viewed with fascination by Western nations interested in finding out what happens if and when they offer aid to premodern and underdeveloped areas.

Western and Japanese scholars alike have begun to replace broad generalizations which have not entirely satisfied them— that modernization was brought off by a handful of leaders; that the initiative was seized by the lower *samurai;* that emergence was possible because of the ability to imitate and the blind obedience of the Japanese people—and to substitute for these cliches

[2] Gabriel A. Almond & James S. Coleman, eds. *The Politics of Developing Areas* (Princeton: Princeton University, 1960), p. 532.

a more vivid description, an understanding in depth of the structure and dynamics of Japanese society. Study of the modernization of Japan is, of course, like the process itself, going forward. Firm conclusions about so complicated a process are therefore inappropriate at this time. Changes in the government of Japan and political behavior of the Japanese even since the reemergence of the country after the treaty of peace in 1952, are part of that continuing process.

Relevance to a General Theory of Politics

For some of the reasons given, it has been justly said that the study of comparative politics has been too historical in emphasis, too legalistic, and too parochial in approach.[3]

At one time, the few treatises available on Japanese government and politics could be called descriptive, formalistic and western-culture biased. Certainly the postwar emphasis in the United States on neglected non-Western politics has, however, done much both to fill such gaps and to cause a serious reconsideration of our general theory of political science.

More recently, books and monographs on Japanese politics have increasingly tried to combine description of governmental institutions with traditional political traits which seem to defy the modernization process. Ever since the war, there have been productive explorations of Japanese national character for its own sake. These have been useful to the student who wishes to understand actual political behavior, as distinct from the formal legal, political process. Their advantage is that they have revealed Japanese politics to be mature, not primitive; to be complex, not simple and copied; to be perhaps unique, not just exotic. With regard to no other country is the national character approach so rewarding.[4]

There have been two disadvantages to the behavioral ap-

[3] "Research in Comparative Politics," *The American Political Science Review*, XLVII, No. 3 (September, 1953); George Kahin, Guy Pauker & Lucien W. Pye, "Comparative Politics of Non-Western Countries," the same review, XLIX, No. 4 (December, 1955).

[4] An enlightening review on the variety of treatment was written by Robert E. Ward, "Theory and Practice in Recent Studies of Japanese Politics," *World Politics*, X, No. 3 (April, 1958). Professor Ward surveyed three different types of approach represented by Harold S. Quigley & John E. Turner, *The New Japan: Government and Politics* (Minneapolis: University of Minnesota, 1956); Chitoshi Yanaga, *Japanese People and Politics* (New York: John Wiley, 1956); and Nobutaka Ike, *Japanese Politics: An Introductory Survey* (New York: Knopf, 1957).

proach. First, it has very often thrown the baby out with the bath: it did not always link the basic characteristics of Japanese society with the more formal governmental structure, through which political behavior must be worked out. And second, it was often blind to the fact that traditional traits of national character were changing fast.

Nevertheless, we are today in much less danger of generalizing superficially; and we are obligated to generalize carefully on political behavior from time to time as Japanese society changes. Since the peace treaty, it is apparent that Japanese political institutions have slowly been modified to be more consistent with traditional political behavior; on the other hand, behavior is set within the continuing modernization process as a result of such long-range forces as industrialization and urbanization. In this sense Japan may be characterized as a state in the advanced stages of transition from a tradition-oriented political system to some sort of modern parliamentary democracy.[5] Corollary characteristics of this transition may be summarized as follows:

Oriental culture roots, technically described, still provide many of the social norms in Japanese society. Japan's ideology is strongly colored by the influence of the recent past. Much of Japan still moves along the well-worn paths of *agraria*.

Occidental characteristics are most prominent in urban Japan. New roads to *industria* are constantly being explored by the Japanese.

Developed Japan has now joined the Western world; nevertheless the *underdeveloped* world of Afro-Asia is close by in fact and in spirit.

Nationalism is not really new to Japan. Japanese political history has provided experience with the clan- and family-nation, even before the advent of the modern nation-state. An emperor myth came first. Experience with decentralized and centralized feudalism came later.

Comparative governments have been the rule in Japan. Both in ancient and in modern times Japanese have experimented with governments of civil, then with governments of military, and then again with governments of civil dominance. Japan went through 2,000 years of independence, even isolation, and built the belief that the Rising Sun would never set. Japan was then defeated and occupied primarily by a young nation, which had never before really occupied or tried to reform a whole nation. In one generation, totalitarian tendencies led observers

[5] For this clear insight, I am grateful to Dr. Nobutaka Ike.

(many of them Japanese) to call Japan's government fascist, but it was not really fascist. In another, Japan submitted to the dubious experiment of being democratized. In yet another, political factions which wanted to continue an alliance with the former Occupiers, also wanted to revise the Occupation-inspired constitution; opponents who wanted no part of the alliance, nevertheless wanted to keep the alien-inspired constitution unchanged at all costs! Japan has had a Liberal-Democratic Party which has not been predominantly liberal or dedicted to democratic principles; it has had Socialist parties which were out of tune with democratic socialism; and it has had communist cliques which were against the Japan Communist Party.

Certainly Japan has thus provided a rich, vividly colorful panoply of political experience for one searching to test any general theory of politics. In fact, today it would be dangerous for the political scientists to generalize at all, without reference to Japan.

Factors of Stability and Order

Democracy can be defined somewhat as follows: (1) government incorporating the consent of the governed; with (2) strict accountability of the government; (3) equality of public opportunity, which leads naturally to (4) rule by the majority; with (5) protection of the minority; and finally, (6) pluralism in the society guarantees against the rise of the all-encompassing, political state.

It is true that before 1945 Japan scarcely approached this rather ideal situation. It is also true that the Occupation tried to approximate the ideal: its policies were, by and large, benevolent, constructive and sound.[6] Furthermore, after independence was gained in 1952, many Japanese found that they had a stake in the perpetuation of a democratic regime. The labor movement had tasted power (sometimes seasoned with irresponsibility) and liked it. Land reform had presented Japanese unprecedented equality and social mobility in the rural areas. For the first time many Japanese, and particularly the women, enjoy legal equality. Japan continued its tradition of a vigorous and independent press.[7]

[6] One of the most sophisticated treatments of this remarkable political experiment to appear so far is Kazuo Kawai, *Japan's American Interlude* (Chicago: University of Chicago, 1960).

[7] Hugh Borton, "Past Limitations and the Future of Democracy in Japan," *Political Science Quarterly*, LXX, No. 3 (September, 1955).

At the time of writing, it was fifteen years since the surrender of Japan, thirteen years since the adoption of the new constitution, and eight years since the achievement once again of independence. One fact often overlooked was that Japanese government and politics continued to operate mainly in the institutional channels established under the Occupation of Japan. This in itself was a political phenomenon of great significance. Central to Japan's institutional structure was the remarkable new (MacArthur) constitution. Enough has been written in this book about its adoption, its contents and its possible revision. It is now time to try to place Japan's organic law within a historical context.

Constitutions of the late eighteenth and early nineteenth centuries were dominated by concepts of liberalism. With the rise of empirical and analytical studies of jurisprudence, in the late nineteenth century, constitutions tended to become national organic laws which avoided ideological coloration. The Meiji Constitution was more of this type. For example, it defined human rights but did so without ringing declarations and it placed rights within the bounds of law. The twentieth century saw a return to constitutions of ideological, particularly socialist, principles.

It may seem strange to Americans to hear it said that the new Japanese Constitution is definitely a document with a strong ideological undertone. Descended partially from the Potsdam Proclamation, the constitution also reflects traditional American ideals, the spirit of more modern New Deal reforms and even socialist principles. It assumes a doctrine of natural law inviolable even by the Diet (in this sense it resembles the West German and Indian constitutions). It synthesizes classic and contemporary human rights. It attempts to achieve wide social and economic gains by means of political manifesto. The practical implementation of all these rights has been left to the realm of politics, an arena in which Japanese conservatives and renovationists have debated ever since. In other words, the constitution is an exhortation to reform. In the view of Takayanagi Kenzo, Chairman of the Constitutional Inquiry committee, "Its construction is rather cubic than plane and rather dynamic than static." [8]

The unique and best-known feature of the new constitution is its strong, clear enunciation of pacifism, at first interpreted as literally banning war potential even for the purpose of defense.

[8] Takayanagi Kenzo, "Character of the Japanese Constitution as Seen from an International Viewpoint," *Jiyu,* February, 1960.

Again in the words of Dr. Takayanagi, "My interpretation of the war-renouncing clause is that it is a rhetorical political manifesto trumpeting pacificism." Yet paradoxically, a majority of Japanese share the aspiration underlying this manifesto.

Nevertheless the Japanese people are undergoing an agonizing reappraisal, attempting to translate the statement of pacifist hopes into a program of security policy. The difficulty is that any and all suggested changes to the "peace constitution" have come up against the public suspicion that elimination of Article 9 will mark Japan's return to militarism. This has been the spirit in which former Premier Katayama Tetsu founded the People's League for Safeguarding the Constitution (*Kempo Yogo Kokumin Rengo*). He stated,

> I believe that the enforcement of the constitution meant a renaissance in Japan. Its significance is immensely great, for it clearly defines the people as the sovereign of the state and guarantees the peaceful life. By the basic principles stipulated in the constitution all political and social institutions have been reformed in a democratic manner.[9]

So very deep was Katayama's conviction that, when the league became involved in partisan political struggles against revision of the American security pact, military bases and nuclear armament, he bolted his own organization. He was determined to start a new movement open to all segments of the population, "including conservatives in order to achieve its primary aim of disseminating the spirit of the constitution."

The constitution, as an exhortation to reform, did contain many technical faults. For example, no one has been satisfied with the definition of the emperor as a symbol instead of a sovereign. The emperor does perform, with the advice of the cabinet, functions of state. Doubtless the document will be formally amended in order to recapture in law the ethos of the Japanese, specifically with regard to the status of the emperor, the structure of the Diet, and the operation of the Supreme Court.

Moreover, a few informal but significant changes in the constitution have already been effected. Most of them are products of the attempt to bring back more centralized national control. Examples include revision of police organization, public finance, and education, all previously assigned to local jurisdiction. These changes may be healthy, for obviously Japan operates best as a unitary rather than a federal state. The massive legal reforms

[9] *Nippon Shuho*, May 5, 1960.

which accompanied the constitution do, however, remain on the statute books and the role of law as an instrument of social control grows steadily stronger.

Of course, the results of the Occupation were not all beneficial. The program of forced democratization and the reintroduction of bureaucratism were at least dubious. The intellectual outlook and behavior of the elite who staffed these democratic institutions have often been inconsistent with the goals set forth in the new constitution.

Nor, on the other hand, can all the gains of stability, order and democracy be attributed solely to the Occupation. The Japanese contribution should not be sold short. Scholars are just beginning to realize how much the modernization of Japan, beginning in the nineteenth century and even before, has contributed. The Restoration in 1868 did provide impetus toward wider representation in government. It allowed the introduction of democratic doctrines and they were never completely wiped out. It called forth the political parties, with all their weaknesses, and the habit of elections. Above all it began the reshuffling of feudal class lines, a basic change which has progressed and accelerated ever since.

On reflection it seems possible that the real, lasting changes inherited from Japan's most recent period of cultural absorption are not different in style from the process of Japanization in the seventh century, which appeared so much like the Sinification of Japan; or from the process of Japanization in the nineteenth century, which appeared so much like a Europeanization of Japan. What is different, in the changes both under and since the Occupation, is the tempo of modernization. The beat has fluctuated, first picking up after the war and then slowing down under "reverse course." As Professor Kazuo Kawai has wisely put it,

Thus the present movement for the revision of the new constitution and for the modification of many of the political reforms of the Occupation period does not represent a trend toward complete repudiation of democracy and reversion to traditionalism.[10]

Factors of Instability and Change

All of the effects of Japan's remarkable modernization do not, of course, lend strength to stability and order. The bewilderingly rapid changes in Japanese society over the last 100 years

[10] Kawai, *op. cit.*, p. 243.

have left many Japanese with no deeply rooted convictions. In 1960, complacent Americans were shocked to discover the harvest of dragon's teeth sown just before and after 1945.

Many of the younger generation in Japan had become potential juvenile delinquents, steeped in extreme self-indulgence, without regard for the society in which they lived and which they despised. Japanese educators—much like American critics of the so-called progressive education—became increasingly alarmed over the misapplication of pragmatism. Doubtless the wholesale importation of an American system of education into a still largely hierarchical Japanese society aggravated the situation. Japanese education came to lack elan, moral tone or a program of its own. It failed to fulfill the promise (which it did at least for the few in the Meiji era) of being an instrument to shape the future course of modernization.

In this same sense, changes in the field of informal relations within the family in Japan of the 1950s were probably of greater significance than alterations of the formal political structure. And they were far more confusing. The individual was being emancipated from traditional social controls. The classic civil liberties were intrenched; but Japanese democracy needed authority too.

More pessimistic observers (including some Japanese) have felt that neither public communication nor the decision-making process in post-treaty Japan has been adequate to the needs of a modern democratic state. Professor Royama Masamichi, for example, has charged that Japanese still discuss without really communicating. Personal exchanges continue to be ritualistic and Japanese openly and frankly come to grips with issues only with difficulty. Part of this has to do with even the modern Japanese language. Part of it has to do with deeply ingrained social mores.

Japanese renovationists and even radicals still engage in elaborate protocol of interpersonal relations, formalities like filters which strain out thought. Japan, it is true, had adopted a parliamentary system long before the Occupation. The success of such a system, however, rests on real debate, eventual division and majority rule. Liberal-Democrats, with a long tradition of bossism and contempt for the public, have increasingly tended to railroad through unpopular measures or doubtful legislation on the sheer strength of their numerical majority. Socialists have in turn taken an all or nothing attitude and simply walked out of the Diet when votes appeared to be going against them. One of the most subtle attributes of a true democracy, nurtured by an open society, is the coupling of majority respect for the minority, regardless of its inferior numbers, with the minority gracefully accepting rule of the majority. One of the best illustrations showing that the Japanese had not learned this lesson was the "great debate" over revision of the American security pact, in which fateful issues were settled without great debate.

The Future

By the 1960s a new political force had begun to make its unmistakable presence felt in Japan. At long last, in the otherwise rapid modernization process, an amorphous middle class was beginning to take shape out of successive economic booms, growth of a consumer economy, and a second spurt of industrialization.[11] Increased urbanization, new images projected by mass media, the further growth of technology, almost an obsession with durable consumer goods and, parallel to these developments, widening of the sphere of the administrative state—these are the corollaries.

Political party platforms, tuned in on the transistor wavelengths of the new middle class, were trying to broadcast what most Japanese seemed to want to hear. This was true of the traditional elite, the Liberal-Democrats, of the new Democratic Socialist Party, and even of the reluctant Socialists. All promised fulfillment of middle-class desires. The significance of the emergence of a true middle class, characteristically making its appearance in Japan after the adoption of many political institutions designed for such a class, is worthy of the keen and steady analysis of all students of political science.

Now the future of Japanese democracy is, of course, dependent to an unfortunate extent on the bare means of subsistence—land, resources, trade—with which it must be supported. In this sense, and aside from any Marxist predeterminations, the nature of the Japanese economy is important.

Modern Japan has inherited a remarkably integrated ethos

[11] In his provocative study, *The Stages of Economic Growth; A Non-Communist Manifesto* (Cambridge: University Press, 1960), W. W. Rostow calls the fifth stage "'the age of high mass-consumption,' whose not unequivocal joys Western Europe and Japan are beginning energetically to probe" (p. 10).

which, despite rapid changes, has always provided a source of stability.[12] This spirit will have to be pitted, once again, against the dangers of the outside world. That outside world the Japanese can no longer hope to control or shut out.

The challenge within Japan arises from the new political force which does not arise from an old elite nor yet from a peasant proletariat. Up to 1960, old-line Japanese political leaders had found the new middle class baffling, a floating vote, apathetic, even apolitical.

With regard to much of Asia, it has become a cliche to speak of peoples with rising expectations. In one part, Japan, the essential political problem is to match the rising expectations of an emergent middle class. If these expectations are frustrated, that class may well turn—really for the first time in Japanese political history—to a form of totalitarianism. The problem is to transport the mundane desires of that class "beyond consumption," to borrow another Rostow phrase, and to complete the fashioning of an indigenous Japanese democracy.

Selected Bibliography*

Bibliographies

Association for Asian Studies. *The Journal of Asian Studies* (quarterly). An annual "Bibliography of Asian Studies" is published as an extra number in September.

Borton, Hugh, Serge Elisseeff, William W. Lockwood, and John C. Pelzel. *A Selected List of Books and Articles on Japan,* rev. and enl. ed. (Cambridge: Harvard University Press, 1954). A basic guide.

Hall, John W. *Japanese History; New Dimensions of Approach and Understanding,* Publication No. 34, Service Center for Teachers of History (Washington: American Historical Association, 1961). A concise summary of publications reflecting research and new interpretations.

Ward, Robert E. *A Guide to Japanese Reference and Research Materials in the Field of Political Science* (Ann Arbor: University of Michigan Press, 1950). Center for Japanese Studies, Bibliographical Series No. 1.

[12] Paul M. A. Linebarger, "The Survival of Historical Japan," *Current History,* XXXIV, No. 200 (April, 1958).

* Only materials available in English are cited.

Government Documents

The Constitution of Japan and the Court Organization Law (Tokyo: Supreme Court, 1958). A useful, brief survey of courts and law.

Daily Summary of the Japanese Press (Tokyo: American Embassy, Translation Services Branch, 1957–   ).

Economic Planning Agency. *New Long-range Economic Plan for Japan (FY1958–FY1962)* (Tokyo: December 17, 1957).

Japan Report (semi-monthly) (New York: Information Office, Consulate-General of Japan, 1952–   ).

Japanese National Commission for UNESCO (comp.). *Japan: Its Land, People and Culture* (Tokyo: Ministry of Finance, 1958). A unique, one-volume encyclopedia on history, geography, economy, and politics; invaluable for reference.

Summaries of Selected Japanese Magazines (weekly) (Tokyo: American Embassy, Translation Services Branch, 1957–   ).

Supreme Commander for the Allied Powers, Report of Government Section. *Political Reorientation of Japan: September 1945 to September 1948*, 2 vols. (Washington: U.S. Government Printing Office, 1959). The only official history of the Occupation.

Books

Almond, Gabriel A., and James S. Coleman (eds.). *The Politics of Developing Areas* (Princeton: Princeton University Press, 1960). Although these essays do not treat specifically of Japan, many of the principles could have been derived from and are applicable to Japan.

Beardsley, Richard K., John W. Hall, and Robert E. Ward. *Village Japan* (Chicago: University of Chicago Press, 1959). The five-year, detailed, interdisciplinary study of a *buraku* (hamlet), in which the author participated.

Benedict, Ruth. *The Chrysanthemum and the Sword: Patterns of Japanese Culture* (Boston: Houghton Mifflin, 1946). A classic on Japanese national character; to be used with some caution since the study is based on Japanese in the United States during World War II.

Borton, Hugh, and others. *Japan between East and West* (New York: Harper, 1957). Edited proceedings of a Council on Foreign Relations Study Group, in which the author participated.

Cohen, Jerome B. *Japan's Postwar Economy* (Bloomington: University of Indiana Press, 1958). A succinct treatment.

Cole, Allan B. *Japanese Society and Politics: The Impact on Social Stratification and Mobility on Politics* (Boston: Boston University, 1956).

Dore, R. P. *City Life in Japan: A Study of a Tokyo Ward* (Berkeley: University of California Press, 1958). A sociological study; should be contrasted with Beardsley, *et al.*, *Village Japan*, above.

Ginsburg, Norton (ed.). *The Pattern of Asia* (Englewood Cliffs, N.J.: Prentice-Hall, 1958). An excellent human geography; see especially Chapters IV–VI on Japan.

Ike, Nobutaka. *Japanese Politics: An Introductory Survey* (New York: Knopf, 1957). An excellent survey of working forces in Japanese politics.

Japan Association of International Law. *Japan and the United Nations* (New York: Manhattan Publishing Co., 1958).

Japan Local Self-Government Institute. *Guide to Local Government in Japan* (Tokyo: Shisei Kaikan, 1959). A brief but authoritative outline.

Kato, Hidetoshi (ed.). *Japanese Popular Culture* (Tokyo: Tuttle, 1959). One of the few studies of aspects of Japan's new mass culture.

Kawai, Kazuo. *Japan's American Interlude* (Chicago: University of Chicago Press, 1960). The most sophisticated treatment of the Occupation and its effects yet to appear.

Linebarger, P. M. A., Djang Chu, and Ardath W. Burks. *Far Eastern Governments and Politics*, 2d ed. (Princeton: Van Nostrand, 1956). East Asian governments and politics, historically considered; see Part II, "Japan."

Mendel, Douglas H., Jr. *Japanese People and Foreign Policy* (Berkeley: University of California Press, 1961).

Nakamura, Kikuo, Yutaka Matsumura. *Political Handbook of Japan 1958* (Tokyo: Tokyo News Service, 1958). A brief but useful reference.

Quigley, Harold S., and John E. Turner. *The New Japan: Government and Politics* (Minneapolis: University of Minnesota Press, 1956). One of the few books on post-treaty government.

Reischauer, Edwin O. *The United States and Japan* (Cambridge: Harvard University Press, 1950). Especially Part III, "The Japanese Character"; the author was appointed Ambassador to Japan in 1961.

Scalapino, Robert A., and Junnosuke Masumi. *Parties and Politics in Contemporary Japan* (Berkeley: University of California Press, 1961).

Tiedemann, Arthur. *Modern Japan: A Brief History* (Princeton: Van Nostrand, 1955). A handy collection of translated documents, with shrewd annotations.

Yanaga, Chitoshi. *Japanese People and Politics* (New York: Wiley, 1956). An excellent survey of the inner workings of politics.

Serials and Articles

Burks, Ardath W. "Japan," *Britannica Book of the Year* (Chicago: Encyclopaedia Britannica, 1957–   ). An annual survey of events.

Burks, Ardath W. "A Note on the Emerging Administrative Structure of the Post-treaty Japanese National Government," *Occasional Papers*, Center for Japanese Studies, 3 (1952).

"Japan Since Recovery of Independence," *The Annals* of The American Academy of Political and Social Science, 308 (November, 1956). A symposium.

Japan Times, The (daily). Tokyo: (1952–   ). The best English-language newspaper published in Japan.

Kawai, Kazuo. "Sovereignty and Democracy in the Japanese Constitution," *American Political Science Review*, XLIX, 3 (September, 1955).

Kyogoku, Jun-ichi, Nobutaka Ike. "Urban-Rural Differences in Voting Behavior in Postwar Japan," *Stanford University Political Science Series*, 66 (1959).

McNelly, Theodore, "The Japanese Constitution: Child of the Cold War," *Political Science Quarterly*, LXXIV, 2 (June, 1959).

Mendel, Douglas H., Jr. "Revisionist Opinion in Post-treaty Japan," *American Political Science Review*, XLVIII, 3 (September, 1954).

"Report on Japan," *Current History*, XXXIV, 200 (April, 1958). A symposium.

Scalapino, Robert A. "Japanese Socialism in Crisis," *Foreign Affairs* (January, 1960).

Ward, Robert E. "The Origins of the Present Japanese Constitution," *American Political Science Review,* L, 4 (December 1956). Professor Ward is now working on a full-length study of the Occupation.

Ward, Robert E. "Theory and Practice in Recent Studies of Japanese Politics," *World Politics,* X, 3 (April, 1958). A review article.

Ward, Robert E. "Urban-Rural Differences and the Process of Political Modernization in Japan: A Case Study," *Economic Development and Cultural Change,* IX, 1 (Part II) (October, 1960.